SPECTRUM®

Math

Grade 8

Published by Spectrum®
an imprint of Carson-Dellosa Publishing
Greensboro, NC

Spectrum®
An imprint of Carson-Dellosa Publishing LLC
P.O. Box 35665
Greensboro, NC 27425 USA

ISBN 978-1-4838-0876-5

02-236157811

Table of Contents Grade 8

Table of Contents, continued

Chapter 6 Statistics and Probability

NAME ________________

Check What You Know

Integers and Exponents

Find the value of each expression.

	a	b	c
1.	$7^3 =$ ______	$8^5 =$ ______	$4^2 =$ ______
2.	$9^4 =$ ______	$1^5 =$ ______	$6^8 =$ ______
3.	$4^{-3} =$ ______	$3^{-5} =$ ______	$7^{-4} =$ ______
4.	$2^{-5} =$ ______	$9^{-3} =$ ______	$10^{-3} =$ ______
5.	$7^4 =$ ______	$3^{-4} =$ ______	$5^9 =$ ______

Rewrite each multiplication or division expression using a base and an exponent.

6.	$4^5 \div 4^2 =$ ______	$6^{-5} \times 6^3 =$ ______	$8^{-4} \div 8^{-2} =$ ______
7.	$9^{11} \div 9^6 =$ ______	$5^{-3} \times 5^{-1} =$ ______	$3^{-6} \div 3^4 =$ ______
8.	$8^2 \times 8^3 =$ ______	$6^4 \times 6^7 =$ ______	$4^{-2} \div 4^{-5} =$ ______
9.	$7^6 \div 7^3 =$ ______	$4^8 \times 4^3 =$ ______	$9^5 \times 9^6 =$ ______
10.	$2^9 \div 2^{-3} =$ ______	$3^8 \div 3^2 =$ ______	$12^4 \times 12^{10} =$ ______
11.	$5^4 \times 5^2 =$ ______	$10^7 \div 10^4 =$ ______	$11^3 \times 11^4 =$ ______
12.	$7^5 \div 7^2 =$ ______	$6^6 \times 6^3 =$ ______	$12^4 \div 12^2 =$ ______

NAME ______________________

Check What You Know

Integers and Exponents

Rewrite each in standard notation.

	a	b	c
13.	9.545×10^3	8.596×10^{-3}	9.318×10^{-3}
14.	8.124×10^6	8.743×10^4	2.961×10^5
15.	1.0428×10^4	7.8543×10^{-2}	4.937×10^{-4}
16.	2.396×10^5	8.352×10^{-6}	3.85×10^7
17.	3.957×10^2	9.389×10^6	4.109×10^{-5}

Rewrite each in scientific notation.

	a	b	c
18.	0.4537	0.006686	133,300
19.	0.7614	0.01087	517,700
20.	892,320	428,200	0.01283
21.	783,000	0.0004642	478,200,000
22.	53,890,000	4,183,200,000	0.00028737

NAME ________________

Lesson 1.1 Using Exponents

A **power** of a number represents repeated multiplication of the number by itself.

$6^4 = 6 \times 6 \times 6 \times 6$ and is read *6 to the fourth power.*

In exponential numbers, the **base** is the number that is multiplied, and the **exponent** represents the number of times the base is used as factor. In 6^4, 6 is the base and 4 is the exponent.

5^5 means 5 is used as a factor 5 times.

$5 \times 5 \times 5 \times 5 \times 5 = 3{,}125$ $\qquad$ $5^5 = 3{,}125$

Write each power as a product of the factors.

	a	b	c
1.	3^3 ________	5^5 ________	6^1 ________
2.	2^{12} ________	3^8 ________	3^6 ________
3.	4^7 ________	4^4 ________	8^3 ________

Use exponents to rewrite these expressions.

	a	b
4.	$24 \times 24 \times 24$ ________	$2 \times 2 \times 2 \times 2$ ________
5.	$3 \times 3 \times 3 \times 3 \times 3$ ________	5×5 ________
6.	$5 \times 5 \times 5 \times 5 \times 5 \times 5$ ________	$4 \times 4 \times 4$ ________

Find the value of each expression.

	a	b	c
7.	$8^3 =$ ________	$9^4 =$ ________	$10^2 =$ ________

NAME ____________________

Lesson 1.1 Using Exponents

Write each power as a product of the factors.

	a	b	c
1.	9^2 ______	58^1 ______	4^3 ______
2.	5^4 ______	8^2 ______	3^4 ______
3.	75^2 ______	6^2 ______	10^{10} ______

Use exponents to rewrite these expressions.

	a	b
4.	8 ______	13×13 ______
5.	$6 \times 6 \times 6 \times 6$ ______	$5 \times 5 \times 5 \times 5$ ______
6.	$2 \times 2 \times 2 \times 2 \times 2 \times 2 \times 2$ ______	$3 \times 3 \times 3$ ______
7.	$86 \times 86 \times 86$ ______	$4 \times 4 \times 4 \times 4 \times 4$ ______
8.	$10 \times 10 \times 10 \times 10 \times 10$ ______	$15 \times 15 \times 15 \times 15 \times 15$ ______

Find the value of each expression.

	a	b	c
9.	$7^1 =$ ______	$3^4 =$ ______	$10^5 =$ ______
10.	$7^5 =$ ______	$5^3 =$ ______	$8^4 =$ ______
11.	$4^2 =$ ______	$2^5 =$ ______	$9^7 =$ ______
12.	$6^4 =$ ______	$12^3 =$ ______	$7^3 =$ ______

NAME ______________________________

Lesson 1.2 Equivalent Expressions with Exponents

To multiply powers with the same base, combine bases, add the exponents, then simplify. $2^2 \times 2^3 = 2^{2+3} = 2^5 = 32$

To divide powers with the same base, combine bases, subtract the exponents, then simplify. $3^5 \div 3^2 = 3^{5-2} = 3^3 = 27$

Find the value of each expression.

	a	b	c
1.	$7^2 =$ ______	$8^3 =$ ______	$4^3 =$ ______
2.	$10^2 =$ ______	$9^4 =$ ______	$11^5 =$ ______
3.	$17^3 =$ ______	$5^6 =$ ______	$6^4 =$ ______
4.	$21^3 =$ ______	$16^4 =$ ______	$12^5 =$ ______

Rewrite each expression as one base and one exponent. Then, find the value.

5.	$8^2 \times 8^3 =$ 8^5; 32768	$3^3 \times 3^3 =$ ______	$2^2 \times 2^2 =$ ______
6.	$7^4 \div 7^2 =$ ______	$9^5 \div 9^3 =$ ______	$16^4 \div 16^2 =$ ______
7.	$6^4 \times 6^1 =$ ______	$4^4 \times 4^2 =$ ______	$3^2 \times 3^2 =$ ______
8.	$10^6 \div 10^4 =$ ______	$8^3 \div 8^2 =$ ______	$7^6 \div 7^3 =$ ______
9.	$5^3 \times 5^2 =$ ______	$10^3 \times 10^4 =$ ______	$15^2 \times 15^1 =$ ______
10.	$2^8 \div 2^3 =$ ______	$3^9 \div 3^7 =$ ______	$6^6 \div 6^3 =$ ______

NAME ____________________

Lesson 1.2 Equivalent Expressions with Exponents

Rewrite each multiplication or division expression using a base and an exponent.

	a	b
1.	$4^3 \times 4^5 =$ ______	$9^2 \times 9^3 =$ ______
2.	$(3 \times 3 \times 3) \times (3 \times 3) =$ ______	$5^6 \div 5^3 =$ ______
3.	$8^5 \div 8 =$ ______	$(2 \times 2 \times 2 \times 2) \div (2 \times 2) =$ ______
4.	$(5 \times 5) \times (5 \times 5) =$ ______	$9^9 \div 9^5 =$ ______
5.	$10^3 \times 10 =$ ______	$6^5 \div 6^2 =$ ______
6.	$4^3 \div 4^2 =$ ______	$(7 \times 7 \times 7) \div 7 =$ ______
7.	$11^5 \times 11^2 =$ ______	$6 \times 6^5 =$ ______
8.	$(8 \times 8 \times 8 \times 8) \div (8 \times 8) =$ ______	$5^3 \times 5^2 =$ ______
9.	$12^9 \times 12^2 =$ ______	$11^{10} \div 11^4 =$ ______
10.	$3^4 \times 3^4 =$ ______	$(4 \times 4 \times 4 \times 4) \div 4 =$ ______
11.	$(5 \times 5 \times 5) \div 5 =$ ______	$6^8 \times 6^4 =$ ______
12.	$4^{12} \div 4^6 =$ ______	$3^3 \times 3^9 =$ ______
13.	$(6 \times 6 \times 6 \times 6) \div (6 \times 6 \times 6) =$ ______	$15^8 \div 15^3 =$ ______
14.	$9^9 \times 9^6 =$ ______	$7^8 \times 7^2 =$ ______
15.	$2^7 \div 2 =$ ______	$4^{11} \times 4 =$ ______

NAME ____________________

Lesson 1.3 Negative Exponents

When a power includes a negative exponent, express the number as 1 divided by the base and change the exponent to positive.

$$4^{-2} = \frac{1}{4^2} = \frac{1}{16} = 0.0625$$

To multiply or divide powers with the same base, combine bases, add or subtract the exponents, and then simplify.

$$2^{-3} \times 2^{-2} = 2^{-5} = \frac{1}{2^5} = 0.03125$$

$$2^{-4} \div 2^{-2} = 2^{-2} = \frac{1}{2^2} = 0.25$$

Rewrite each expression with a positive exponent. Then, solve. Round your answer to four decimal places.

	a	b	c
1.	3^{-2} = ______	6^{-3} = ______	8^{-2} = ______
2.	7^{-3} = ______	3^{-3} = ______	9^{-2} = ______
3.	4^{-3} = ______	5^{-2} = ______	2^{-3} = ______
4.	2^{-4} = ______	10^{-3} = ______	1^{-4} = ______

Find each product. Round your answer to five decimal places.

5.	$4^{-2} \times 4^{-3}$ = ______	$2^{-4} \times 2^{-1}$ = ______	$3^{-2} \times 3^{-3}$ = ______
6.	$6^{-2} \times 6^{-2}$ = ______	$5^{-2} \times 5^{-4}$ = ______	$3^{-2} \times 3^{-2}$ = ______
7.	$8^{-6} \times 8^{4}$ = ______	$7^{-5} \times 7^{2}$ = ______	$2^{-7} \times 2^{4}$ = ______

Find each quotient. Round your answer to five decimal places.

8.	$4^{-4} \div 4^{-2}$ = ______	$8^{-5} \div 8^{-3}$ = ______	$3^{-5} \div 3^{-2}$ = ______
9.	$2^{-8} \div 2^{-4}$ = ______	$5^{-6} \div 5^{-4}$ = ______	$6^{-7} \div 6^{-4}$ = ______
10.	$3^{-3} \div 3^{2}$ = ______	$4^{-3} \div 4^{1}$ = ______	$2^{-6} \div 2^{-3}$ = ______

NAME ______________________

Lesson 1.3 Negative Exponents

Rewrite each multiplication or division expression using a base and an exponent.

	a	b
1.	$3^{-4} \times 3^{-6} =$ ______	$9^{-3} \div 9^{-5} =$ ______
2.	$4^{3} \div 4^{-2} =$ ______	$5^{5} \times 5^{-6} =$ ______
3.	$12^{-3} \times 12^{-4} =$ ______	$4^{-6} \times 4^{4} =$ ______
4.	$7^{6} \div 7^{-3} =$ ______	$2^{-3} \div 2^{3} =$ ______
5.	$11^{4} \times 11^{-3} =$ ______	$6^{-5} \times 6^{-4} =$ ______
6.	$8^{-5} \div 8^{3} =$ ______	$12^{-4} \div 12 =$ ______
7.	$7^{5} \times 7^{-4} =$ ______	$5^{-3} \times 5^{2} =$ ______
8.	$2^{5} \div 2^{-3} =$ ______	$3^{-12} \times 3^{-4} =$ ______
9.	$6^{3} \div 6^{-4} =$ ______	$7^{-3} \div 7^{4} =$ ______
10.	$9^{-3} \times 9^{4} =$ ______	$10^{-5} \times 10^{-2} =$ ______
11.	$8^{-4} \div 8^{-2} =$ ______	$2^{-2} \times 2^{-12} =$ ______
12.	$3^{-6} \times 3^{-3} =$ ______	$8^{-6} \div 8^{4} =$ ______
13.	$10^{-2} \div 10^{3} =$ ______	$4^{-5} \times 4^{-2} =$ ______
14.	$9^{-6} \div 9^{-3} =$ ______	$11^{4} \div 11^{-2} =$ ______
15.	$6^{-5} \div 6^{3} =$ ______	$5^{-12} \times 5^{-4} =$ ______
16.	$12^{-6} \div 12 =$ ______	$4^{-4} \times 4^{-3} =$ ______

NAME ______________________

Lesson 1.4 Scientific Notation

Scientific notation is most often used as a concise way of writing very large and very small numbers. It is written as a number between 1 and 10 multiplied by a power of 10. Any number can be expressed in scientific notation.

$1{,}503 = 1.503 \times 10^3$ (+3) $\quad$ $0.0376 = 3.76 \times 10^{-2}$ (−2) $\quad$ $85 = 8.5 \times 10$ (+1)

Translate numbers written in scientific notation into standard form by reading the exponent.

$7.03 \times 10^5 = 703000$ Move the decimal right 5 places. $\quad$ $5.4 \times 10^{-4} = 0.00054$ Move the decimal left 4 places.

Write each number in scientific notation.

	a	b	c
1.	0.013 = ______	4105 = ______	27.3 = ______
2.	810.4 = ______	0.684 = ______	0.017 = ______
3.	0.0006 = ______	427.5 = ______	36,054 = ______
4.	50,210 = ______	0.0005 = ______	256.21 = ______
5.	36.25 = ______	0.892 = ______	0.00065 = ______
6.	0.027 = ______	1,416.3 = ______	0.0049 = ______

Write each number in standard form.

7.	2.6×10^{-3} = ______	8.46×10^5 = ______	4.65×10^{-1} = ______
8.	9.02×10^4 = ______	5.15×10^{-2} = ______	8.45×10^3 = ______
9.	7.25×10^{-4} = ______	1.06×10^3 = ______	9.06×10^{-5} = ______
10.	9.7×10^{-3} = ______	3.02×10^4 = ______	1.56×10^4 = ______

NAME ____________________

Lesson 1.4 Scientific Notation

Write each number in scientific notation.

	a	b	c
1.	32.5 = ________	6,708 = ________	387 = ________
2.	0.569 = ________	67,345 = ________	0.027 = ________
3.	0.079 = ________	0.51 = ________	6,791 = ________
4.	98.25 = ________	2,385 = ________	0.413 = ________
5.	7,831 = ________	418 = ________	75.183 = ________
6.	0.0004 = ________	7,301.4 = ________	0.0018 = ________
7.	5,624 = ________	23.65 = ________	0.965 = ________
8.	0.0045 = ________	523 = ________	0.355 = ________

Write each number in standard form.

9.	9.13×10^5 = ________	4.02×10^{-3} = ________	2.43×10^4 = ________
10.	1.124×10^{-1} = ________	8.48×10^3 = ________	5.12×10^{-2} = ________
11.	9.47×10^3 = ________	3.28×10^{-4} = ________	6.73×10^{-3} = ________
12.	5.3×10^{-5} = ________	4.13×10^4 = ________	3.78×10^4 = ________
13.	3.12×10^3 = ________	1.329×10^5 = ________	8.69×10^2 = ________
14.	4.5×10^{-4} = ________	9.8×10^{-6} = ________	3.56×10^5 = ________
15.	5.42×10^{-2} = ________	9.08×10^{-8} = ________	2.7×10^3 = ________
16.	7.3×10^2 = ________	1.25×10^4 = ________	8.8×10^{-8} = ________

NAME ______________________

Check What You Learned

Integers and Exponents

Find the value of each expression.

	a	b	c
1.	$3^7 =$ ________	$4^8 =$ ________	$5^2 =$ ________
2.	$12^9 =$ ________	$4^5 =$ ________	$8^4 =$ ________
3.	$3^{-6} =$ ________	$4^{-3} =$ ________	$5^{-7} =$ ________
4.	$10^{-4} =$ ________	$6^{-3} =$ ________	$8^{-5} =$ ________
5.	$8^{-6} =$ ________	$7^4 =$ ________	$3^{-9} =$ ________
6.	$10^7 =$ ________	$9^{-2} =$ ________	$2^8 =$ ________

Rewrite each multiplication or division expression using a base and an exponent.

7.	$8^2 \times 8^3 =$ ________	$5^{-5} \times 5^{-2} =$ ________	$6^2 \times 6^4 =$ ________
8.	$4^{-1} \times 4^3 =$ ________	$3^4 \div 3^{-3} =$ ________	$12^{-2} \div 12^4 =$ ________
9.	$5^4 \times 5^7 =$ ________	$8^{-2} \times 8^{-6} =$ ________	$5^8 \times 5^{-3} =$ ________
10.	$9^{-2} \times 9^{-5} =$ ________	$7^8 \div 7^{-3} =$ ________	$6^{-2} \div 6^{-4} =$ ________
11.	$7^{-1} \times 7^{-3} =$ ________	$9^4 \div 9^8 =$ ________	$3^{-8} \div 3^4 =$ ________
12.	$10^{-3} \times 10^3 =$ ________	$8^6 \div 8^{-3} =$ ________	$7^4 \times 7^2 =$ ________

NAME ________________

Check What You Learned

Integers and Exponents

Rewrite each number in standard notation.

	a	b	c
13.	3.04×10^{-3}	4.26×10^{2}	8.1×10^{-4}
14.	6.5×10^{5}	2.4×10^{-2}	7.15×10
15.	3.286×10^{-5}	8.2734×10^{6}	7.362×10^{-6}
16.	8.23×10^{7}	4.602×10^{-3}	2.382×10^{5}
17.	9.12×10^{7}	7.292×10^{-3}	8.153×10^{-4}

Rewrite each number in scientific notation.

18.	1,985	10.32	414.1
19.	0.0003954	95.45	8,524
20.	239,390	0.003121	43,100
21.	0.0283	0.000273	3,476,000
22.	37,120,000	374,200	0.005283

NAME ______________________

Check What You Know

Rational and Irrational Number Relationships

CHAPTER 2 PRETEST

Evaluate each each expression.

	a	b	c
1.	$\sqrt{25}$ = ________	$\sqrt{9}$ = ________	$\sqrt{100}$ = ________
2.	$\sqrt{\frac{4}{16}}$ = ________	$\sqrt{81}$ = ________	$\sqrt{\frac{9}{25}}$ = ________
3.	$\sqrt[3]{343}$ = ________	$\sqrt[3]{729}$ = ________	$\sqrt[3]{64}$ = ________
4.	$\sqrt[3]{216}$ = ________	$\sqrt[3]{\frac{27}{512}}$ = ________	$\sqrt[3]{\frac{64}{729}}$ = ________

Approximate the value of each expression.

5. The value of $\sqrt{10}$ is between ______ and ______.

6. The value of $\sqrt[3]{74}$ is between ______ and ______.

7. The value of $\sqrt{43}$ is between ______ and ______.

8. The value of $\sqrt[3]{17}$ is between ______ and ______.

9. The value of $\sqrt[3]{2}$ is between ______ and ______.

10. The value of $\sqrt{24}$ is between ______ and ______.

Use roots or exponents to solve each equation. Write fractions in simplest form.

	a	b	c
11.	$x^2 = 64$	$\sqrt{x} = 9$	$x^3 = 343$
	$x =$ ________	$x =$ ________	$x =$ ________
12.	$\sqrt[3]{x} = 6$	$x^2 = 121$	$\sqrt[3]{x} = 10$
	$x =$ ________	$x =$ ________	$x =$ ________

NAME ______________________

Check What You Know

Rational and Irrational Number Relationships

Compare using <, >, or =.

	a	b	c
13.	$\sqrt{\frac{4}{9}}$ ______ $\frac{2}{3}$	$\sqrt{10}$ ______ 5	$\sqrt[3]{25}$ ______ 3
14.	1.2 ______ $\sqrt{4}$	$\sqrt[3]{62}$ ______ 3.5	$\sqrt[3]{37}$ ______ 4
15.	$0.\overline{33}$ ______ $\sqrt{\frac{1}{3}}$	$\frac{5}{6}$ ______ $\sqrt{2}$	$\sqrt{5}$ ______ 3

Put the values below in order from least to greatest along a number line.

16. 14, $\sqrt{18}$, 4π

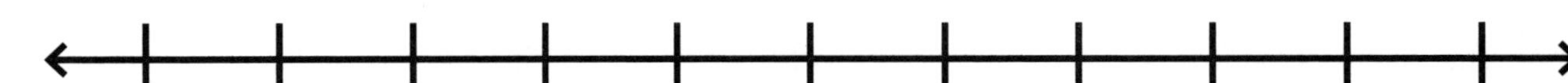

17. $\sqrt{15}$, $\sqrt{21}$, $\sqrt{12}$

18. $\sqrt{5}$, 2, 5

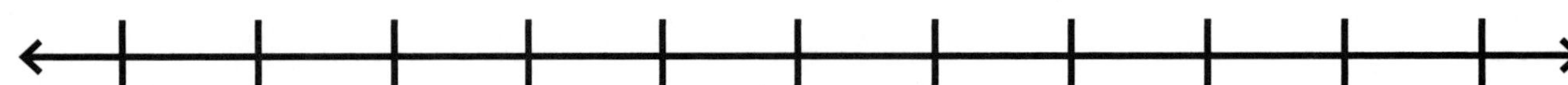

NAME ____________________

Lesson 2.1 Understanding Rational and Irrational Numbers

A **rational number** is a number that either terminates or repeats a pattern. It can be written as a fraction, $\frac{a}{b}$, where *a* and *b* are both whole number integers and *b* does not equal zero.

Here are some examples of rational numbers: 3, -5, $\frac{1}{3}$, $4.\overline{66}$, $\frac{5}{11}$, 3.25

An **irrational number** is any decimal that does not terminate and never repeats. These numbers are often represented by symbols.

Here are some examples of irrational numbers: 5.23143..., $\sqrt{5}$, π

Tell if each number is *rational* or *irrational*.

	a	b	c
1.	$\frac{1}{5}$ ________	$\sqrt{5}$ ________	-5 ________
2.	$\sqrt[3]{27}$ ________	$\frac{1}{3}$ ________	2.354 ________
3.	$\sqrt{36}$ ________	$3.\overline{45}$ ________	$\frac{7}{9}$ ________
4.	$\sqrt{20}$ ________	19.294153 ________	$-\frac{4}{5}$ ________
5.	$\sqrt{15}$ ________	π ________	$-\frac{7}{10}$ ________

NAME ______________________

Lesson 2.2 Square Roots

The **square** of a number is that number times itself. A square is expressed as $\mathbf{6^2}$, which means 6×6, or 6 squared. The **square root** of a number is the number that, multiplied by itself, equals that number. The square root of 36 is 6: $\sqrt{36} = 6$.

Not all square roots of numbers are whole numbers like 6. Numbers that have a whole number as their square root are called **perfect squares**.

The expression of a square root is called a **radical**. The symbol $\sqrt{}$ is called a **radical sign**. When a number is not a perfect square, you can estimate its square root by determining which perfect squares it comes between.

$\sqrt{50}$ is a little more than 7, because $\sqrt{49}$ is exactly 7. $\sqrt{60}$ is between 7 and 8 but closer to 8, because 60 is closer to 64 than to 49.

Identify the square root of these perfect squares.

	a	b	c
1.	$\sqrt{16}$ = ______	$\sqrt{64}$ = ______	$\sqrt{25}$ = ______
2.	$\sqrt{100}$ = ______	$\sqrt{1}$ = ______	$\sqrt{9}$ = ______
3.	$\sqrt{36}$ = ______	$\sqrt{81}$ = ______	$\sqrt{4}$ = ______

Estimate the following square roots.

4. $\sqrt{85}$ is between ______ and ______ but closer to ______.

5. $\sqrt{20}$ is between ______ and ______ but closer to ______.

6. $\sqrt{35}$ is between ______ and ______ but closer to ______.

7. $\sqrt{70}$ is between ______ and ______ but closer to ______.

8. $\sqrt{45}$ is between ______ and ______ but closer to ______.

NAME ______________________

Lesson 2.2 Square Roots

Identify the square root of these perfect squares.

	a	b	c
1.	$\sqrt{64}$ = ________	$\sqrt{36}$ = ________	$\sqrt{49}$ = ________
2.	$\sqrt{100}$ = ________	$\sqrt{25}$ = ________	$\sqrt{1}$ = ________
3.	$\sqrt{9}$ = ________	$\sqrt{4}$ = ________	$\sqrt{169}$ = ________
4.	$\sqrt{121}$ = ________	$\sqrt{81}$ = ________	$\sqrt{400}$ = ________

Estimate the following square roots.

5. $\sqrt{78}$ is between ________ and ________ but closer to ________.

6. $\sqrt{108}$ is between ________ and ________ but closer to ________.

7. $\sqrt{90}$ is between ________ and ________ but closer to ________.

8. $\sqrt{175}$ is between ________ and ________ but closer to ________.

9. $\sqrt{3}$ is between ________ and ________ but closer to ________.

10. $\sqrt{52}$ is between ________ and ________ but closer to ________.

11. $\sqrt{132}$ is between ________ and ________ but closer to ________.

12. $\sqrt{80}$ is between ________ and ________ but closer to ________.

13. $\sqrt{125}$ is between ________ and ________ but closer to ________.

14. $\sqrt{28}$ is between ________ and ________ but closer to ________.

NAME ____________________

Lesson 2.3 Cube Roots

The **cube** of a number is that number multiplied by itself three times. A cube is expressed as n^3, which means $n \times n \times n$ or n cubed. The cube root of a number is the number that, multiplied by itself and by itself again, equals that number. The cube root of 27 is 3: $\sqrt[3]{27} = 3$.

The expression of a cube root is called a **radical**. The symbol $\sqrt[3]{}$ is called a **radical sign**. The *3* on the radical sign shows that this is a cube root.

Identify the cube root.

	a	b	c
1.	$\sqrt[3]{1{,}728}$ = ______	$\sqrt[3]{729}$ = ______	$\sqrt[3]{42{,}875}$ = ______
2.	$\sqrt[3]{3{,}375}$ = ______	$\sqrt[3]{512}$ = ______	$\sqrt[3]{15{,}625}$ = ______
3.	$\sqrt[3]{8{,}000}$ = ______	$\sqrt[3]{125}$ = ______	$\sqrt[3]{343}$ = ______
4.	$\sqrt[3]{8}$ = ______	$\sqrt[3]{64}$ = ______	$\sqrt[3]{1{,}000}$ = ______
5.	$\sqrt[3]{27}$ = ______	$\sqrt[3]{216}$ = ______	$\sqrt[3]{64{,}000}$ = ______
6.	$\sqrt[3]{125{,}000}$ = ______	$\sqrt[3]{343{,}000}$ = ______	$\sqrt[3]{216{,}000}$ = ______
7.	$\sqrt[3]{1}$ = ______	$\sqrt[3]{1{,}000{,}000}$ = ______	$\sqrt[3]{27{,}000}$ = ______
8.	$\sqrt[3]{512{,}000}$ = ______	$\sqrt[3]{729{,}000}$ = ______	$\sqrt[3]{8{,}000{,}000}$ = ______

NAME ____________________

Lesson 2.3 Cube Roots

Cube roots can be estimated by finding cube roots on either side of the desired root. $\sqrt[3]{130}$ is between 5 and 6 because $\sqrt[3]{125}$ is 5 and $\sqrt[3]{216}$ is 6. Therefore, $\sqrt[3]{130}$ is between 5 and 6, but closer to 5 because 130 is closer to 125 than it is to 216.

Fractions can also have cube roots. For example, $\sqrt[3]{\frac{1}{8}} = \frac{1}{2}$ because $\frac{1}{2} \times \frac{1}{2} \times \frac{1}{2} = \frac{1}{8}$.

Find the cube root of each number.

	a	b	c
1.	$\sqrt[3]{\frac{1}{64}} =$ ______	$\sqrt[3]{\frac{8}{27}} =$ ______	$\sqrt[3]{512} =$ ______
2.	$\sqrt[3]{0} =$ ______	$\sqrt[3]{\frac{64}{125}} =$ ______	$\sqrt[3]{1} =$ ______
3.	$\sqrt[3]{\frac{8}{216}} =$ ______	$\sqrt[3]{\frac{125}{343}} =$ ______	$\sqrt[3]{64} =$ ______

Estimate the following cube roots.

4. $\sqrt[3]{10}$ is between ______ and ______ but closer to ______.

5. $\sqrt[3]{110}$ is between ______ and ______ but closer to ______.

6. $\sqrt[3]{500}$ is between ______ and ______ but closer to ______.

7. $\sqrt[3]{155}$ is between ______ and ______ but closer to ______.

8. $\sqrt[3]{1,322}$ is between ______ and ______ but closer to ______.

NAME ______________________

Lesson 2.4 Using Roots to Solve Equations

Equations with exponential variables can be solved using the inverse operation. In this case, using roots will help to solve the problem.

$x^2 = 121$	**Step 1:** Evaluate the problem to find out which root to use. In this case, the exponent is 2, so you would use the square root as the inverse operation.
$\sqrt{x^2} = \sqrt{121}$	**Step 2:** Find the root of both sides of the equation.
$x = 11$	**Step 3:** Solve the problem.

Solve each problem by using roots. Show your work and write fractions in simplest form.

	a	b	c
1.	$x^2 = \frac{16}{169}$	$729 = x^3$	$x^2 = \frac{8}{125}$
	$x =$ ______	$x =$ ______	$x =$ ______
2.	$25 = x^2$	$x^2 = \frac{25}{64}$	$x^3 = 512$
	$x =$ ______	$x =$ ______	$x =$ ______
3.	$\frac{9}{36} = x^2$	$x^3 = 512$	$x^2 + 2 = 38$
	$x =$ ______	$x =$ ______	$x =$ ______
4.	$68 - 4 = x^3$	$x^2 - 5 = 44$	$x^3 + 4 = 5$
	$x =$ ______	$x =$ ______	$x =$ ______

NAME ______________________

Lesson 2.4 Using Roots to Solve Equations

Equations with exponential variables can be solved using the inverse operation. In this case, using exponents will help to solve the problem.

$\sqrt{x} = 6$ **Step 1:** Evaluate the problem to decide which exponent to use. In this case, since we are solving for the square root, the appropriate exponent to use will be 2 (or square).

$(\sqrt{x})^2 = 6^2$ **Step 2:** Square both sides of the equation.

$x = 36$ **Step 3:** Solve the problem.

Solve each problem by using roots. Show your work and write fractions in simplest form.

	a	b	c
1.	$\sqrt{x} = 25$	$5 = \sqrt{x}$	$\sqrt[3]{x} = 6$
	$x =$ ______	$x =$ ______	$x =$ ______
2.	$\sqrt{x - 4} = 4$	$\sqrt[3]{x} = 19$	$7 = \sqrt{x}$
	$x =$ ______	$x =$ ______	$x =$ ______
3.	$\sqrt[3]{78 - x} = 4$	$18 = \sqrt{x}$	$6 = \sqrt{42 - x}$
	$x =$ ______	$x =$ ______	$x =$ ______
4.	$8 = \sqrt[3]{x - 6}$	$\sqrt{x} = 14$	$7 = \sqrt[3]{x}$
	$x =$ ______	$x =$ ______	$x =$ ______

NAME ____________________

Lesson 2.5 Comparing Rational and Irrational Numbers

Compare rational and irrational numbers by using a best guess for irrational numbers.

$\sqrt{3} < 2$ This statement is true because $\sqrt{3}$ is between 1 and 2.

$5 > \sqrt{20}$ This statement is true because $\sqrt{20}$ is between 4 and 5.

Compare using <, >, or =.

	a	b	c
1.	$\sqrt{9}$ ______ π	4.5 ______ $\sqrt{25}$	3.9 ______ $\sqrt{10}$
2.	$\sqrt{2}$ ______ 1	$\sqrt[3]{\frac{8}{27}}$ ______ $\frac{2}{3}$	1.1 ______ $\sqrt{2}$
3.	$0.\overline{66}$ ______ $\frac{2}{3}$	$\sqrt{8}$ ______ 3	1 ______ $\sqrt{\frac{16}{25}}$
4.	$\sqrt{36}$ ______ 6.5	1 ______ $0.\overline{45}$	$\frac{3}{5}$ ______ $\sqrt{\frac{9}{5}}$
5.	$\sqrt[3]{343}$ ______ 7.2	$0.\overline{77}$ ______ $\frac{7}{9}$	7 ______ $\sqrt{52}$
6.	$\sqrt{5}$ ______ 4	$\frac{3}{4}$ ______ $0.\overline{75}$	$\sqrt[3]{32}$ ______ 3.5
7.	$\frac{5}{10}$ ______ $\sqrt{1}$	$\sqrt[3]{6}$ ______ 2	1.4 ______ $\sqrt{2}$
8.	$\sqrt[3]{\frac{27}{125}}$ ______ 0.6	$\frac{1}{2}$ ______ 0.55	$\sqrt[3]{18}$ ______ 2.5

NAME ______________________

Lesson 2.6 Approximating Irrational Numbers

Approximate the value of an irrational number by exploring values.

The value of $\sqrt{2}$ is something between 1 and 2.

Look at the squares of 1.4 and 1.5.

$1.4^2 = 1.96$

$1.5^2 = 2.25$

By looking at these squares, it is evident that $\sqrt{2}$ is between 1.4 and 1.5.

Approximate the value of each root to the tenths place.

1. The value of $\sqrt{7}$ is between ______ and ______.

2. The value of $\sqrt{10}$ is between ______ and ______.

3. The value of $\sqrt{26}$ is between ______ and ______.

4. The value of $\sqrt[3]{25}$ is between ______ and ______.

5. The value of $\sqrt[3]{99}$ is between ______ and ______.

6. The value of $\sqrt[3]{514}$ is between ______ and ______.

7. The value of $\sqrt{78}$ is between ______ and ______.

8. The value of $\sqrt[3]{824}$ is between ______ and ______.

NAME ______________________

Lesson 2.6 Approximating Irrational Numbers

You can approximate the value of an irrational number to the hundredths place as well.

The value of $\sqrt{3}$ is something between 1 and 2.

Look at the squares of 1.7 and 1.8.

$1.7^2 = 2.89$

$1.8^2 = 3.24$

By looking at these squares, it is evident that $\sqrt{3}$ is between 1.7 and 1.8.

Now, narrow explore to the hundredths place.

$1.73^2 = 2.99$

$1.74^2 = 3.03$

By looking at these squares, it is evident that $\sqrt{3}$ is between 1.73 and 1.74.

Approximate each value to the hundredths place.

1. The value of $\sqrt{8}$ is between ______ and ______.

2. The value of $\sqrt{11}$ is between ______ and ______.

3. The value of $\sqrt{90}$ is between ______ and ______.

4. The value of $\sqrt[3]{72}$ is between ______ and ______.

5. The value of $\sqrt[3]{81}$ is between ______ and ______.

6. The value of $\sqrt{27}$ is between ______ and ______.

7. The value of $\sqrt[3]{33}$ is between ______ and ______.

8. The value of $\sqrt{23}$ is between ______ and ______.

NAME ____________________

Lesson 2.7 Comparing and Ordering Irrational Numbers

Rational and irrational numbers can be compared by approximating their value and placing them along a number line.

Place these numbers on a number line: $\sqrt{5}$, 2.5, $\sqrt{3}$

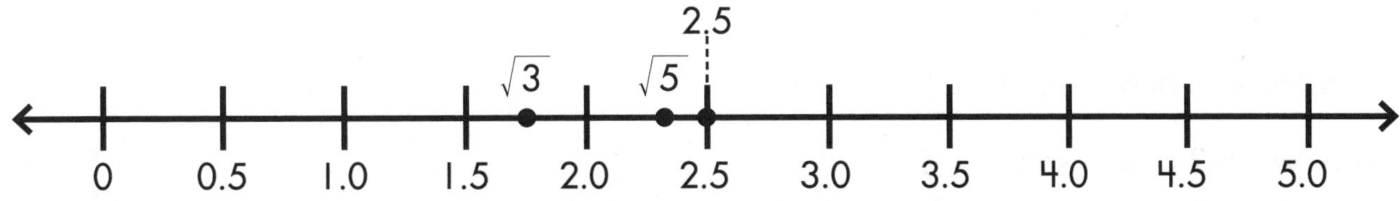

Put the values below in order from least to greatest along a number line.

1. π^2, 10, $\sqrt{75}$

2. $\sqrt{7}$, $\frac{\sqrt{7}}{2}$, 2

3. $\sqrt{10}$, 3.5, 2^2

4. 4, $\sqrt{15}$, 5.2

5. $\frac{1}{3}$, $\sqrt{1}$, 0.45

6. $\sqrt{72}$, 9, 8^2

NAME ___________________________

Lesson 2.7 Comparing and Ordering Irrational Numbers

Expressions and equations containing irrational numbers can be approximated by testing values.

Compare using <, >, or =.

$\sqrt{3} + 5$ ________ $3 + \sqrt{5}$

$\sqrt{3}$ is between 1 and 2, so use 1.5.

$\sqrt{5}$ is between 2 and 3, so use 2.5.

$(1.5) + 5$ ________ $3 + (2.5)$

$4.5 < 5.5$

Approximate the value of each expression and then compare using <, >, or =.

	a	b
1.	$\sqrt{10} + 2$ ________ $10 + \sqrt{2}$	$4 + \sqrt{2}$ ________ $\sqrt{4} + 2$
	Approximation: ____________	Approximation: ____________
2.	$12 + \sqrt{6}$ ________ $\sqrt{12} + 6$	$\sqrt[3]{8} + 6$ ________ $8 + \sqrt[3]{6}$
	Approximation: ____________	Approximation: ____________
3.	$15 + \sqrt{12}$ ________ $\sqrt{15} + 12$	$\sqrt{7} + 3$ ________ $7 + \sqrt{3}$
	Approximation: ____________	Approximation: ____________
4.	$4 + \sqrt[3]{7}$ ________ $\sqrt[3]{4} + 7$	$\sqrt{3} + 5$ ________ $3 + \sqrt{5}$
	Approximation: ____________	Approximation: ____________

NAME ________________

Check What You Learned

Rational and Irrational Number Relationships

Evaluate each expression.

	a	b	c
1.	$\sqrt{36}$ = ________	$\sqrt{16}$ = ________	$\sqrt{121}$ = ________
2.	$\sqrt{\frac{9}{36}}$ = ________	$\sqrt{144}$ = ________	$\sqrt{\frac{100}{121}}$ = ________
3.	$\sqrt[3]{512}$ = ________	$\sqrt[3]{1{,}000}$ = ________	$\sqrt[3]{125}$ = ________
4.	$\sqrt[3]{216}$ = ________	$\sqrt[3]{\frac{64}{512}}$ = ________	$\sqrt[3]{\frac{8}{729}}$ = ________

Approximate the value of each expression to the tenths place.

5. The value of $\sqrt{12}$ is between ______ and ______.

6. The value of $\sqrt[3]{76}$ is between ______ and ______.

7. The value of $\sqrt{46}$ is between ______ and ______.

8. The value of $\sqrt[3]{21}$ is between ______ and ______.

9. The value of $\sqrt[3]{7}$ is between ______ and ______.

10. The value of $\sqrt{30}$ is between ______ and ______.

Use roots or exponents to solve each equation. Write fractions in simplest form.

	a	b	c
11.	$\sqrt{x} = 7$	$x^3 = 512$	$x^2 = 81$
	x = ________	x = ________	x = ________
12.	$x^2 = 144$	$\sqrt[3]{x} = 4$	$\sqrt[3]{x} = 9$
	x = ________	x = ________	x = ________

NAME ______________________

Check What You Learned

Rational and Irrational Number Relationships

Compare using <, >, or =.

	a	b	c
13.	$\sqrt{\frac{9}{10}}$ ______ $\frac{3}{4}$	$\sqrt{12}$ ______ 3	$\sqrt[3]{27}$ ______ 3
14.	2.1 ______ $\sqrt{4}$	$\sqrt[3]{76}$ ______ 5.5	$\sqrt[3]{48}$ ______ 4
15.	$0.\overline{66}$ ______ $\sqrt[3]{\frac{8}{27}}$	$\frac{6}{7}$ ______ $\sqrt{3}$	$\sqrt{7}$ ______ 3

Put the values below in order from least to greatest along a number line.

16. 2π, $\sqrt{38}$, $\sqrt{52}$

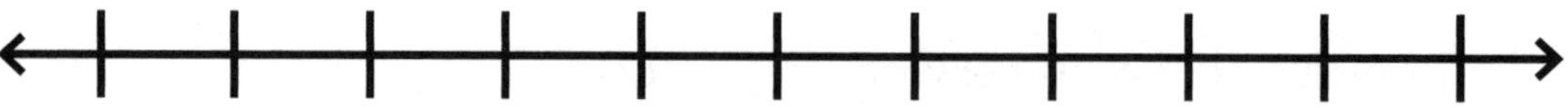

17. 2.75, $\sqrt{18}$, $\sqrt[3]{27}$

18. $\sqrt{3}$, 1.4, $\frac{3}{2}$

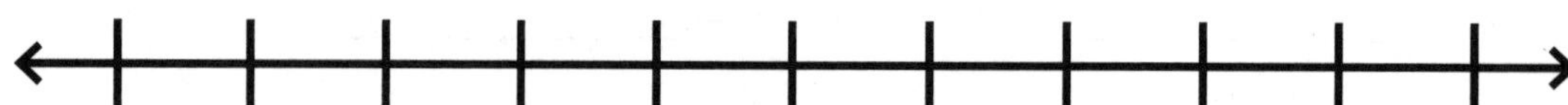

NAME ____________________

Check What You Know

Linear Equations

Find the rate of change, or slope, for the situation.

1. A cell-phone company charges per minute for each call.

Time (minutes)	10	15	20	25
Cost ($)	1.00	1.50	2.00	2.50

The rate of change, or slope, for this situation is __________.

Find the value of the variable in each equation.

	a	b	c
2.	$a + 13 = 27$ ________	$2n - 2 = 10$ ________	$\frac{x}{4} + 4 = 12$ ________
3.	$18 - 2p = 10$ ________	$\frac{n}{24} = 3$ ________	$n - 33 = 19$ ________
4.	$f + 22 = 45$ ________	$\frac{r}{16} + 3 = 6$ ________	$s \times 4 + 2 = 46$ ________

Use the slope-intercept form of equations to draw lines on the grids below.

5.

a $y = 3x + 2$

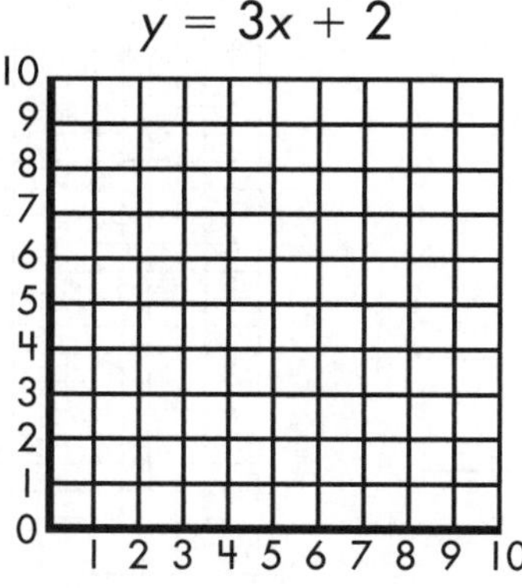

b $y = -2x + 8$

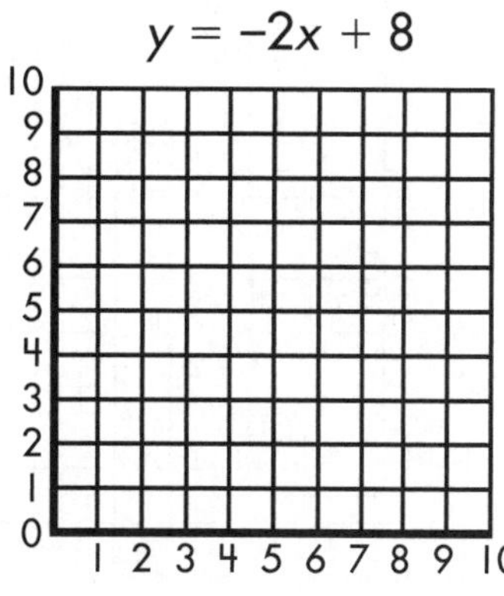

Complete the table. Then, graph the equation.

6. $y = 2x - 3$

x	y

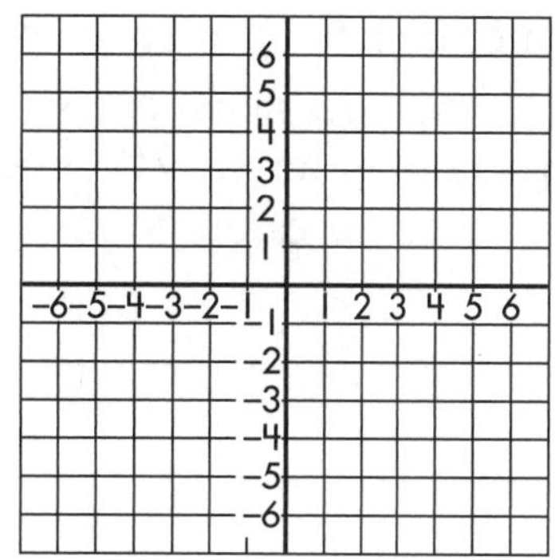

NAME ______________________________

CHAPTER 3 PRETEST

Check What You Know

Linear Equations

Solve each system of equations.

	a	b
7.	$-4x - 15y = -17$	$-x - 7y = 14$
	$-x + 5y = -13$	$-4x - 14y = 28$
	$x =$ ______, $y =$ ______	$x =$ ______, $y =$ ______
8.	$y = -1\frac{1}{8} - \frac{7}{8}x$	$y = \frac{1}{3}x + 2$
	$-4x + 9y = -22$	$5x + 4y = -30$
	$x =$ ______, $y =$ ______	$x =$ ______, $y =$ ______

Use slope-intercept form to graph each system of equations and solve the system.

a

9. $y = 2x + 3$

$y = 3$

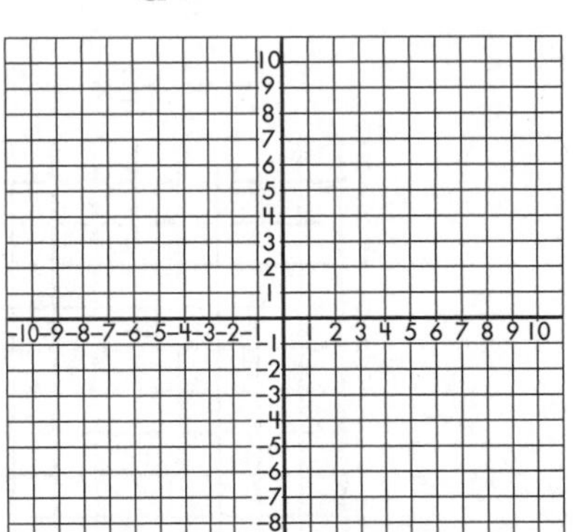

x: ______;

y: ______

b

$y = -\frac{1}{2}x + 4$

$y = x - 2$

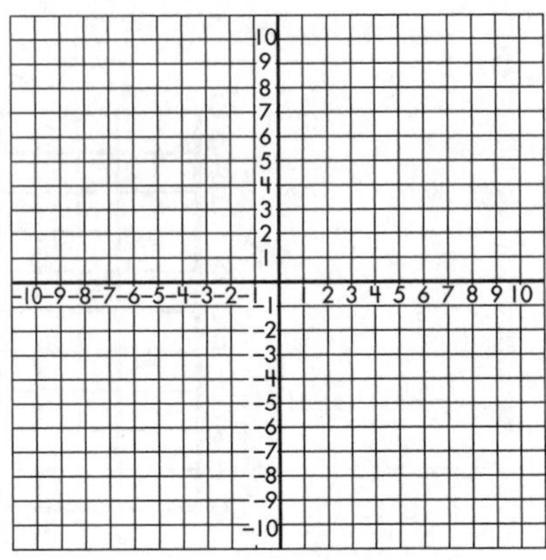

x: ______;

y: ______

Set up a system of equations to solve the word problem.

10. At Billy's school, 80 students come to school by bicycle or by car. Together, the vehicles they arrive to school in have 270 wheels. How many of each are used? Use b to represent the number of bicycles and c to represent the number of cars.

Equation 1: ______________________________

Equation 2: ______________________________ $b =$ ______; $c =$ ______

NAME ______________________

Lesson 3.1 Understanding Slope

The **slope** of a line on a coordinate grid can be found by determining the **rate of change**.

Michael keeps track of the number of yards he mows for 5 days.

	Day 1	Day 2	Day 3	Day 4	Day 5
Number of Lawns	1	3	6	8	13
Amount Earned ($)	20	60	120	160	260

Find the slope, or rate of change, by dividing the rate of change for the dependent variable (amount earned) by the rate of change for the independent variable (number of lawns).

$\frac{\text{change in money earned}}{\text{change in \# of lawns}} = \frac{60 - 20}{3 - 1} = \frac{40}{2} = 20$ $\frac{\text{change in money earned}}{\text{change in \# of lawns}} = \frac{260 - 160}{13 - 8} = \frac{100}{5} = 20$

The rate of change, or slope, in this situation is 20 and is **constant**.

Find the slope, or rate of change for each situation. Be sure to show your work.

1. Students are buying tickets for the fall dance. The student council keeps track of how many tickets they sell in one week.

	Monday	Tuesday	Wednesday	Thursday	Friday
Number of Tickets Sold	10	15	23	28	32
Amount Earned ($)	50	75	115	140	160

The rate of change, or slope, for this situation is ____________.

2. Jean planted a sunflower. She decided to measure how much it grew each week.

Time (weeks)	1	2	3	4
Height (cm)	16.2	20.4	24.6	28.8

The rate of change, or slope, for this situation is ____________.

NAME ______________________________

Lesson 3.1 Understanding Slope

Sometimes a rate of change is **variable**, or changes as data is collected.

Samantha kicks a ball and records a video of the ball's path so she can observe its path.

Time (s)	0	1	2	3	4
Height (m)	0	5.5	9.1	6	2

Find the slope, or rate of change, by dividing the rate of change for the dependent variable (time) by the rate of change for the independent variable (height).

$\frac{\text{change in time}}{\text{change in height}} = \frac{2 - 1}{9.1 - 5.5} = \frac{1}{3.6}$ $\frac{\text{change in time}}{\text{change in height}} = \frac{4 - 3}{6 - 2} = -\frac{1}{4}$

The rate of change, or slope, in this situation is **variable** because it changes from one data collection point to another.

Determine if each slope, or rate of change, is *constant* or *variable*. Show your work.

1. Eric walks to his friend's house.

Time (minutes)	5	10	15	20
Distance Traveled (miles)	0.25	0.5	0.75	1

The rate of change for this situation is ____________.

2. Cindy went for a bike ride through town.

Time (minutes)	5	10	15	20
Distance Traveled (miles)	1.0	1.5	2.3	2.5

The rate of change for this situation is ____________.

NAME ______________________

Lesson 3.1 Understanding Slope

Determine if each slope, or rate of change, is *constant* or *variable*. Show your work.

1. Johnson is ordering t-shirts for his school. The more he orders, the lower the cost per shirt is.

Number of T-Shirts	100	200	300	400	500
Total Cost ($)	500	900	1200	1400	1500

The rate of change for this situation is ____________.

2. Bike rental costs $10 per hour.

Time (hours)	1	2	3	4	5
Cost ($)	10	20	30	40	50

The rate of change for this situation is ____________.

3. Miles a plane traveled while flying.

Time (minutes)	20	40	60	80	100
Distance (miles)	180	360	540	720	900

The rate of change for this situation is ____________.

NAME ______________________

Lesson 3.2 Graphing Linear Equations Using Slope

If the **slope** of a line and the place it **intercepts** (or crosses) the *y*-axis are known, a line can be graphed using an equation with *x* and *y* variables.

Graph $y = -2x + 5$.

slope (points to $-2x$) **intercept** (points to 5)

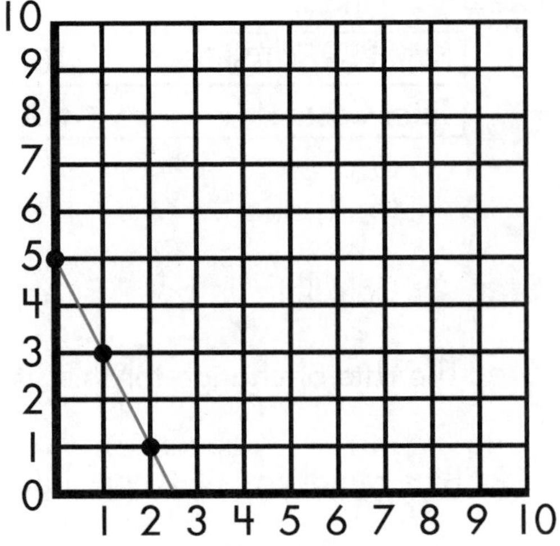

Step 1: Find the point where the line crosses the y-axis. (0, 5)

Step 2: Find the slope: -2.
In fraction form, the slope is $\frac{-2}{1}$.

Step 3: Starting at the intercept, mark the slope by using the numerator to count along the *y*-axis, and the denominator to count along the *x*-axis: Move down 2, and to the right 1.

Step 4: Draw a line to connect the points.

Use the slope-intercept form of equations to draw lines on the grids below.

	a	b
1.	$y = \frac{1}{4}x + 1$	$y = -x + 2$
2.	$y = \frac{4}{3}x + 4$	$y = 2x + 3$

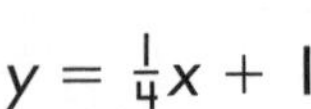

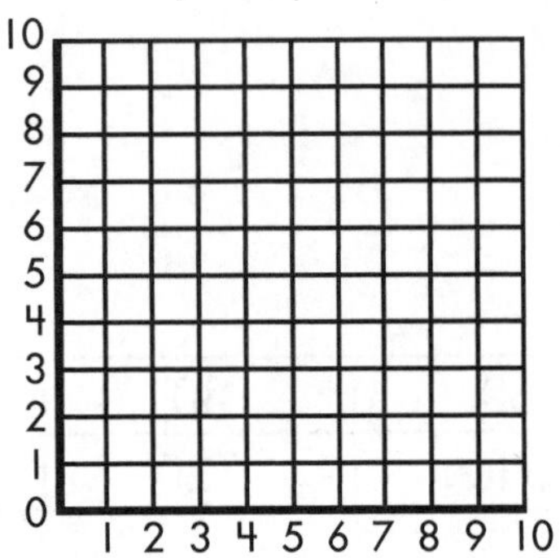

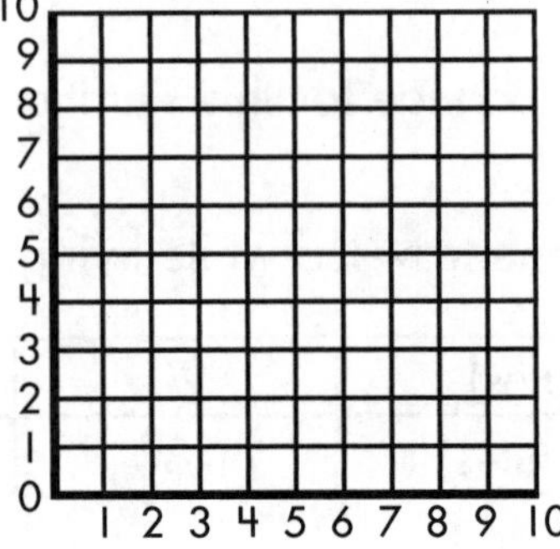

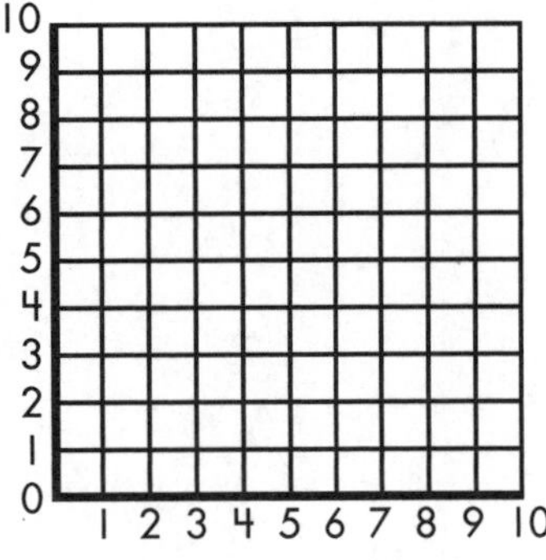

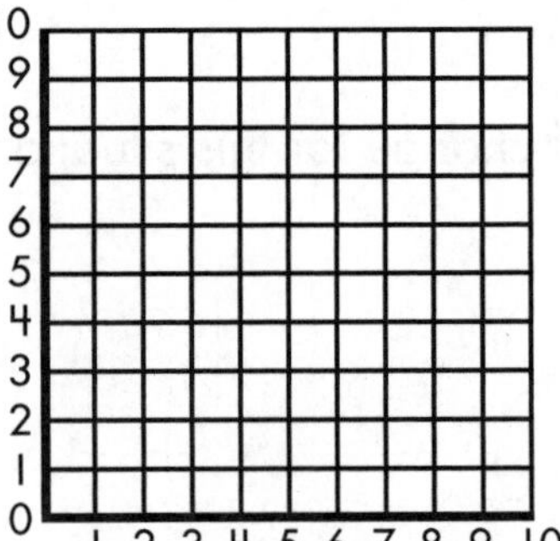

NAME ___________________________

Lesson 3.2 Graphing Linear Equations Using Slope

When a linear equation is graphed, the equation that was used to create the line can be found by using the slope-intercept equation.

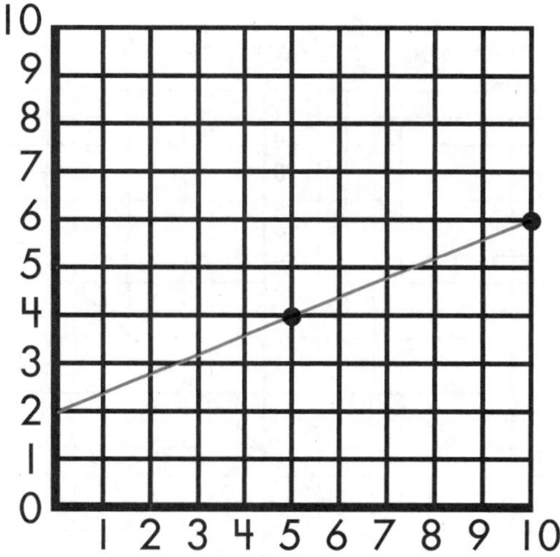

Step 1: Find the point where the line crosses the y-axis. (0, 2)

Step 2: Mark points on the line where it crosses at exact locations that correspond to an ordered pair. (5, 4) and (10, 6)

Step 3: Calculate the slope using $\frac{\text{change in } y}{\text{change in } x}$. $\frac{4-2}{5-0} = \frac{2}{5}$

Step 4: Use $y = slope{\cdot}x + intercept$ to create the equation for the line in slope-intercept form.

$y = \frac{2}{5}x + 2$

Use the pictures below to create equations for the lines in slope-intercept form.

a **b**

1.

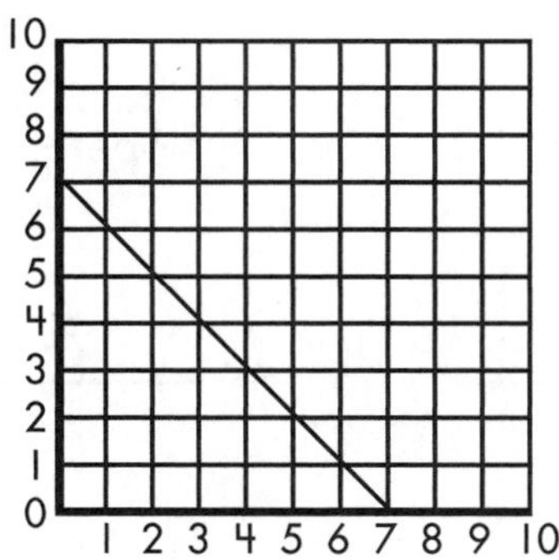

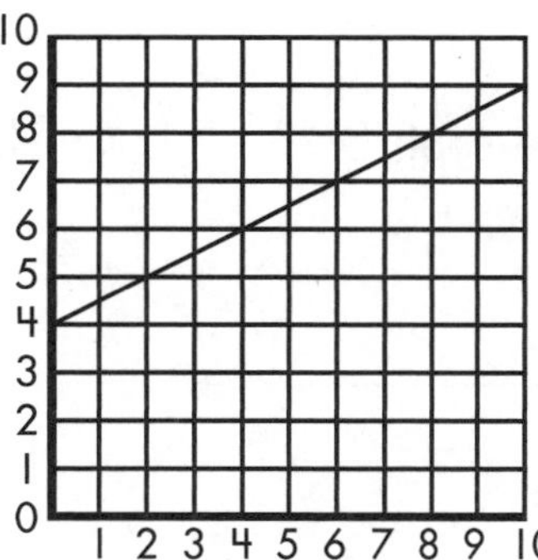

2.

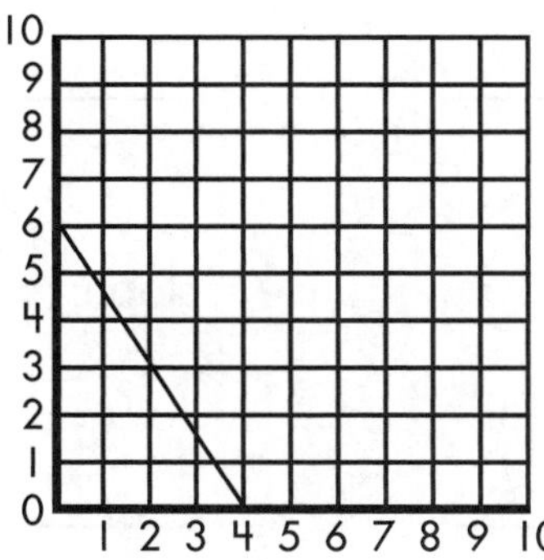

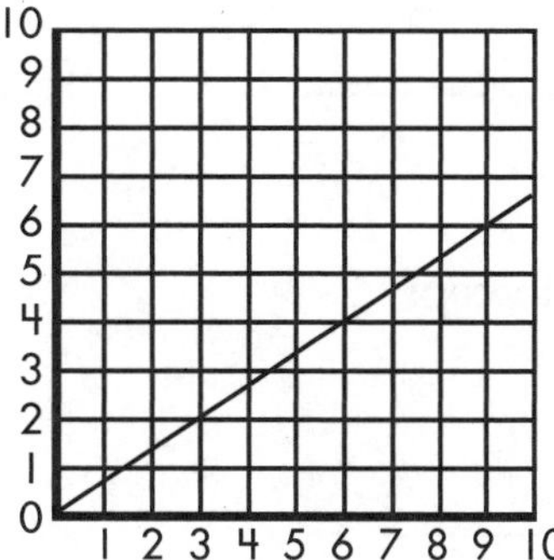

NAME ______________________________

Lesson 3.2 Graphing Linear Equations Using Slope

When given the slope and intercept of any straight line, a linear equation can be created using the slope-intercept form.

Slope: $\frac{5}{6}$; Intercept: -2

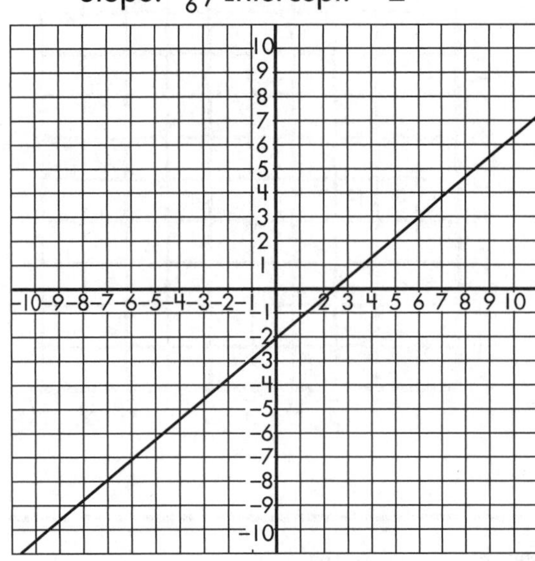

Step 1: Use the equation $y = mx + b$, where m equals slope and b is the y-intercept.

Step 2: Substitute the known quantities for the slope and the y-intercept.

$y = \frac{5}{6}x - 2$

Use slope-intercept form to write equations given the conditions below.

	a	b	c
1.	slope: $\frac{4}{3}$; intercept: 3	slope: -2; intercept: 4	slope: $-\frac{1}{2}$; intercept: 7
	______________	______________	______________
2.	slope: 3; intercept: -5	slope: $\frac{2}{5}$; intercept: 0	slope: $-\frac{3}{4}$; intercept: -2
	______________	______________	______________
3.	slope: -4; intercept: 6	slope: $\frac{5}{2}$; intercept: -3	slope: $\frac{1}{2}$; intercept: 1
	______________	______________	______________

NAME ______________________

Lesson 3.3 Solving 1-Variable Equations

The **Addition and Subtraction Properties of Equality** state that when the same number is added to both sides of an equation, the two sides remain equal:

$$4 + 17 = 21 \quad 4 + 17 + 5 = 21 + 5 \quad (26 = 26)$$

When the same number is subtracted from both sides of an equation, the two sides remain equal:

$$32 = 16 + 16 \quad 32 - 4 = 16 + 16 - 4 \quad (28 = 28)$$

Use these properties to determine the value of variables:

$x + 17 = 23$	$40 - n = 19$	$y - 14 = 3$
$x + 17 - 17 = 23 - 17$	$40 - n - 40 = 19 - 40$	$y - 14 + 14 = 3 + 14$
$x + 0 = 6 \quad x = 6$	$0 - n = -29 \quad n = 29$	$y + 0 = 17 \quad y = 17$

Find the value of the variable in each equation.

	a	b	c
1.	$a + 12 = 25$ ______	$48 + d = 60$ ______	$y - 19 = 18$ ______
2.	$31 - x = 16$ ______	$11 + n = 25$ ______	$m - 21 = 34$ ______
3.	$28 + b = 50$ ______	$p - 16 = 32$ ______	$t + 22 = 57$ ______
4.	$33 + c = 54$ ______	$e + 19 = 37$ ______	$16 + r = 40$ ______
5.	$52 - n = 24$ ______	$y - 15 = 18$ ______	$21 + n = 49$ ______
6.	$m - 5 = 18$ ______	$36 + s = 45$ ______	$21 - a = 7$ ______
7.	$17 + d = 29$ ______	$x - 23 = 9$ ______	$27 + f = 35$ ______
8.	$r - 15 = 24$ ______	$27 - p = 3$ ______	$34 - x = 18$ ______
9.	$y + 12 = 20$ ______	$n - 24 = 31$ ______	$16 + p = 38$ ______
10.	$18 + q = 25$ ______	$m + 17 = 32$ ______	$e + 29 = 36$ ______
11.	$39 - r = 34$ ______	$42 + x = 56$ ______	$q - 21 = 35$ ______
12.	$18 + p = 22$ ______	$s - 32 = 9$ ______	$43 + n = 49$ ______

NAME ______________________________

Lesson 3.3 Solving 1-Variable Equations

The **Multiplication and Division Properties of Equality** state that when each side of the equation is multiplied by the same number, the two sides remain equal:

$$3 + 4 = 7 \quad (3 + 4) \times 5 = 7 \times 5 \quad (35 = 35)$$

When each side of the equation is divided by the same number, the two sides remain equal:

$$2 \times 6 = 12 \quad \frac{(2 \times 6)}{3} = \frac{12}{3} \quad (4 = 4)$$

Use these properties to determine the value of variables:

$n \div 5 = 4$	$3n = 18$	$\frac{60}{n} = 4$
$n \div 5 \times 5 = 4 \times 5$	$\frac{3n}{3} = \frac{18}{3}$	$\frac{60n}{n} = 4n$ or $60 = 4n$
$n = 20$	$n = 6$	$\frac{60}{4} = \frac{4n}{4}$ $15 = n$

Find the value of the variable in each equation.

	a	b	c
1.	$5b = 35$ ______	$\frac{a}{4} = 16$ ______	$f \times 12 = 72$ ______
2.	$x \div 4 = 7$ ______	$3k = 33$ ______	$\frac{42}{b} = 7$ ______
3.	$9 \times n = 72$ ______	$44 \div m = 22$ ______	$12a = 60$ ______
4.	$\frac{n}{20} = 4$ ______	$a \times 12 = 60$ ______	$6p = 90$ ______
5.	$x \div 7 = 11$ ______	$t \div 25 = 8$ ______	$\frac{x}{15} = 6$ ______
6.	$b \times 16 = 64$ ______	$11d = 132$ ______	$\frac{65}{m} = 5$ ______
7.	$\frac{n}{14} = 3$ ______	$f \times 9 = 99$ ______	$4n = 60$ ______
8.	$e \times 5 = 120$ ______	$\frac{120}{m} = 10$ ______	$b \div 9 = 7$ ______
9.	$8t = 104$ ______	$\frac{b}{9} = 6$ ______	$m \times 18 = 54$ ______
10.	$\frac{a}{6} = 12$ ______	$7m = 84$ ______	$a \div 4 = 18$ ______

NAME ___________________________

Lesson 3.3 Solving 1-Variable Equations

One-variable equations can be solved by isolating the variable on one side of the equation by performing inverse operations.

Addition	Subtraction	Multiplication	Division
$t + 4 = 16$ $t + 4 - 4 = 16 - 4$ $t = 12$	$28 - r = 15$ $28 - r - 28 = 15 - 28$ $-r = -13 \quad r = 13$	$5n = 65$ $5n \div 5 = 65 \div 5$ $n = 13$	$72 \div r = 9$ $72 \div r \times r = 9 \times r$ $72 = 9r$ $72 \div 9 = 9r \div 9$ $r = 8$

Find the value of the variable in each equation.

	a	b	c
1.	$r \times 13 = 13$ ________	$w + 18 = 22$ ________	$17 \times v = 153$ ________
2.	$f \div 12 = 7$ ________	$y \div 8 = 17$ ________	$24 - q = 13$ ________
3.	$d \times 7 = 35$ ________	$t \div 11 = 18$ ________	$v + 19 = 36$ ________
4.	$q + 8 = 16$ ________	$66 \div w = 11$ ________	$y \div 9 = 8$ ________
5.	$v - 8 = 9$ ________	$17 + d = 29$ ________	$4 + s = 20$ ________
6.	$300 \div d = 20$ ________	$15u = 135$ ________	$\frac{x}{5} = 12$ ________
7.	$q \times 3 = 27$ ________	$28 \div r = 4$ ________	$11x = 77$ ________
8.	$w \div 4 = 13$ ________	$x - 16 = 20$ ________	$20 - d = 13$ ________
9.	$29 - y = 19$ ________	$d \times 15 = 75$ ________	$27 \div t = 9$ ________
10.	$y \div 18 = 11$ ________	$w \times 20 = 20$ ________	$w + 14 = 22$ ________
11.	$j \div 20 = 3$ ________	$12c = 156$ ________	$n + 16 = 31$ ________
12.	$\frac{225}{r} = 15$ ________	$12 - q = 8$ ________	$x - 19 = 1$ ________

NAME ____________________

Lesson 3.4 Solving Complex 1-Variable Equations

Some problems with variables require more than one step to solve. Use the properties of equality to undo each step and find the value of the variable.

$2n - 7 = 19$

First, undo the subtraction by adding.

$2n - 7 + 7 = 19 + 7 \quad 2n = 26$

Then, undo the multiplication by dividing.

$n = 13$

$\frac{n}{3} + 5 = 11$

First, undo the addition by subtracting.

$\frac{n}{3} + 5 - 5 = 11 - 5 \quad \frac{n}{3} = 6$

Then, undo the division by multiplying.

$\frac{n}{3} \times 3 = 6 \times 3 \quad n = 18$

Find the value of the variable in each equation.

	a	b	c
1.	$2n + 2 = 16$ ______	$\frac{a}{3} - 1 = 4$ ______	$\frac{b}{4} + 2 = 11$ ______
2.	$11p - 5 = 28$ ______	$8b + 12 = 52$ ______	$\frac{r}{20} - 3 = 3$ ______
3.	$\frac{m}{16} + 7 = 10$ ______	$6n + 4 = 64$ ______	$4s - 5 = 39$ ______
4.	$\frac{a}{9} - 3 = 6$ ______	$5d + 6 = 71$ ______	$\frac{m}{8} + 5 = 14$ ______
5.	$9a - 11 = 61$ ______	$\frac{e}{12} - 7 = 3$ ______	$\frac{i}{4} + 5 = 73$ ______
6.	$3p + 12 = 54$ ______	$\frac{n}{3} + 12 = 27$ ______	$5b - 7 = 93$ ______
7.	$\frac{s}{15} + 1 = 5$ ______	$6x + 25 = 73$ ______	$\frac{a}{3} - 3 = 11$ ______
8.	$3r - 11 = 43$ ______	$\frac{x}{7} + 14 = 22$ ______	$5m + 13 = 68$ ______
9.	$\frac{n}{5} - 5 = 8$ ______	$\frac{a}{6} + 4 = 20$ ______	$3p - 15 = 48$ ______

NAME ____________________

Lesson 3.4 Solving Complex 1-Variable Equations

Find the value of the variable in each equation.

	a	b	c
1.	$\frac{a}{10} + 4 = 5$ ______	$\frac{c}{2} + 5 = 3$ ______	$3e - 2 = -29$ ______
2.	$1 - g = -5$ ______	$\frac{h - 10}{2} = -7$ ______	$\frac{j - 5}{2} = 5$ ______
3.	$-9 + \frac{f}{4} = -7$ ______	$\frac{9 + n}{3} = 2$ ______	$\frac{-5 + p}{22} = -1$ ______
4.	$4q - 9 = -9$ ______	$\frac{s + 9}{2} = 3$ ______	$\frac{-12 + u}{11} = -3$ ______
5.	$\frac{-4 + w}{2} = 6$ ______	$-5 + \frac{y}{3} = 0$ ______	$\frac{b}{4} + 8 = 7$ ______
6.	$9 + \frac{d}{4} = 15$ ______	$6 + \frac{f}{2} = 15$ ______	$\frac{h + 11}{3} = -2$ ______
7.	$\frac{j - 10}{3} = -4$ ______	$-12k + 4 = 100$ ______	$\frac{m}{16} - 9 = -8$ ______
8.	$-7 + 4o = -15$ ______	$\frac{q - 13}{2} = -8$ ______	$-5r + 13 = -17$ ______
9.	$\frac{t + 10}{-2} = 5$ ______	$\frac{v + 8}{-2} = 10$ ______	$-14x - 19 = 303$ ______
10.	$6z - 3 = 39$ ______	$\frac{45}{w} - 3 = 6$ ______	$9d + 4 = 31$ ______
11.	$3y + 9 = 5$ ______	$12n - 2 = 4$ ______	$v + \frac{8}{9} = 10$ ______
12.	$10 - 7y = 3$ ______	$3 - \frac{q}{5} = 4$ ______	$\frac{m}{12} = -7$ ______
13.	$5g - 2 = 10$ ______	$28 - \frac{d}{70} = 56$ ______	$\frac{r}{93} = 84$ ______
14.	$4v + 37 = 44$ ______	$6u - 40 = 54$ ______	$\frac{6b}{14} = 24$ ______
15.	$\frac{a}{46} = 88$ ______	$83 - \frac{a}{27} = 37$ ______	$5z + 80 = 45$ ______
16.	$58 - \frac{d}{90} = 93$ ______	$30 - \frac{r}{95} = 3$ ______	$\frac{4u}{32} = 13$ ______

NAME ______________________

Lesson 3.4 Solving Complex 1-Variable Equations

Sometimes like terms in equations have to be combined in order to solve the problem. When terms have the same variable raised to the same exponent, they can be added or subtracted. Other times, you can use the Distributive Property to combine terms.

Adding or Subtracting Like Terms	Using the Distributive Property to Combine Terms
$2x + 3x = 75$	$2(x + 3) = 46$
$5x = 75$	$2x + 6 = 46$
$5x \div 5 = 75 \div 5$	$2x + 6 - 6 = 46 - 6$
$x = 15$	$2x \div 2 = 40 \div 2$
	$x = 20$

Find the value of the variable in each equation by combining like terms.

	a	b
1.	$3x + 4 + 2x + 5 = 34$ ________	$2(x + 1) + 4 = 12$ ________
2.	$\frac{1}{2}(x + 8) - 15 = -3$ ________	$2x - 5 + 3x + 8 = 18$ ________
3.	$-185 = -3r - 4(-5r + 8)$ ________	$-5t - 2(5t + 10) = 100$ ________
4.	$-4b - 4(-6b - 8) = 172$ ________	$-3p + 2(5p - 12) = -73$ ________
5.	$-3f + 3(-3f + 5) = -81$ ________	$-43 = -5c + 4(2c + 7)$ ________
6.	$-5s + 3(5s + 2) = 126$ ________	$4d + 2(4d + 7) = -106$ ________
7.	$103 = -2u + 3(-3u + 5)$ ________	$-2n + 2(3n + 14) = -20$ ________
8.	$-11 = 5y + 4(-y - 4)$ ________	$-5a - 2(-7a - 10) = 128$ ________
9.	$\frac{1}{2}(c + 5) - 10 = -4$ ________	$-4f + 2(4f - 5) = -19$ ________
10.	$2(v + 4) + 6 = 24$ ________	$-9 = 6h + 3(-h - 3)$ ________
11.	$-6p - 8(4p + 8) = 98$ ________	$7c + 3(3c + 5) = -103$ ________
12.	$-4s + 2(4s + 1) = 125$ ________	$-3n + 3(4n + 15) = -21$ ________

NAME ______________________

Lesson 3.5 Graphing Linear Equations

A **linear equation** is an equation that creates a straight line when graphed on a coordinate plane. To graph a linear equation, create a function table with at least 3 ordered pairs. Then, plot these ordered pairs on a coordinate plane. Draw a line through the points. In the table are some points for this linear function:

$$y = \frac{x}{2} + 1$$

x	y
−2	0
0	1
2	2
4	3

These points are plotted on the line graph at the far right.

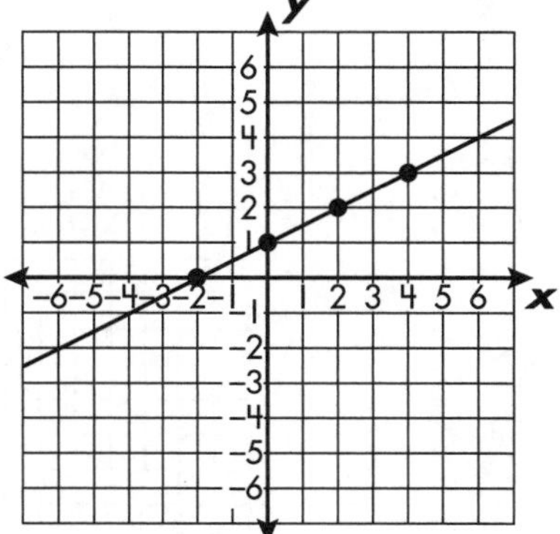

Complete the function table for each function. Then, graph the function.

a

1. $y = x - 3$

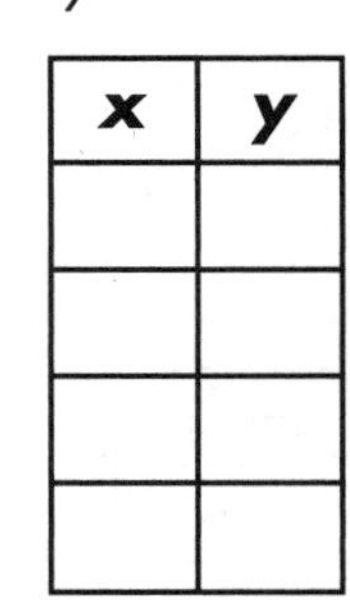

x	y

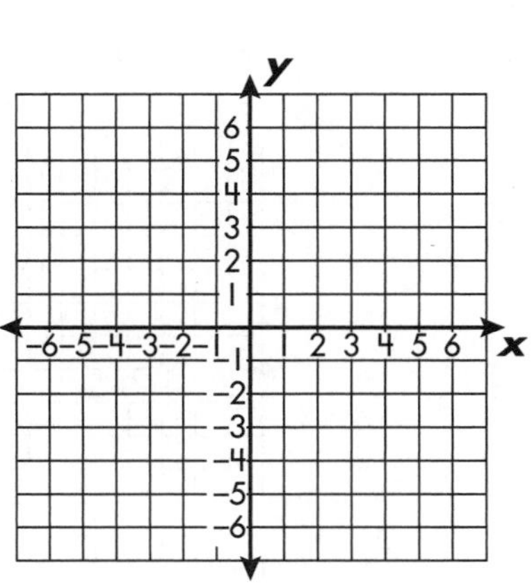

b

$y = 2x + 1$

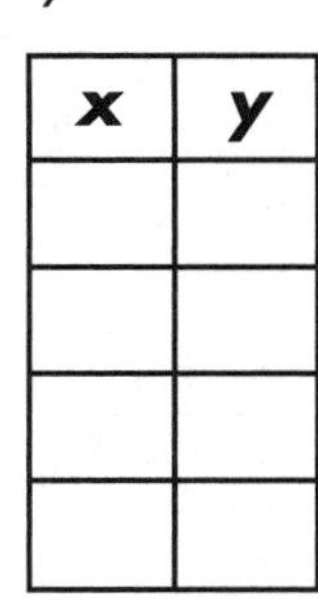

x	y

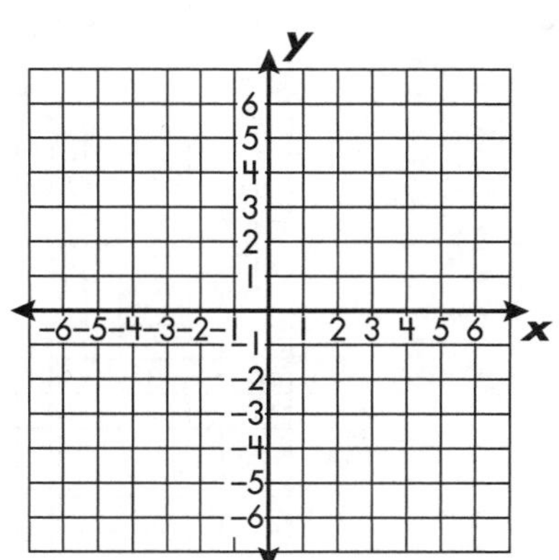

2. $y = \frac{x}{2} - 2$

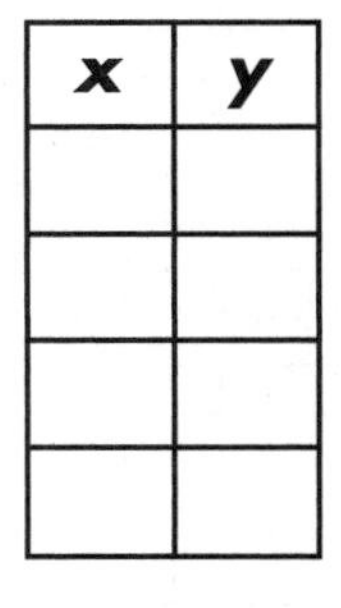

x	y

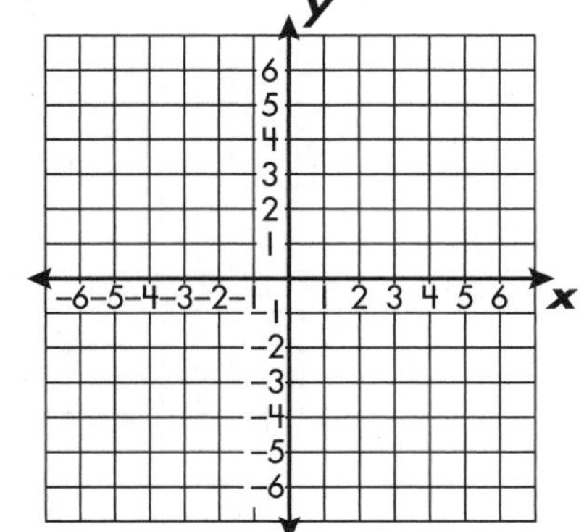

$y = \frac{x - 2}{3}$

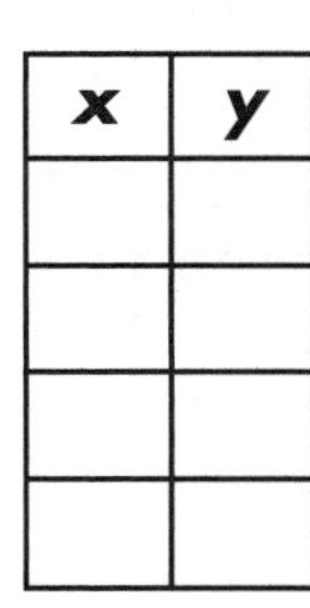

x	y

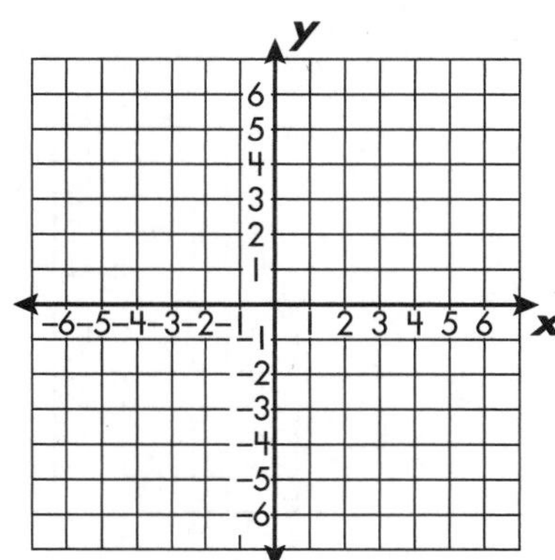

NAME ____________________

Lesson 3.5 Graphing Linear Equations

Graph each linear equation using a function table to find the necessary values.

	a	b
1.	$y = 2x - 4$	$y = \frac{2x}{3}$

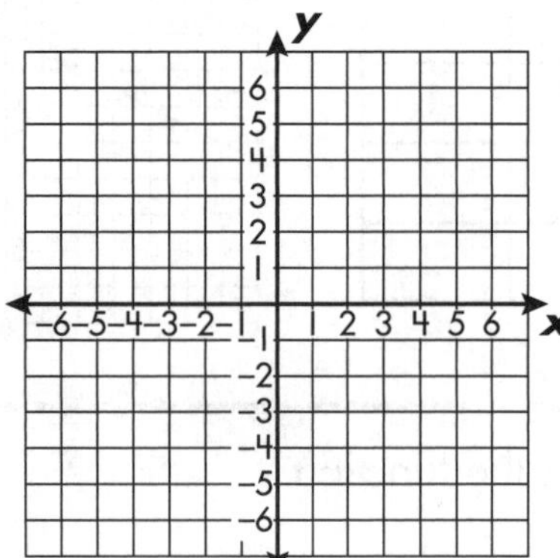
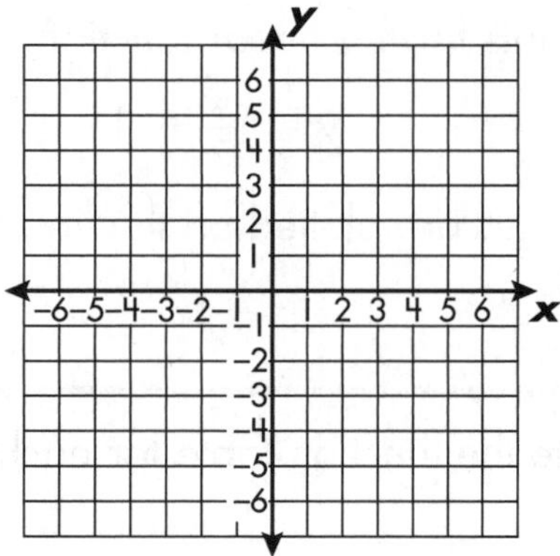

	a	b
2.	$y = \frac{x}{4} + 2$	$y = 3x - 3$

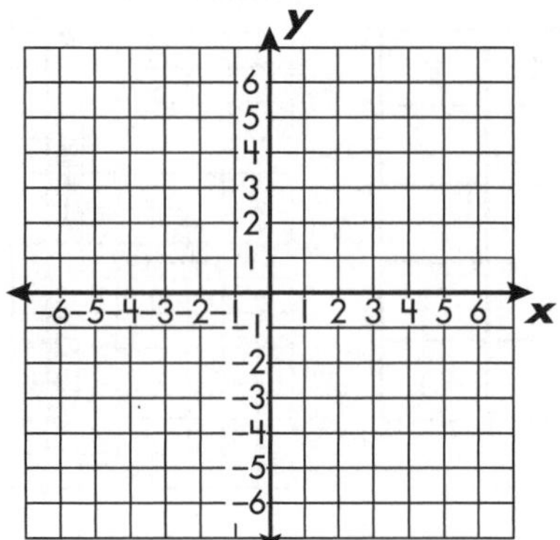
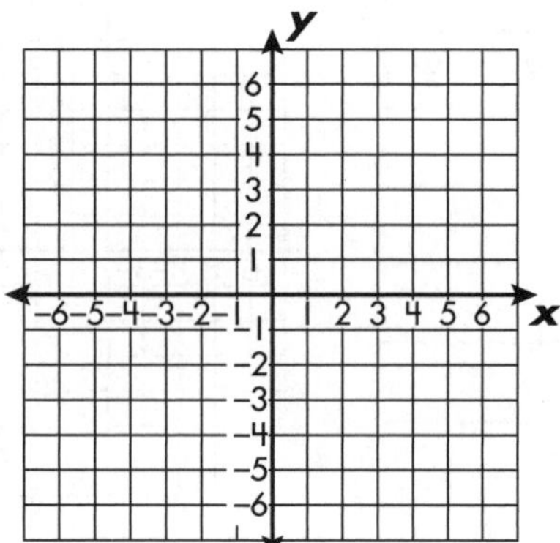

	a	b
3.	$y = 2x + 1$	$y = 3 - \frac{x}{2}$

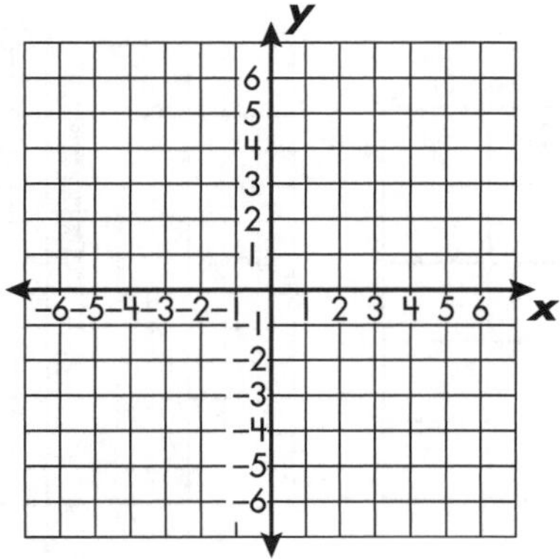
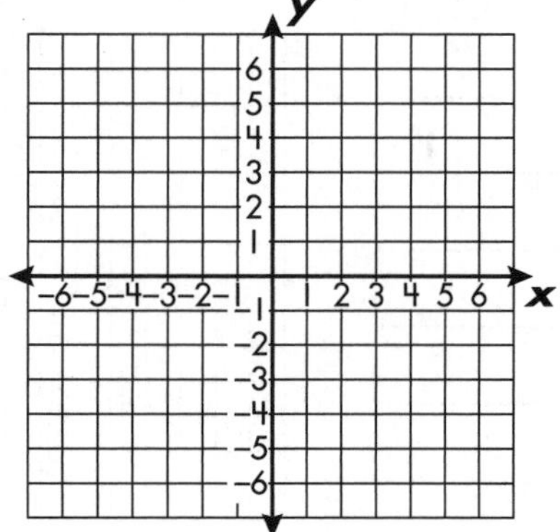

NAME ______________________

Lesson 3.6 Understanding Linear Equation Systems

A **system of linear equations** is a set of equations that have the same variables. Graphing the solutions of the equations results in a set of lines in the coordinate plane. If the lines intersect at a single point, that point represents the one ordered pair that satisfies the equation.

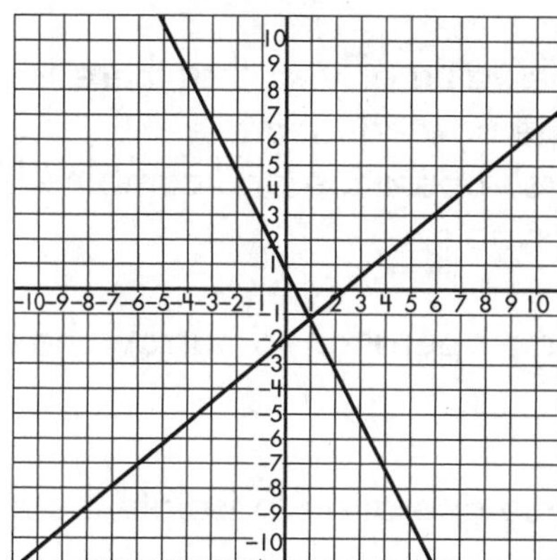

This represents a system because the lines intersect.

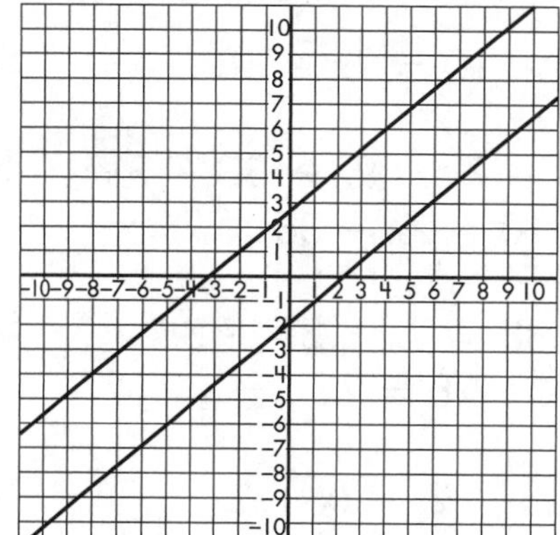

This is not a system because the lines do not intersect.

Tell if each graph represents a system of linear equations by writing *yes* or *no*.

a | **b**

1.

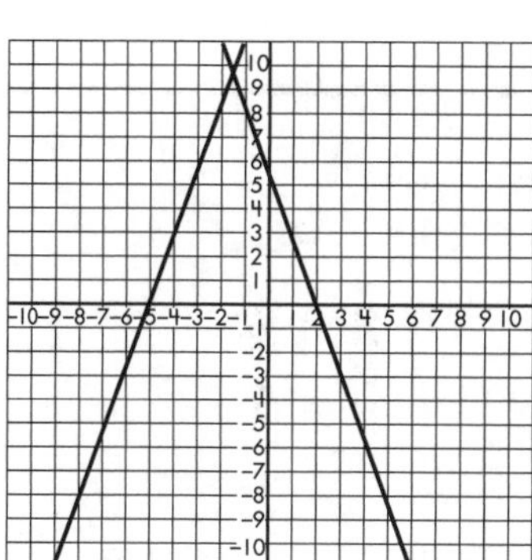

____

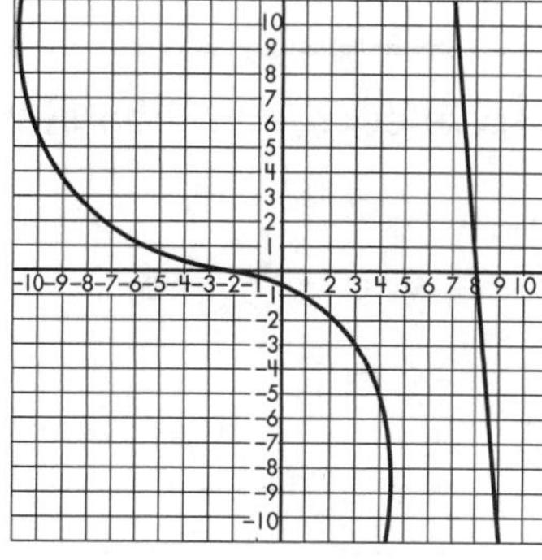

____

2.

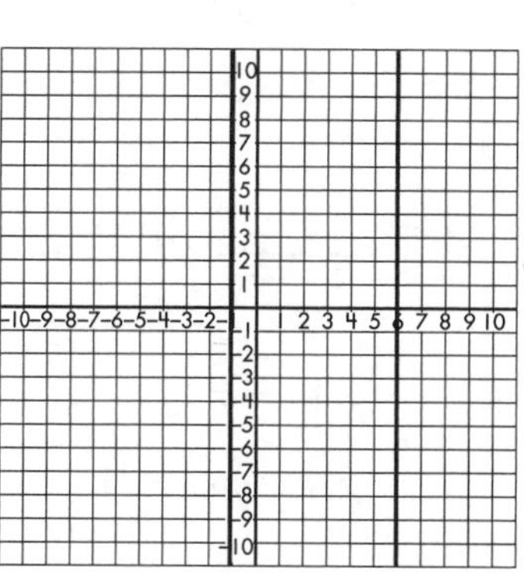

____

____

NAME ______________________

Lesson 3.7 Solving 2-Variable Linear Equation Systems

Systems of equations can be solved by using the method of substitution following the steps below.

$y = 7x + 10$
$y = 9x + 38$

Work	Step
$7x + 10 = 9x + 38$	**Step 1:** Substitute one value of y so that there is only one variable in the new equation.
$7x + 10 - 7x = 9x + 38 - 7x$ $10 = 2x + 38$	**Step 2:** Use the inverse operation and combine like terms with the x variable.
$10 - 38 = 2x + 38 - 38$ $-28 = 2x$	**Step 3:** Use the inverse operation to narrow the equation to 2 terms.
$-28 \div 2 = 2x \div 2$	**Step 4:** Use the inverse operation to isolate the x variable.
$x = -14$	**Step 5:** Find the value of the x variable.
$y = 7(-14) + 10$	**Step 6:** Substitute the value of the x variable in one of the equations.
$y = -98 + 10$ $y = -88$	**Step 7:** Solve to find the value of the y variable.

Use substitution to solve each equation system.

	a	b
1.	$y = -\frac{4}{3x} + 6$ $y = 2$ $x =$ ______, $y =$ ______	$y = \frac{1}{2x} + 3$ $y = 5$ $x =$ ______, $y =$ ______
2.	$y = 4x + 5$ $y = -\frac{1}{3}x - 8$ $x =$ ______, $y =$ ______	$y = \frac{7}{2}x - 5$ $y = -5$ $x =$ ______, $y =$ ______
3.	$y = \frac{1}{3}x - 4$ $y = -\frac{7}{3}x + 4$ $x =$ ______, $y =$ ______	$y = -\frac{5}{2}x + 10$ $y = \frac{1}{2}x + 4$ $x =$ ______, $y =$ ______

NAME ______________________

Lesson 3.7 Solving 2-Variable Linear Equation Systems

Systems of equations can be solved by using the **method of elimination** following the steps below.

$$3x + 4y = 31$$
$$2x - y = 6$$

$$2x - y = 6$$
$$2x - y - 2x = 6 - 2x$$
$$-y = 6 - 2x$$
$$y = -6 + 2x$$

Step 1: Use inverse operations to isolate one variable on one side of the equation.

$$3x + 4(-6 + 2x) = 31$$
$$3x - 24 + 8x = 31$$
$$11x - 24 = 31$$

Step 2: Substitute the new equation in place of the appropriate variable so there is only one variable in the new equation.

$$11x - 24 + 24 = 31 + 24$$
$$11x = 55$$
$$11x \div 11 = 55 \div 11$$
$$x = 5$$

Step 3: Use inverse operations and the distributive property to find a solution for the variable.

$$y = -6 + 2(5)$$
$$y = 4$$

Step 4: Substitute the value of the variable in one of the equations and solve.

Use elimination to solve each system of equations.

	a	b
1.	$-4x - 2y = -12$ $4x + 8y = -24$ $x =$ ______, $y =$ ______	$4x + 8y = 20$ $-4x + 2y = -30$ $x =$ ______, $y =$ ______
2.	$x - y = 11$ $2x + y = 19$ $x =$ ______, $y =$ ______	$-6x + 5y = 1$ $6x + 4y = -10$ $x =$ ______, $y =$ ______
3.	$-2x - 9y = -25$ $-4x - 9y = -23$ $x =$ ______, $y =$ ______	$8x + y = -16$ $-3x + y = -5$ $x =$ ______, $y =$ ______

NAME ______________________

Lesson 3.7 Solving 2-Variable Linear Equation Systems

Use substitution or elimination to solve each system of equations.

	a	b
1.	$y = \frac{2}{3}x - 5$ $y = -x + 10$	$x + y = -3$ $x - y = 1$
	$x =$ ______, $y =$ ______	$x =$ ______, $y =$ ______
2.	$3x - y = 0$ $\frac{1}{4}x + \frac{3}{4}y = \frac{5}{2}$	$-6x + 6y = 6$ $-6x + 3y = -12$
	$x =$ ______, $y =$ ______	$x =$ ______, $y =$ ______
3.	$y = 3 - x$ $y - 3x = 5$	$-4x + 9y = 9$ $x = -6 + 3y$
	$x =$ ______, $y =$ ______	$x =$ ______, $y =$ ______
4.	$3g + f = 15$ $g + 2f = 10$	$3b + 5t = 17$ $2b + t = 9$
	$g =$ ______, $f =$ ______	$b =$ ______, $t =$ ______
5.	$y = 4 - 2x$ $y = -5 + 4x$	$5h + 2e = 32$ $6h + 6e = 42$
	$x =$ ______, $y =$ ______	$h =$ ______, $e =$ ______

NAME ____________________

Lesson 3.8 Graphing Linear Equation Systems

Graphing both lines that make up an equation system can solve the system.

$y = 3x + 2$

$y = 2x + 1$

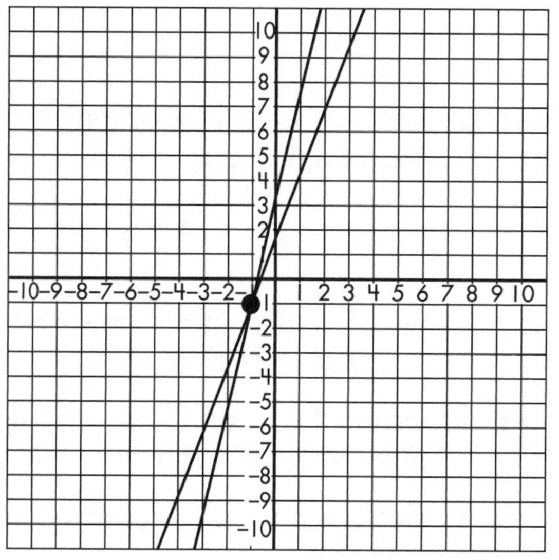

Step 1: Graph the first line in the system using slope intercept form as a guide.

Step 2: Graph the second line in the system using slope-intercept form as a guide.

Step 3: Find the point of intersection to solve the equation system.

$(-1, -1)$

Use slope-intercept form to graph each system of equations and solve the system.

a

1. $y = -x + 4$

$y = 3x$

x: ______;

y: ______

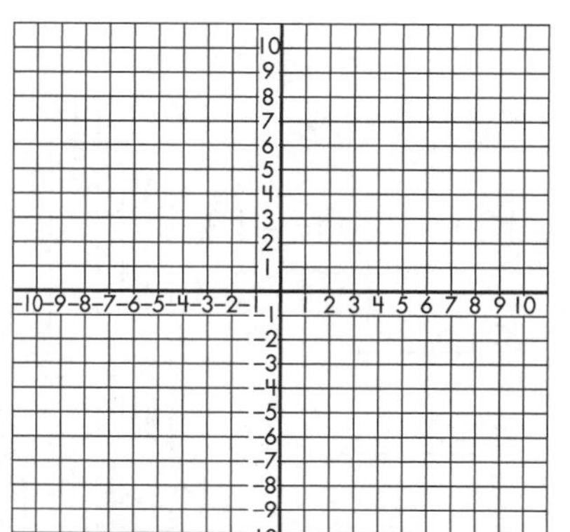

b

$y = 2x + 4$

$y = 3x + 2$

x: ______;

y: ______

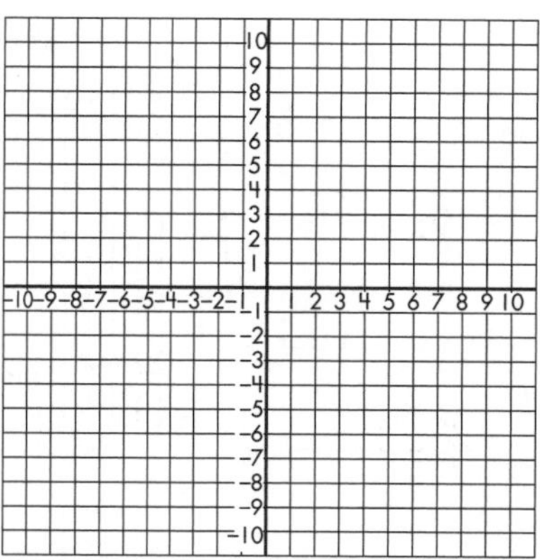

2. $y = -2x - 4$

$y = -4$

x: ______;

y: ______

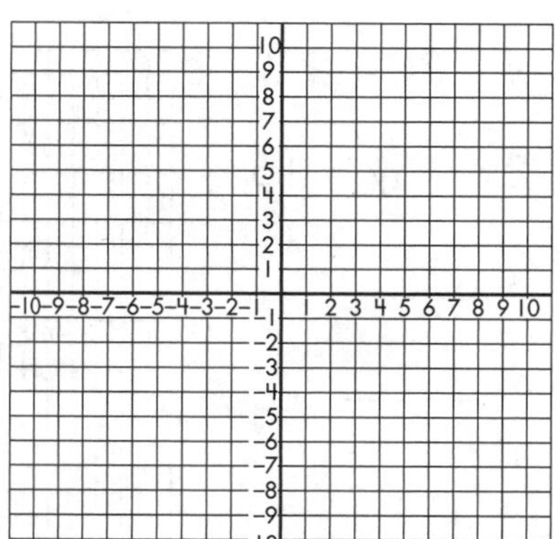

$y = 2x - 2$

$y = -x - 5$

x: ______;

y: ______

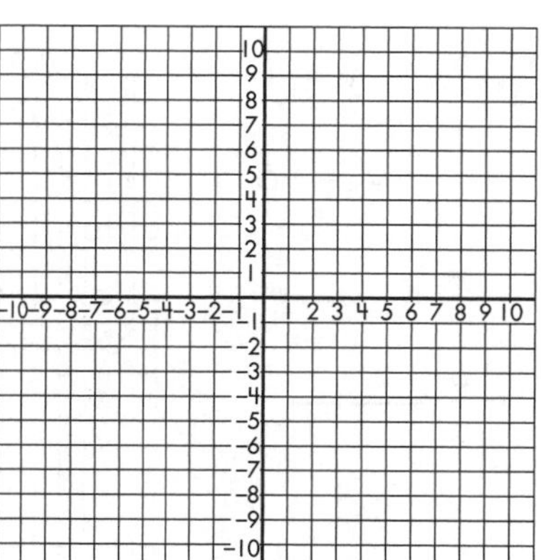

NAME ____________________

Lesson 3.8 Graphing Linear Equation Systems

In some cases, you must first isolate the y before you can solve the system.

$$2x - 4y = 10$$
$$x + y = 2$$

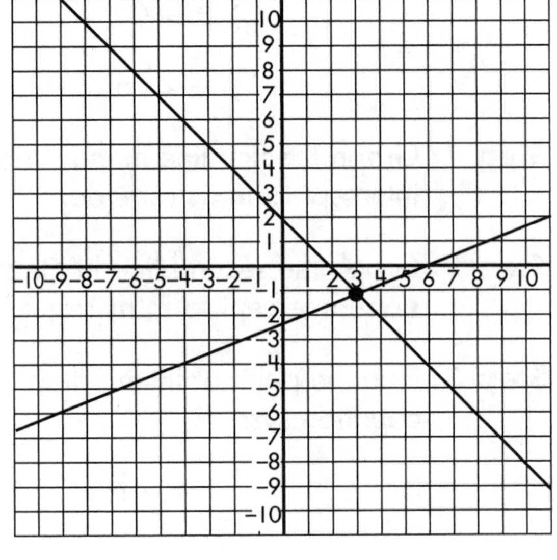

Step 1: Isolate y in both equations by using inverse operations to create slope-intercept form.

$$y = \frac{1}{2}x - 2\frac{1}{2}$$
$$y = -x + 2$$

Step 2: Graph the first line in the system using slope intercept form as a guide.

Step 3: Graph the second line in the system using slope-intercept form as a guide.

Step 4: Find the point of intersection to solve the equation system.

$$(3, -1)$$

Use slope-intercept form to graph each system of equations and solve the system.

a

1. $x + y = 2$

$-9x + 4y = 8$

x: ______;

y: ______

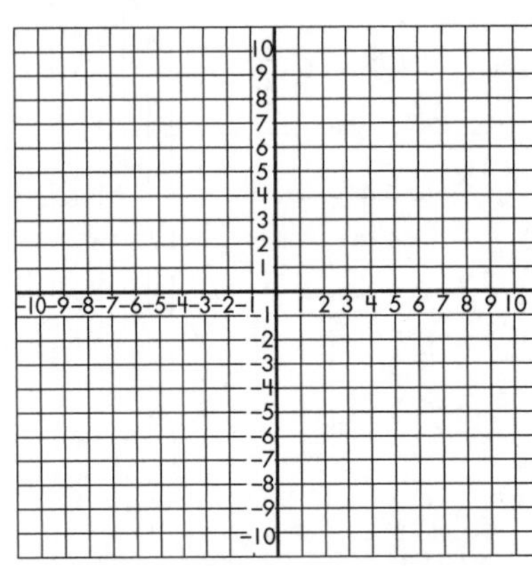

b

$5x + y = 9$

$10x - 7y = -18$

x: ______;

y: ______

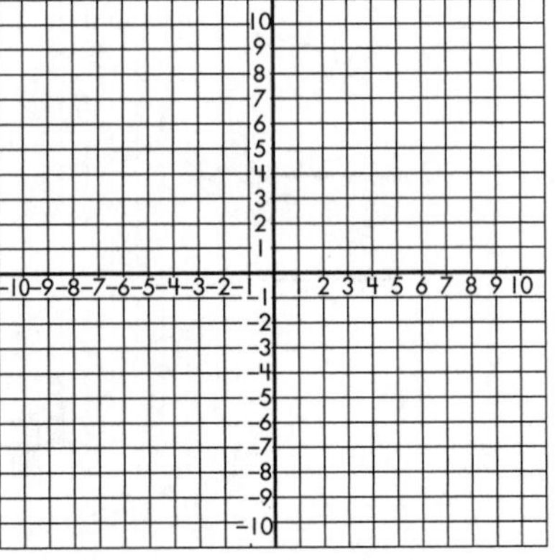

2. $2x - y = 0$

$x + y = -6$

x: ______;

y: ______

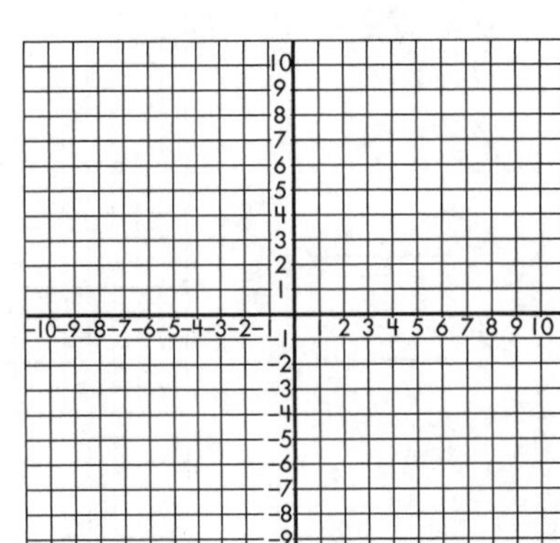

$x - 3y = 2$

$2x + 5y = 15$

x: ______;

y: ______

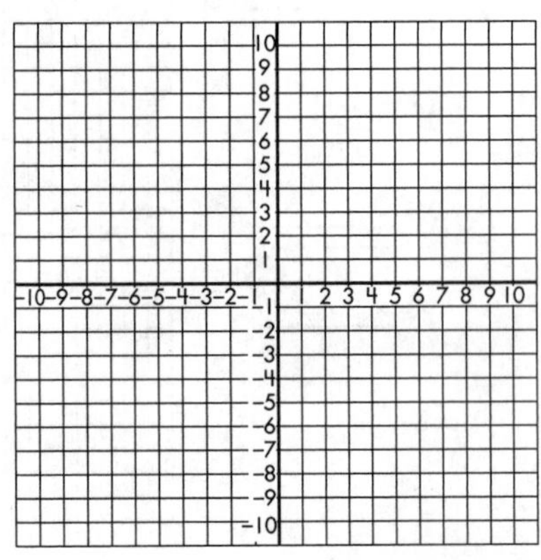

NAME ______________________

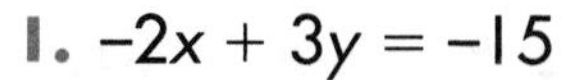

Lesson 3.8 Graphing Linear Equation Systems

Use slope-intercept form to graph each system of equations and solve the system.

a

1. $-2x + 3y = -15$

$y = -x + 10$

x: ______;

y: ______

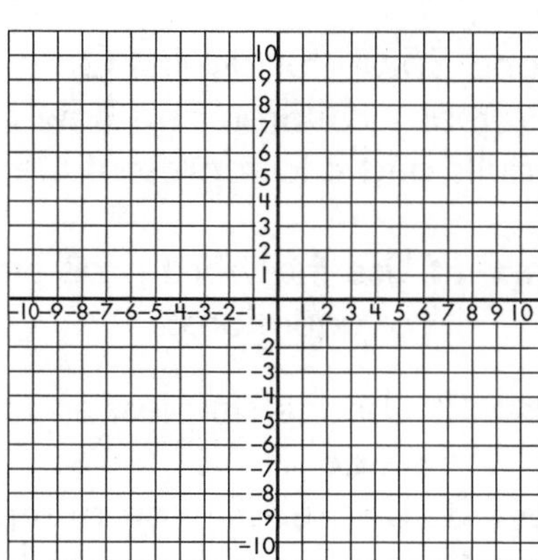

b

$3x + 2y = 9$

$y = 4x - 1$

x: ______;

y: ______

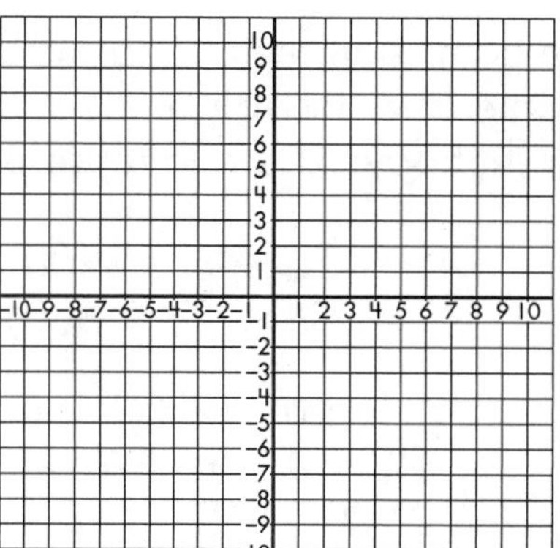

2. $5x - 2y = 4$

$y = 2x - 1$

x: ______;

y: ______

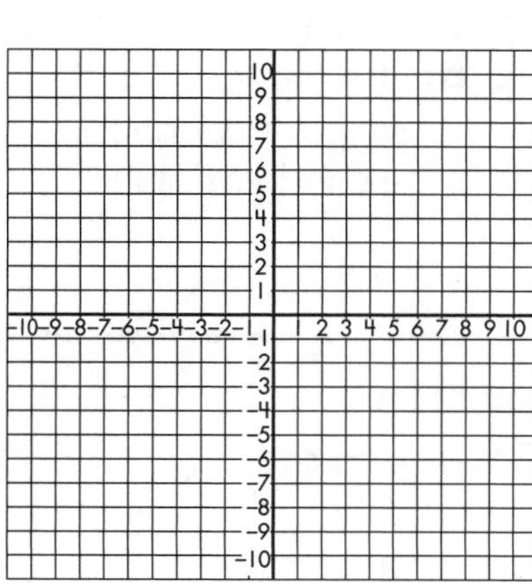

$y = -2x - 4$

$4x - 2y = -8$

x: ______;

y: ______

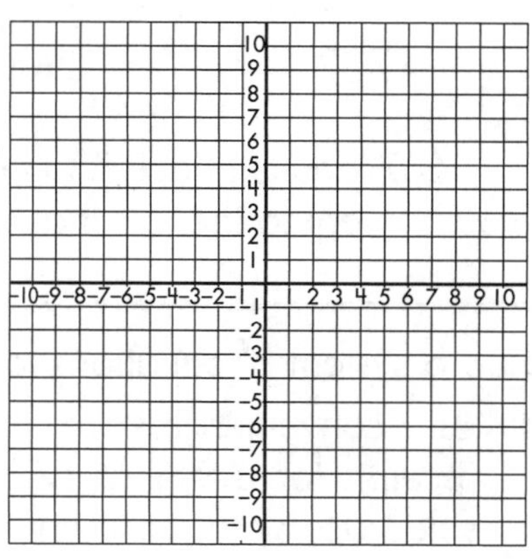

3. $2y - 4x = 2$

$y = x + 4$

x: ______;

y: ______

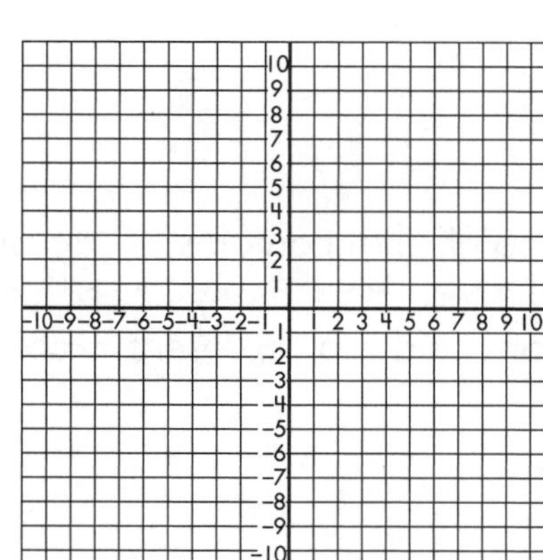

$x + y = 6$

$-3x + y = 2$

x: ______;

y: ______

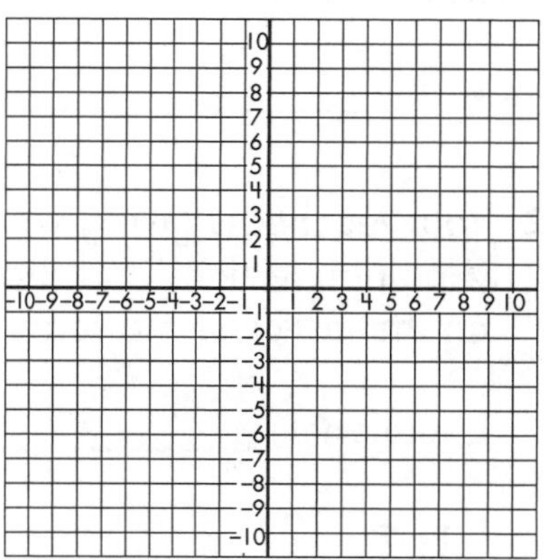

NAME ____________________

Lesson 3.9 Problem-Solving With Linear Equation Systems

Linear equation systems can be used to find solutions to word problems that have a constant relationship between two variables.

The admission fee at a fair is \$2.00 for children and \$5.00 for adults. On a certain day, 2,400 people enter the fair and \$6,801 is collected. How many children and how many adults went to the fair that day? Use *a* to represent the number of adults and *c* to represent the number of children.

$a + c = 2400$
$5a + 2c = 6801$

Step 1: Use the word problem to set up the system of equations.

$a = 2400 - c$

Step 2: Use the simplest equation to isolate one variable.

$5(2400 - c) + 2c = 6801$

Step 3: Use substitution to replace one of variables.

$12{,}000 - 5c + 2c = 6801$
$12{,}000 - 3c = 6801$
$12{,}000 - 3c - 12{,}000 = 6801 - 12{,}000$
$-3c \div (-3) = -5199 \div (-3)$

Step 4: Use combination of like terms and inverse operations to isolate the variable in the equation.

$c = 1{,}733$

Step 5: Find the value of one variable.

$a + 1733 = 2400$
$a + 1733 - 1733 = 2400 - 1733$
$a = 667$

Step 6: Use the value of the first variable in the simplest equation to find the value of the second variable.

667 adults and 1,733 children went to the fair that day.

Set up a system of equations to solve each word problem.

1. At a convenience store, bottled water costs \$1.10 and sodas cost \$2.35. One day, the receipts for a total of 172 waters and sodas were \$294.20. How many of each kind were sold? Use *w* to represent bottled water and *s* to represent soda.

Equation 1: ____________________

Equation 2: ____________________

$w =$ ________; $s =$ ________

2. Your teacher is giving you a test worth 100 points that contains 40 questions. There are 2-point questions and 4-point questions on the test. How many of each type of question are on the test? Use *t* to represent 2-point questions and *f* to represent 4-point questions.

Equation 1: ____________________

Equation 2: ____________________

$t =$ ________; $f =$ ________

NAME ____________________

Lesson 3.9 Problem-Solving With Linear Equation Systems

Set up a system of equations to solve each word problem.

1. Jonathan has saved 57 coins in his bank. The coins are a mixture of quarters and dimes. He has saved $12.00 so far. How many quarters and how many dimes are in Jonathan's bank? Use q to represent the number of quarters and d to represent the number of dimes.

Equation 1: ____________________

Equation 2: ____________________

q = ________; d = ________

2. Members of the drama club held a car wash to raise funds for their spring musical. They charged $3 to wash a car and $5 to wash a pick-up truck or a sport utility vehicle. If they earned a total of $425 by washing a total of 125 vehicles, how many of each did they wash? Use c to represent the number of cars and t to represent the number of trucks.

Equation 1: ____________________

Equation 2: ____________________

c = ________; t = ________

3. Last Saturday 2,200 people attended an event at Fairway Gardens. The admission fee was $1.50 for children and $4.00 for adults. If the total amount of money collected at the event was $5,050, how many children and how many adults attended the event? Use c to represent the number of children and a to represent the number of adults.

Equation 1: ____________________

Equation 2: ____________________

c = ________; a = ________

NAME ____________________

Check What You Learned

Linear Equations

Find the rate of change, or slope, for the situation.

1. A sales person earns commission based on total sales

Sale Amount ($)	100	250	500	700
Commission ($)	5	12.50	25	35

The rate of change, or slope, for this situation is ____________.

Find the value of the variable in each equation.

	a	b	c
2.	$12 + n = 37$ ______	$\frac{a}{3} = 15$ ______	$3x + 2 = 56$ ______
3.	$p - 17 = 26$ ______	$9 - \frac{m}{4} = 4$ ______	$q + 27 = 35$ ______
4.	$7b - 5 = 44$ ______	$n \times 4 = 52$ ______	$\frac{e}{8} + 4 = 11$ ______

Use the slope-intercept form of equations to draw lines on the grids below.

5. **a** $y = -\frac{1}{3}x + 7$

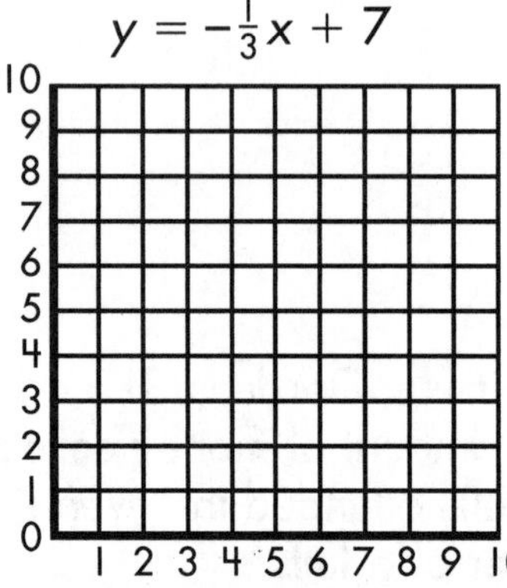

b $y = 3x + 1$

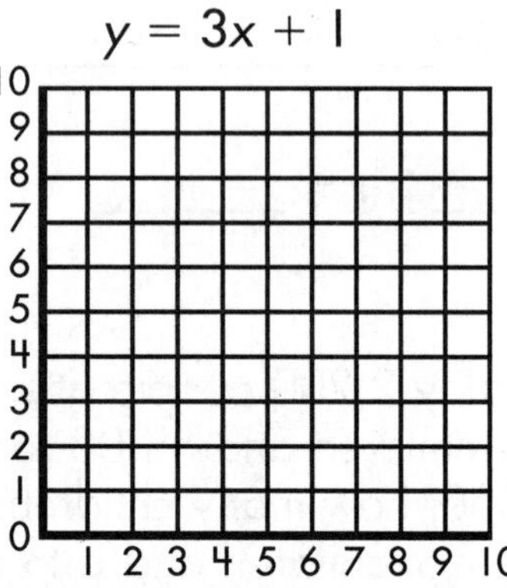

Complete the table. Then, graph the equation.

6. $y = -x + 3$

x	y
–5	
–3	
0	
3	
5	

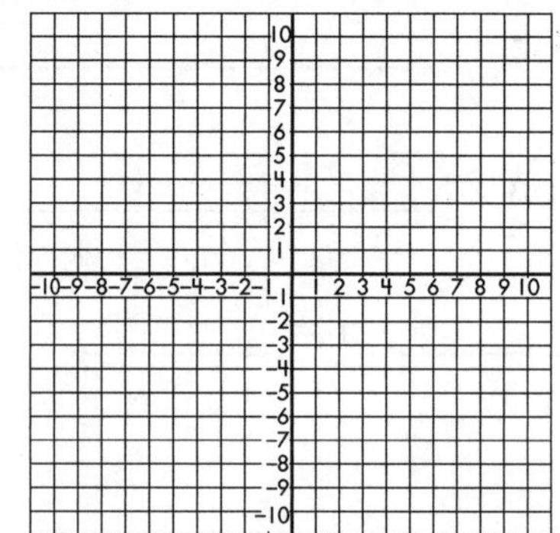

NAME ____________________

Check What You Learned

Linear Equations

Solve each system of equations.

	a	b
7.	$-4x - 2y = 14$ $-10x + 7y = -25$	$y = \frac{3}{2}x - 2$ $y = x + 2$
	$x =$ ______, $y =$ ______	$x =$ ______, $y =$ ______
8.	$5x + 4y = -14$ $y = 1 - \frac{1}{2}x$	$-20y - 7x = -14$ $10y - 2x = -4$
	$x =$ ______, $y =$ ______	$x =$ ______, $y =$ ______

Use slope-intercept form to graph each system of equations and solve the system.

9. $-2x + 5y = 15$

$y = -x - 4$

x: ______;

y: ______

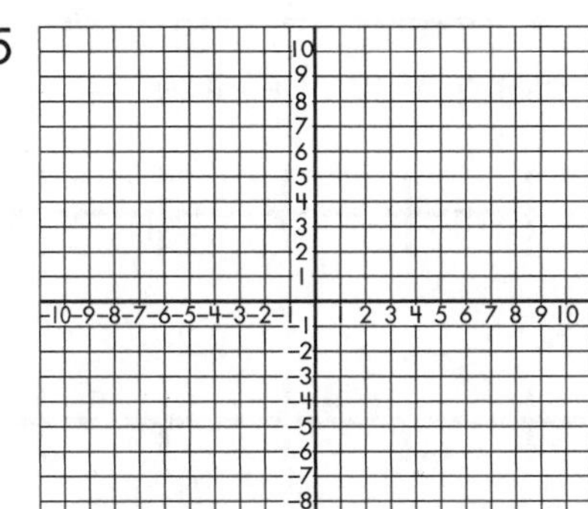

$-x + 5y = 30$

$10x + 6y = 9$

x: ______;

y: ______

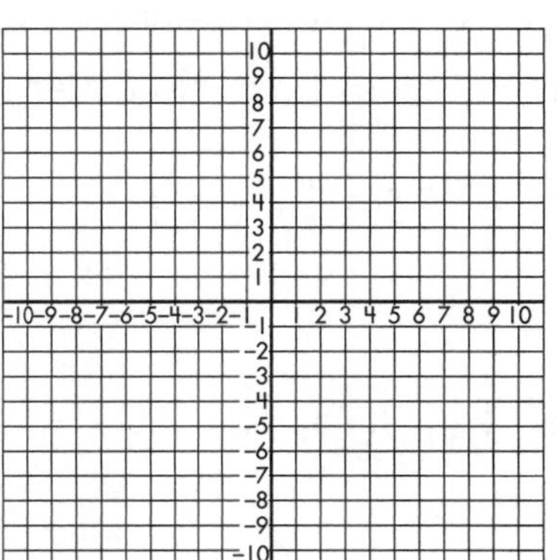

Set up a system of equations to solve the word problem.

10. Kim scored 33 points at her basketball game with a combination of 2-point shots and 3-point shots. If she made a total of 15 baskets, how many of each kind of shot did Kim make? Use t to represent 2-point shots and x to represent 3-point shots.

Equation 1: ______________________

Equation 2: ______________________ $t =$ ______; $x =$ ______

NAME ______________________

Mid-Test Chapters 1–3

Evaluate each expression. Simplify fractions.

	a	b	c
1.	$\sqrt{49}$ = ______	$\sqrt[3]{0}$ = ______	$\sqrt{\frac{1}{16}}$ = ______
2.	$\sqrt[3]{\frac{64}{216}}$ = ______	$\sqrt{\frac{9}{81}}$ = ______	$\sqrt{64}$ = ______
3.	$\sqrt{121}$ = ______	$\sqrt[3]{343}$ = ______	$\sqrt[3]{27}$ = ______

Approximate each value to the hundredths place.

4. The value of $\sqrt{3}$ is between ______ and ______.

5. The value of $\sqrt{15}$ is between ______ and ______.

6. The value of $\sqrt{78}$ is between ______ and ______.

Put the values below in order from least to greatest along a number line.

7. $-1.75, -\frac{1}{2}, \pi, \sqrt{2}$

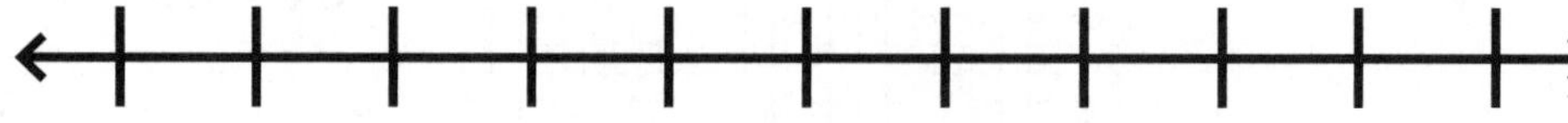

8. $1\frac{1}{4}, 0.98, \sqrt{3}, 0.05$

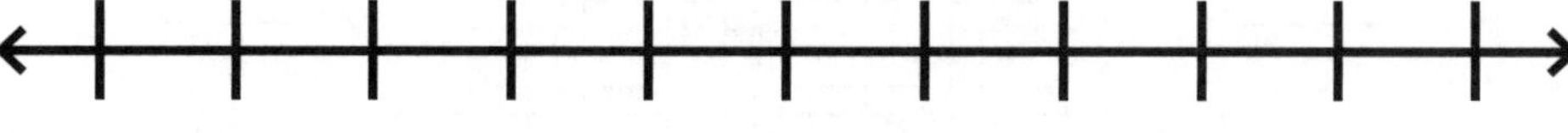

9. $\sqrt{\frac{1}{4}}, \frac{3}{4}, 0.7, 0.25$

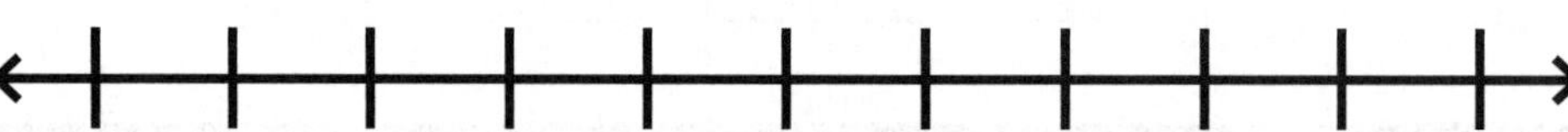

Find the value of each expression.

	a	b	c
10.	2^4 = ______	5^2 = ______	8^3 = ______
11.	9^{-4} = ______	12^{-3} = ______	8^{-5} = ______

Write each number in scientific notation.

12.	15.67 = ______	9,247 = ______	422 = ______
13.	0.75 = ______	15,295 = ______	0.034 = ______

CHAPTERS 1–3 MID-TEST

NAME ______________________

Mid-Test Chapters 1–3

Solve each problem by using roots. Write fractions in simplest form.

	a	b	c
14.	$x^2 = \frac{4}{25}$	$512 = x^3$	$x^3 = \frac{27}{343}$
	$x =$ ________	$x =$ ________	$x =$ ________
15.	$\sqrt{x} = 9$	$15 = \sqrt{x}$	$\sqrt[3]{x} = 9$
	$x =$ ________	$x =$ ________	$x =$ ________

Find the slope, or constant rate of change, for each situation. Be sure to show your work.

16. Students are buying tickets for rides at the fall carnival. The student council keeps track of how many tickets they sell in one week.

	Monday	Tuesday	Wednesday	Thursday	Friday
Number of Tickets Sold	100	123	245	182	124
Amount Earned ($)	150	184.50	367.50	273	186

The rate of change, or slope, for this situation is ____________.

Find the value of the variable in each equation.

	a	b	c
17.	$x - 7 = 8$ ________	$x + 5 = 15$ ________	$s + 7 = -5$ ________
18.	$r - 7 = -4$ ________	$\frac{t}{5} + 5 = 9$ ________	$4x = -12$ ________
19.	$6x - 5 = 13$ ________	$7 - 6t = -5$ ________	$10x - 7 = 7$ ________

Solve each system of equations.

	a	b	c
20.	$y = \frac{5}{3}x - 1$	$6x + 4y = 6$	$y = \frac{1}{3}x - 4$
	$y = -6$	$3x = -15$	$y = -\frac{7}{3}x + 4$
	$x =$ ______, $y =$ ______	$x =$ ______, $y =$ ______	$x =$ ______, $y =$ ______

CHAPTERS 1–3 MID-TEST

NAME ______________________

Mid-Test Chapters 1–3

Use the slope-intercept form of equations to draw lines on the grids below.

21.

a $y = 3x + 7$

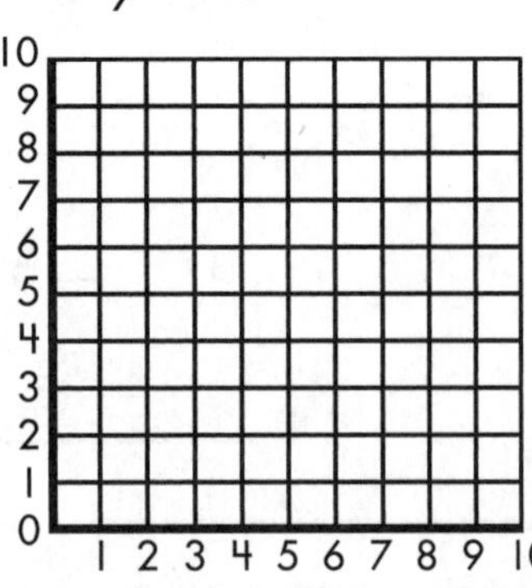

b $y = \frac{1}{2}x + 1$

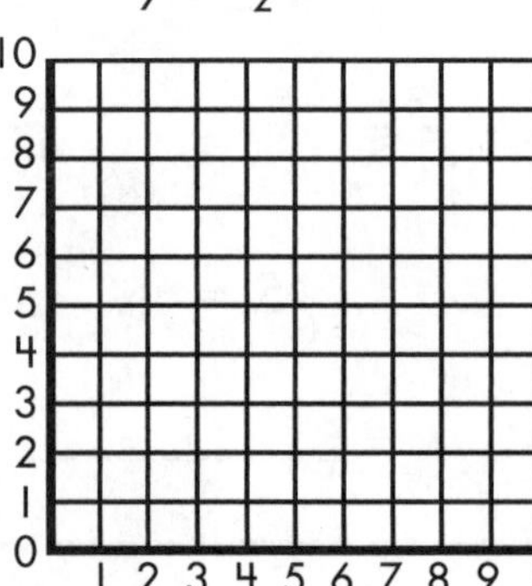

c $y = -2x + 8$

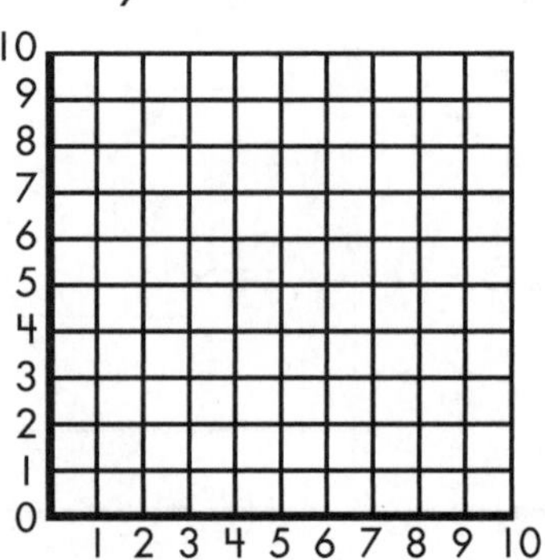

Complete the tables. Then, graph the equations.

22. $y = -\frac{1}{2}x - 2$

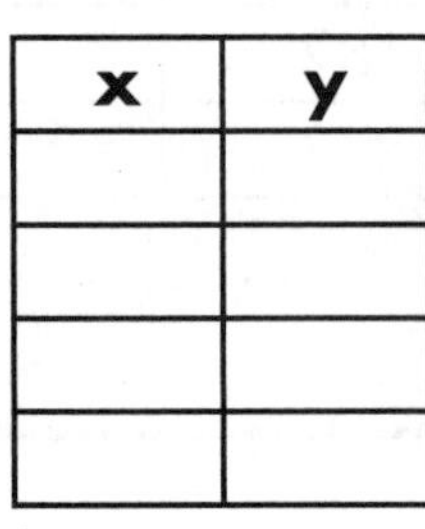

x	y

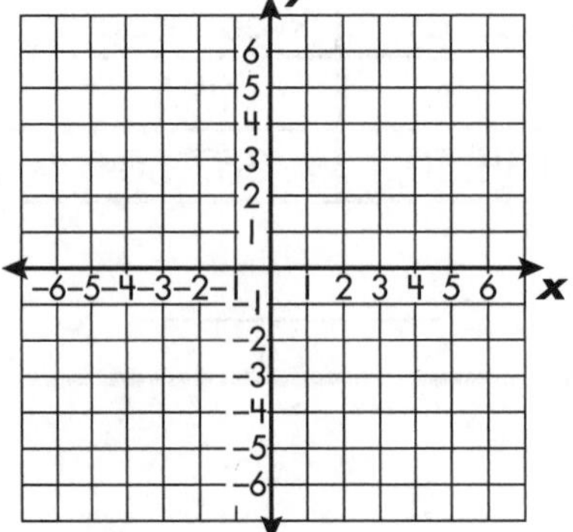

23. $y = -\frac{1}{3}x + 5$

x	y

Graph the systems of equations.

24. $y = \frac{7}{4}x - 3$

$y = 4$

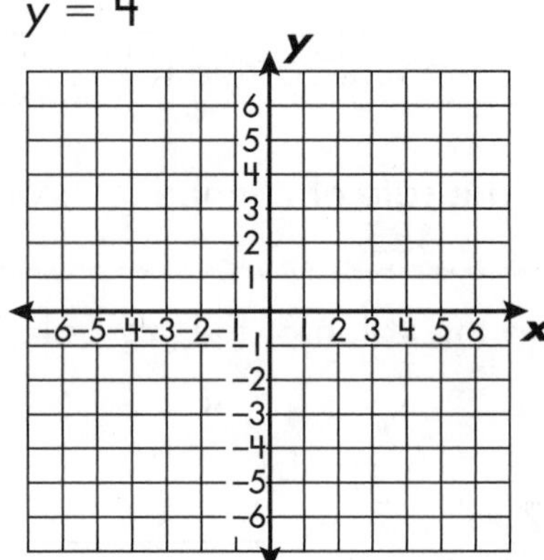

25. $2x - y = 4$

$x - y = 2$

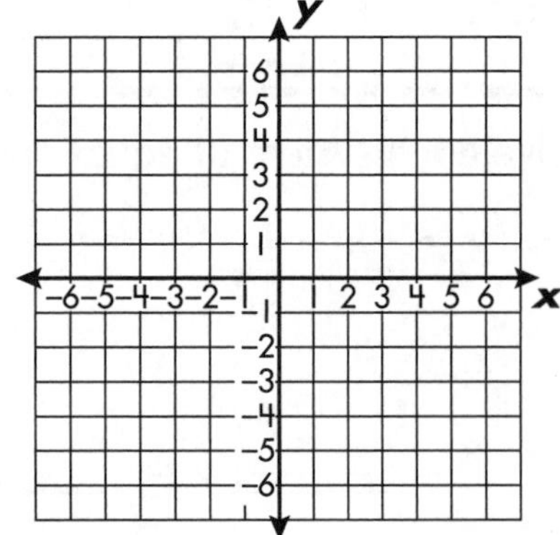

CHAPTERS 1-3 MID-TEST

NAME ____________________

Mid-Test Chapters 1–3

Rewrite each multiplication or division expression using a base and an exponent.

	a	b	c
26.	$5^6 \div 5^3$ ________	$4^{12} \div 4^6$ ________	$3^3 \times 3^9$ ________
27.	$15^2 \times 15^1$ ________	$7^4 \div 7^2$ ________	$6^6 \div 6^3$ ________
28.	$10^3 \times 10^4$ ________	$2^2 \times 2^2$ ________	$7^6 \div 7^3$ ________

Tell if each number is *rational* or *irrational.*

	a	b	c
29.	$\frac{7}{4}$ ________	π ________	$\sqrt{99}$ ________
30.	3.635 ________	$\sqrt{77}$ ________	$\sqrt{255}$ ________
31.	5.6 ________	$\frac{1}{9}$ ________	$2.\overline{756}$ ________

Compare the values using <, >, or =.

	a	b	c
32.	$\sqrt{36}$ ________ 6.5	1.4 ________ $\sqrt{2}$	$\frac{1}{2}$ ________ 0.55
33.	3.9 ________ $\sqrt{10}$	$\sqrt{5}$ ________ 4	$\sqrt{8}$ ________ 3
34.	1 ________ $\sqrt{\frac{16}{25}}$	$\sqrt[3]{343}$ ________ 7.2	$\sqrt[3]{6}$ ________ 2

CHAPTERS 1–3 MID-TEST

NAME ___________________

Check What You Know

Functions

Decide if each table represents a function by stating *yes* or *no*.

1.

a

input	output
3	4, 2
4	−6
5	−7
−2	5

____

b

input	output
−4	6
−3	2
1	0
7	6

____

c

input	output
−3	4
−2	5
0	0
4	8

____

Complete each function table for the given function.

2. $y = 18x - 4$

x	y
−15	
−11	
5	
9	
12	

$y = x - 19$

x	y
−63	
−42	
−28	
37	
55	

$y = 12x + 3$

x	y
−13	
−6	
−4	
10	
12	

Find the relationship for each function table and then complete the table.

3.

a

x	y
3	
4	40
9	
10	94

Function: _______________

b

x	y
14	−3
63	
70	
77	6

Function: _______________

Find the rate of change, or slope, for points on the function table and decide if it represents a *linear* or *nonlinear* relationship.

4.

x	y	Rate
0	14	
2	10	
3	8	
5	12	

Relationship: _______________

x	y	Rate
−2	−17	
−1	−11	
0	−5	
1	1	

Relationship: _______________

NAME ____________________

Check What You Know

Functions

Find the rate of change for each function table. Write fractions in simplest form.

5.

a

input	output
3	8
7	12
12	17

rate of change: ____________

b

input	output
27	3
54	6
90	10

rate of change: ____________

c

input	output
6	2
10	7
14	12

rate of change: ____________

Find the initial value of each function represented below.

6.

input	output
2	3
6	11
10	19

$b =$ ____________

input	output
0	2
2	10
4	18

$b =$ ____________

input	output
0	3
2	7
4	11

$b =$ ____________

Use the information given to find the function models for the linear functions shown.

7.

a

(4, 2) and (8, 5)

$y=$ ____________

b

input	output
6	1
18	3
30	5

$y=$ ____________

c

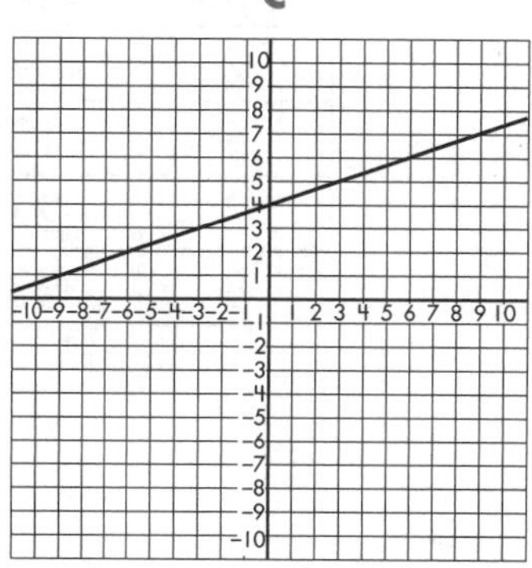

$y=$ ____________

Compare the rate of change for the equation and table and decide which has a greater rate of change by writing *equation* or *table*.

8.

$y = 6x - 2$ or

x	–3	2	6
y	5	–5	–13

____

NAME ____________________

Lesson 4.1 Defining Functions

A **function** is a relationship between two variables which results in only one output value for each input value. If one input has more than one output, then a function does not exist.

input	output
3	−2
4	−3
5	−1

This table represents a function because for every input variable, there is one and only one output variable.

input	output
3	10, 20
6	15

This table does not represent a function because one of the input variables has more than one output variable.

Decide if each table represents a function by stating *yes* or *no*.

1.

a

input	output
−9	c
−5	c
1	b
6	a

____

b

input	output
2	4
4	6
6	8

____

c

input	output
−4	0
−1	6, −6
0	4

____

2.

input	output
2	17, −7
3	−13
7	−27
8	−43

____

input	output
1	c
5	a
8	b

____

input	output
13	14, 5
16	7
18	13

____

NAME ______________________

Lesson 4.2 Input/Output Tables

In a function, each value of **x** relates to only one value of **y**. For example, if $y = x + 6$, whatever x is, y must be greater than x by the number 6.

A **function table** shows the values for each pair of variables as the result of the particular function.

Complete each function table for the given function.

1.

a $y = x + 6$

x	y
−10	−4
−2	4
0	
3	
5	
8	

b $y = 2x - 2$

x	y
0	
1	
3	
5	
8	
10	

c $y = x - 7$

x	y
0	
2	
5	
7	
10	
15	

2.

$y = x^2 - 3$

x	y
−3	
−2	
−1	
0	
3	

$y = \frac{x}{4}$

x	y
−8	
−4	
4	
8	
12	

$y = \frac{x}{2} - 1$

x	y
−10	
−6	
−2	
2	
4	

3.

$y = 3x + 2$

x	y
−3	
−2	
0	
2	
5	

$y = (2 + x) \div 3$

x	y
−8	
−5	
1	
4	
7	

$y = \frac{x}{3} + 3$

x	y
−9	
−6	
−3	
3	
6	

NAME ___________________________

Lesson 4.2 Input/Output Tables

Complete each function table for the given function.

1.

a $y = 9x - 4$

x	y
−10	−94
−6	−58
−2	
5	
12	

b $y = \frac{x}{2} + 2$

x	y
−22	
−8	
2	
12	
22	

c $y = x - 4$

x	y
−23	
−11	
−4	
11	
22	

2.

a $y = x + 3$

x	y
−15	
−9	
2	
8	
14	

b $y = 2x - 6$

x	y
−21	
−16	
−7	
13	
24	

c $y = \frac{x}{10} + 5$

x	y
−120	
−80	
30	
90	
100	

3.

a $y = 7x + 5$

x	y
−11	
−8	
−5	
−2	
1	

b $y = x \div 13$

x	y
−182	
−91	
−26	
104	
195	

c $y = 3x + 24$

x	y
−29	
−16	
11	
19	
26	

NAME ______________________

Lesson 4.2 Input/Output Tables

Read each function. Experiment with values of x. Look for whole number values of x that create a whole number value for y (positive or negative). Once you find 5 numbers for x, fill in the function table for x and for y. Put the values of x in numerical order.

1. $y = \frac{x}{2} - 7$

x	y

$y = \frac{x}{3} - 7$

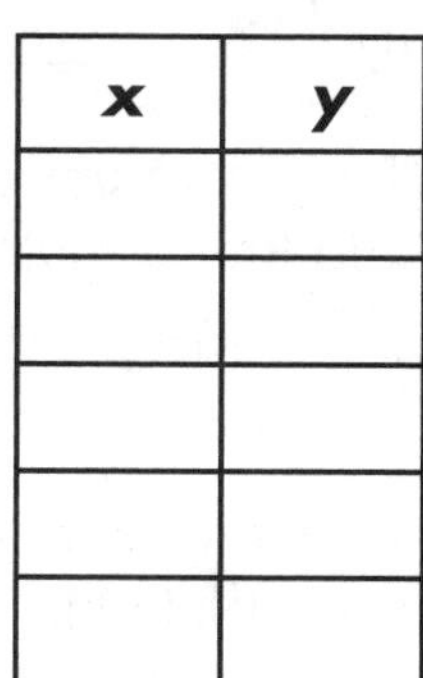

x	y

$y = \frac{x + 4}{5}$

x	y

2. $y = 9x - 3$

x	y

$y = \frac{x^2}{2}$

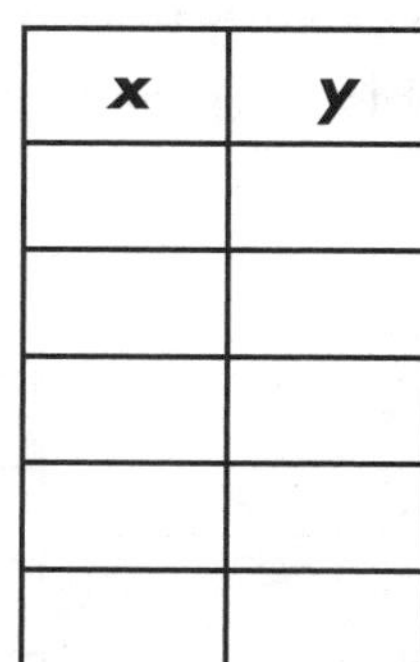

x	y

$y = 2 - \frac{x}{6}$

x	y

Read each function table. See if you can identify the function it represents.

3.

x	y
−2	−3
−1	−2
0	−1
1	0
2	1

$y =$ ________

x	y
0	0
1	−3
2	−6
3	−9
5	−15

$y =$ ________

x	y
−4	−1
−2	0
0	1
2	2
4	3

$y =$ ________

x	y
−3	9
−2	4
0	0
1	1
2	4

$y =$ ________

NAME ______________________

Lesson 4.3 Functions and Linear Relationships

Data in tables can be used to create equations. If the table of values represents a function, a linear relationship in the form of $y = mx + b$ exists.

x	y
99	9
72	6
54	4
27	1

Step 1: Find the rate of change by calculating the slope, or rate of change, between the two variables. $\frac{y_2 - y_1}{x_2 - x_1}$

$$\frac{9 - 1}{99 - 27} = \frac{8}{72} = \frac{1}{9}$$

Step 2: Substitute known values of x and y with the slope into the formula $y = mx + b$.

$$9 = \left(\frac{1}{9}\right)(99) + b$$
$$9 = \left(\frac{1}{9}\right)(99) + b$$
$$9 - 11 = 11 + b - 11$$
$$-2 = b$$

Step 3: Use the found values in the linear function to complete the table.

$$y = \left(\frac{1}{9}\right)(72) - 2$$
$$y = 8 - 2 = 6$$
$$y = \left(\frac{1}{9}\right)(54) - 2$$
$$y = 6 - 2 = 4$$

Find the relationship for each function table and then complete the table.

a

1.

x	y
12	
24	
84	7
120	10

Function: ______________

b

x	y
2	
4	7
5	
11	14

Function: ______________

2.

x	y
3	12
6	36
7	
9	

Function: ______________

x	y
2	
4	50
5	60
10	

Function: ______________

3.

x	y
2	19
3	26
5	
10	

Function: ______________

x	y
8	
12	1
24	4
48	

Function: ______________

NAME ____________________

Lesson 4.3 Functions and Linear Relationships

Find the relationship for each function table and then complete the table.

a

1.

x	y
2	11
3	18
5	
10	

Function: ____________

b

x	y
8	
12	5
24	8
48	

Function: ____________

2.

x	y
15	
20	7
40	11
50	

Function: ____________

x	y
1	
2	
4	40
10	106

Function: ____________

3.

x	y
2	2
6	18
7	
12	

Function: ____________

x	y
14	
28	8
56	12
63	

Function: ____________

4.

x	y
4	10
6	
9	15
12	

Function: ____________

x	y
0	1
3	
6	3
9	

Function: ____________

NAME ______________________

Lesson 4.4 Functions and Nonlinear Relationships

Not all function tables represent a linear relationship. If the rate of change, or slope, is not constant, then the function does not represent a linear relationship.

Test the rate of change in a function table by using the slope formula, $\frac{y_2 - y_1}{x_2 - x_1}$, across multiple points on the table.

Linear Relationship

x	y	Rate
1	217	217
2	434	
3	651	217
4	868	

Nonlinear Relationship

x	y	Rate
–1	0	–5
0	–5	
1	–8	–1
2	–9	

Find the rate of change, or slope, for points on the function table and decide if it represents a *linear* or *nonlinear* relationship.

1.

a

x	y	Rate
–10	–10	
–5	–7	
0	–4	
5	–1	

Relationship: ______________

b

x	y	Rate
–3	–15	
1	–8	
5	–1	
9	6	

Relationship: ______________

2.

a

x	y	Rate
0	2	
1	4	
2	10	
3	28	

Relationship: ______________

b

x	y	Rate
1	6	
2	5	
3	4	
4	5	

Relationship: ______________

3.

a

x	y	Rate
10	327	
20	342	
30	357	
40	372	

Relationship: ______________

b

x	y	Rate
0	100,000	
1	102,000	
2	104,040	
3	106,120	

Relationship: ______________

NAME ____________________

Lesson 4.5 Calculating Rate of Change in Functions

The rate of change that exists in a function can be calculated by finding the ratio of the amount of change in the output variable to the amount of change in the input variable.

$$\frac{\text{change in output}}{\text{change in input}} = \text{rate of change}$$

Function tables can be used to find this rate of change.

input	output
1	4
2	8
3	12

$$\frac{12 - 4}{3 - 1} = \frac{8}{2} = 4$$

The rate of change for this function table is 4.

Find the rate of change for each function table. Write fractions in simplest form.

1.

a

input	output
2	3
6	11
10	19

____

b

input	output
0	2
2	10
4	18

____

c

input	output
0	3
2	7
4	11

____

2.

a

input	output
1	4.5
3	5.5
5	6.5

____

b

input	output
1	−2
3	−18
5	−34

____

c

input	output
1	40
3	10
5	−20

____

3.

a

input	output
30	15
60	25
90	35

____

b

input	output
30	5
60	10
90	15

____

c

input	output
0	4
2	7
4	10

____

NAME ____________________

Lesson 4.5 Calculating Rate of Change in Functions

Find the rate of change for each function table. Write fractions in simplest form.

1.

a

input	output
3	8
7	12
12	17

____

b

input	output
27	3
54	6
90	10

____

c

input	output
6	2
10	7
12	12

____

2.

a

input	output
2	2
5	12
7	22

____

b

input	output
3	14
8	19
12	23

____

c

input	output
8	0
10	–2
12	–4

____

3.

a

input	output
1	9
5	27
10	45

____

b

input	output
1	10
2	12
3	14

____

c

input	output
6	0
8	1
9	2

____

4.

a

input	output
–6	–8
–4	–7
–2	–6

____

b

input	output
–6	–6
0	–1
6	4

____

c

input	output
2	13
3	18
4	23

____

NAME ______________________

Lesson 4.6 Initial Values of Linear Functions

Where a linear function crosses the y-axis is considered its initial value. One way to find the initial value of a linear function is to solve the equation for when the input, or x, equals 0. Use the formula $y = mx + b$, where m represents the rate of change and b represents the initial value of the linear function, to solve.

input	output
2	6
4	12
6	18

$\frac{18 - 6}{6 - 2} = \frac{12}{4} = 3$ **Step 1:** Find the rate of change for the function table.

$6 = (3)(2) + b$ **Step 2:** Substitute values of x, y, and m in the linear equation.

$6 - 6 = 6 - 6 + b$
$b = 0$ **Step 3:** Solve for b to find the initial value of the function.

Find the initial value of each function.

1.

a

input	output
3	8
7	12
12	17

$b =$ ____________

b

input	output
27	3
54	6
90	10

$b =$ ____________

c

input	output
6	2
10	7
12	12

$b =$ ____________

2.

a

input	output
2	2
5	14
7	22

$b =$ ____________

b

input	output
3	14
8	19
12	23

$b =$ ____________

c

input	output
8	0
10	–2
12	–4

$b =$ ____________

3.

a

input	output
1	9
5	27
10	45

$b =$ ____________

b

input	output
1	10
2	12
3	14

$b =$ ____________

c

input	output
6	0
8	1
9	2

$b =$ ____________

NAME ____________________

Lesson 4.6 Initial Values of Linear Functions

Sometimes the initial value of a linear function can be immediately found when it is described in the context of a real-world problem.

Joe's Pizza and Subs sells a 14-inch cheese pizza for $10.00. Toppings can be added to the pizza for $0.50 each. How much will a pizza cost if it has three toppings?

Initial Value: $10.00

Step 1: Identify the output variable. In this case, the price of the pizza is the output and the number of toppings is the input variable.

Step 2: Reread the problem to find the described output starting point. In this problem, it is $10.00.

Find the initial value in each real-world problem below.

1. Julie is trying to grow her hair out so she can donate it to be made into a wig. When she first measures it, it is six inches long. It is growing at a rate of one inch each month. How long will her hair be in 5 months?

   Initial Value: ____________________

2. Nina bought a new fish tank that holds 25 gallons of water. If she fills up the tank at a rate of 1 gallon per 30 seconds, how full will the tank be after 5 minutes?

   Initial Value: ____________________

3. Michael has to mow his grass when it gets too long. He likes for the grass to be 3 inches long. If it grows at a rate of 1 inch every 2 days, how long will his grass be after 8 days without mowing?

   Initial Value: ____________________

4. Phillip has been assigned 50 pages of reading. If he still has 35 pages of reading left after he has been reading for 10 minutes, how many pages will he have left after he has been reading for 40 minutes?

   Initial Value: ____________________

5. Jack pulls the plug from a bathtub that is holding 25 gallons of water. After 40 seconds, there are 15 gallons of water left in the tub. How much water will be left in the bathtub one minute after Jack pulls the plug?

   Initial Value: ____________________

6. Penelope lives 10 miles from her school. After 5 minutes of driving, she still has 7 miles left before she gets to school. How far will she have traveled after 8 minutes of driving?

   Initial Value: ____________________

NAME ____________________

Lesson 4.7 Constructing Function Models

Function models, or equations, can be constructed by using known values of input (x) and output (y) variables, the rate of change (m), and the initial value of the output variable (b) in the format, $y = mx + b$.

Step 1: Calculate the rate of change. $\frac{12 - 5}{5 - 2} = \frac{7}{3}$

Step 2: Substitute known values of x and y into the slope-intercept form of the equation. $y = mx + b$

$(2) = \left(\frac{7}{3}\right)(2) + b$

Step 3: Solve to find the initial value of the output variable (b). $2 = \frac{14}{3} + b$

$b = 2 - \frac{14}{3} = -\frac{8}{3}$

Step 4: Write the equation using the found values of m and b. $y = \frac{7}{3}x + \left(-\frac{8}{3}\right)$ or $\frac{7}{3}x - \frac{8}{3}$

Construct a function model, or equation, for each table below.

1.

a

input	output
1	3
2	6
3	9

Function Model: ____________

b

input	output
3	1
6	2
9	3

Function Model: ____________

c

input	output
1	6
3	18
5	30

Function Model: ____________

2.

input	output
2	2
3	4
4	6

Function Model: ____________

input	output
2	1
4	4
6	7

Function Model: ____________

input	output
12	4
16	8
20	12

Function Model: ____________

3.

input	output
2	−1
4	1
6	3

Function Model: ____________

input	output
1	3
2	7
3	11

Function Model: ____________

input	output
0	6
1	8
3	12

Function Model: ____________

NAME ______________________________

Lesson 4.7 Constructing Function Models

Function models can be constructed by observing points on a graph, calculating the rate of change (or slope), and plugging known values into the equation, $y = mx + b$.

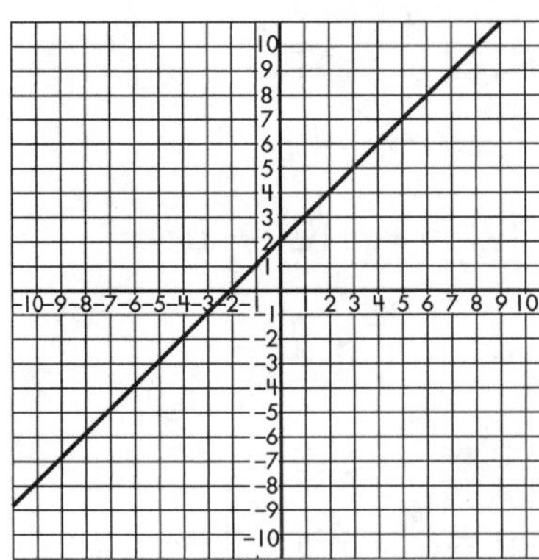

Step 1: Find and name two points on the line. — (4, 6) and (2, 4)

Step 2: Calculate the rate of change. — $m = \frac{4-6}{2-4} = \frac{-2}{-2} = 1$

Step 3: Use the found points and calculated slope to find the initial value of the output if it cannot be determined based on the graph. — Based on the graph, the initial value of the output variable is 2.

Step 4: Write the formula for all values of x and y using the equation. — $y = (1)x + 2$
$y = x + 2$

Use the graphs to write function models, or equations, in the form of $y = mx + b$.

	a	b
1.	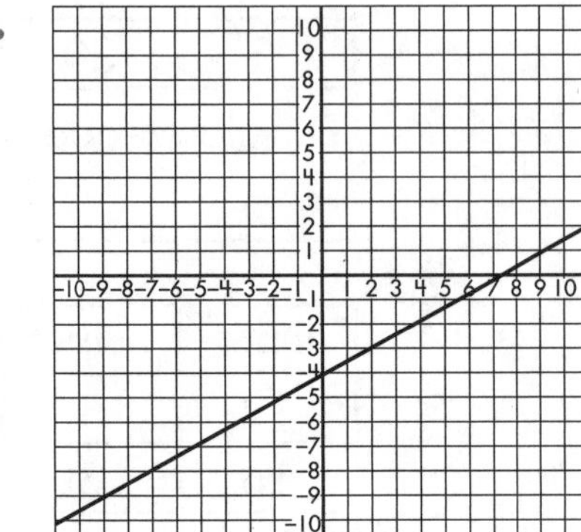 Function Model: ______________	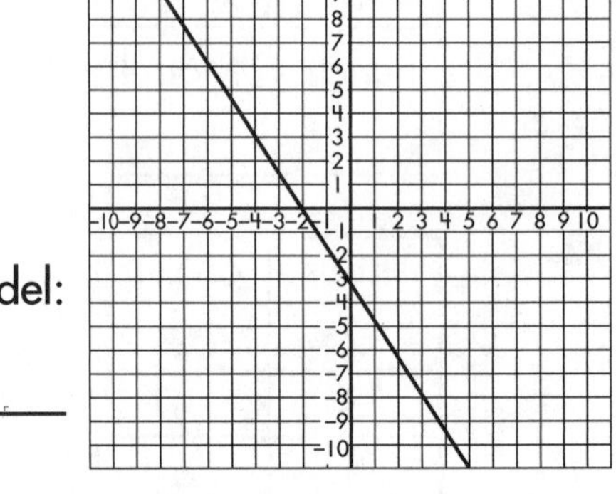 Function Model: ______________
2.	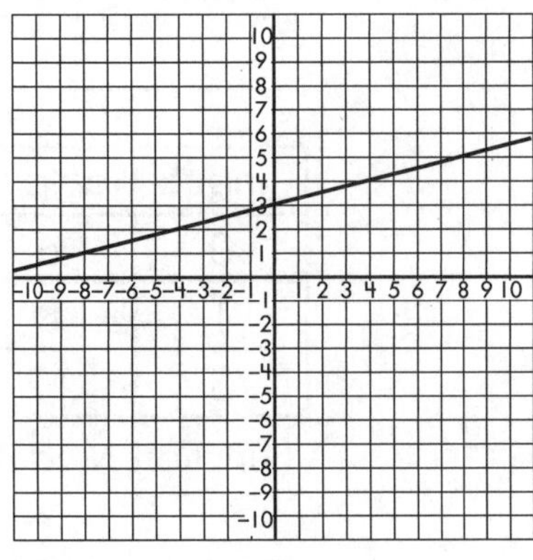 Function Model: ______________	Function Model: ______________

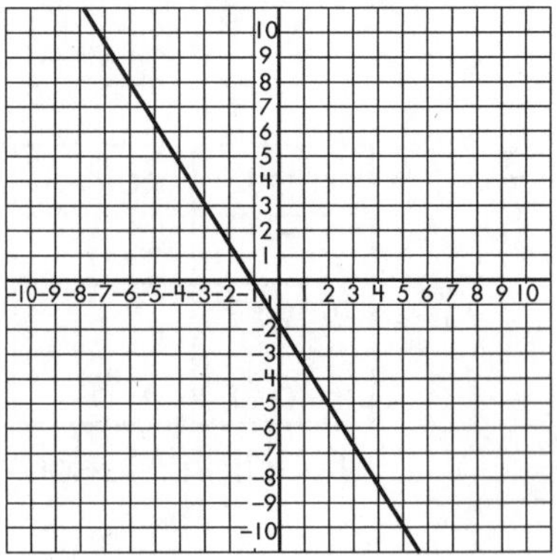

NAME ______________________

Lesson 4.7 Constructing Function Models

Function models can be constructed when two points on the line representing the function are given, provided the function is linear. First, calculate the rate of change, or slope, using the points given. Then, plug one set of the known x and y values into the equation, $y = mx + b$, to find the initial value of the output variable.

Find the equation of a line that runs through points (2, 3) and (5, 6).

Step 1: Find the rate of change, or slope, m. $m = \frac{3-6}{2-5} = \frac{-3}{-3} = 1$

Step 2: Plug in known values of x and y to calculate b.
$3 = (1)(2) + b$
$3 = 2 + b$
$1 = b$

Step 3: Write the equation that will allow all values of x and y to be found.
$y = 1x + 1$
$y = x + 1$

Use the points given to find the function model for the linear function they represent.

	a	b	c
1.	(3, 4) and (5, 8) $y =$ ________	(4, 5) and (8, 3) $y =$ ________	(1, 2) and (5, 10) $y =$ ________
2.	(2, 7) and (0, 1) $y =$ ________	(2, 0) and (0, 3) $y =$ ________	(−1, 2) and (7, 6) $y =$ ________
3.	(1, 1) and (3, 5) $y =$ ________	(1, 3) and (2, 4) $y =$ ________	(2, 6) and (−2, 4) $y =$ ________
4.	(2, 16) and (−1, 7) $y =$ ________	(2, 13) and (1, 8) $y =$ ________	(4, 3) and (8, 1) $y =$ ________

NAME ______________________________

Lesson 4.8 Analyzing Function Graphs

Models of real-life situations can be drawn on non-specific graphs—or ones without titles or labeled *x* and *y* axes—in order to see the relationship between two variables that are being examined along different points.

Situation:

Mike rides a bike to Sam's house. When he arrives, he and Sam wait for Sam's mom who then drives them to the bus stop. Sam and Mike wait for the bus, and then get on the bus, which then takes them to school.

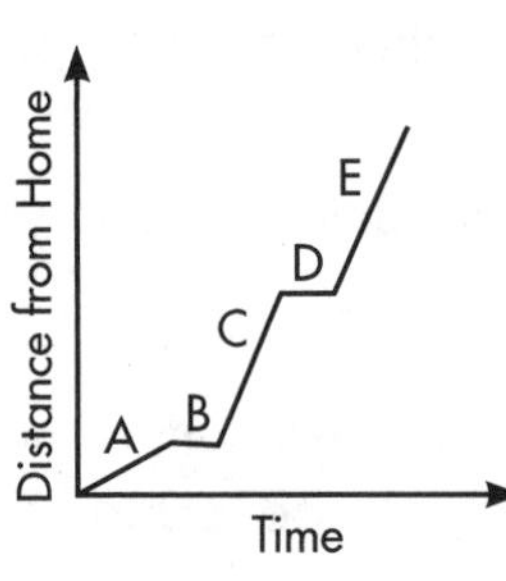

Relationships:

Mike travels at a constant rate to Sam's house (A).

Mike and Sam do not travel while they wait for Sam's mom to drive them to the bus stop (B).

Sam's mom takes Mike and Sam to the bus stop (C).

Mike and Sam do not travel while they are waiting at the bus stop (D).

Mike and Sam appear to travel at the same constant rate both in the car and on the bus (E).

Use the situation and graph to describe 3 relationships that exist in each function.

1. Situation:

An amusement park is open from April to November each year. The graph shows the number of visitors it receives.

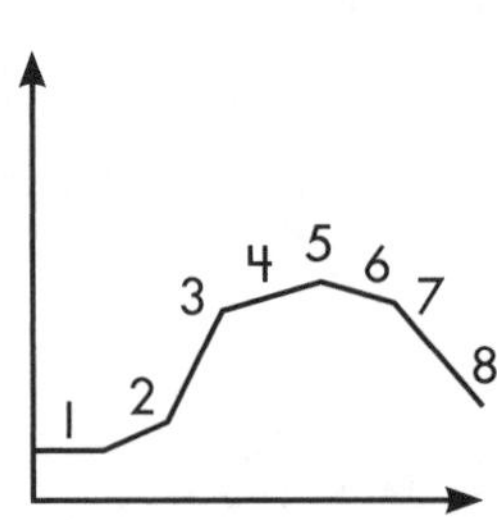

Relationships:

____

____

____

____

____

2. Situation:

Grace is studying words for a spelling bee. She has 4 weeks to learn as many as she can.

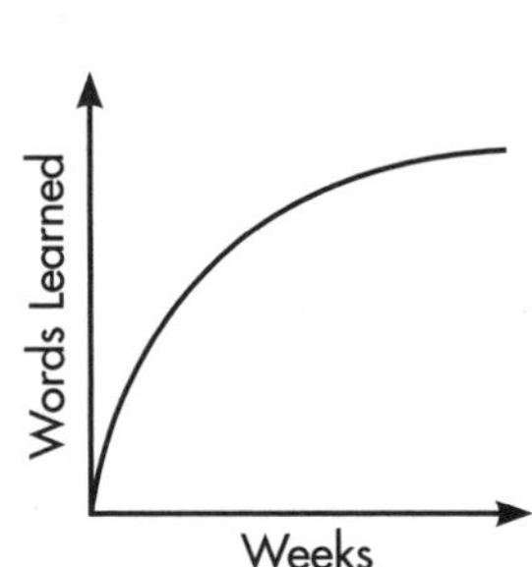

Relationships:

____

____

____

____

____

3. Situation:

A family is taking a 500 mile trip to visit family.

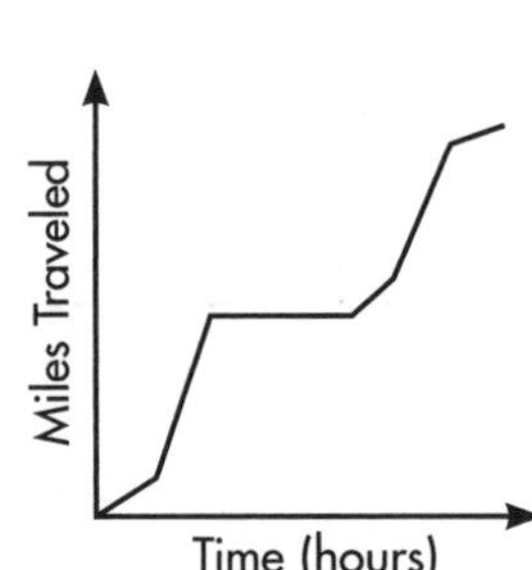

Relationships:

____

____

____

____

____

NAME ____________________

Lesson 4.9 Graphing Functions

The slope-intercept form of a linear function, $y = mx + b$, can be used to create a graph of that function.

$y = 2x - 7$

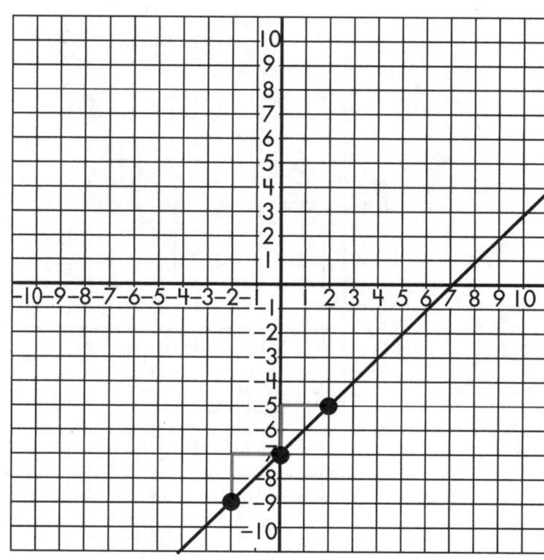

Step 1: Mark the point where the line will cross the y-axis ($b = -7$).

Step 2: From the point which crosses the y-axis, use the slope (m) to find other points on both sides. Remember that slope is found by $\frac{\text{change in } y}{\text{change in } x}$.

Step 3: Draw a line that goes directly through the points found.

Sketch each linear function shown.

1.

a $y = -3x + 4$

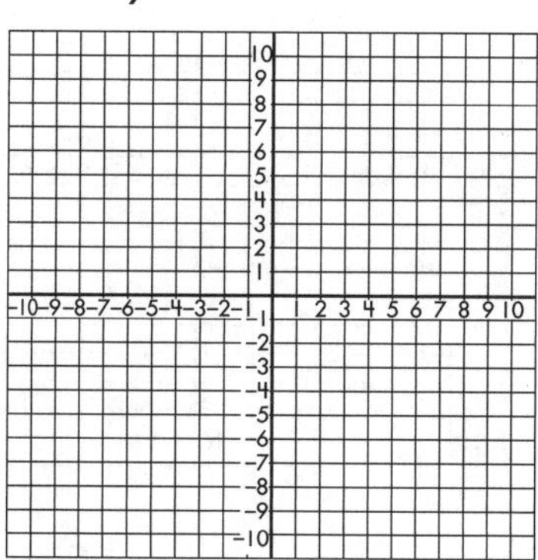

b $y = \frac{1}{6}x$

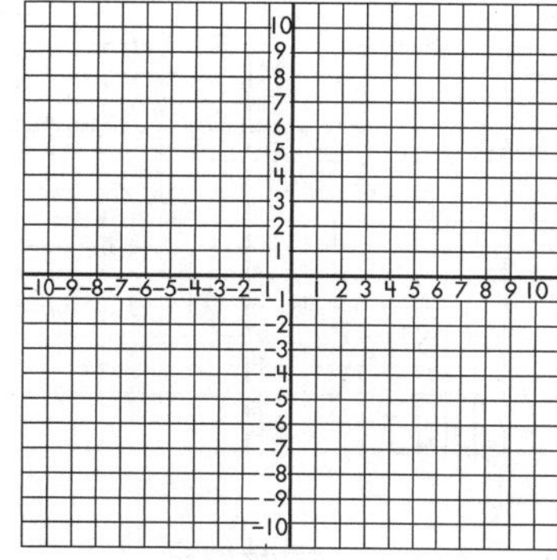

2.

a $y = 3x - 1$

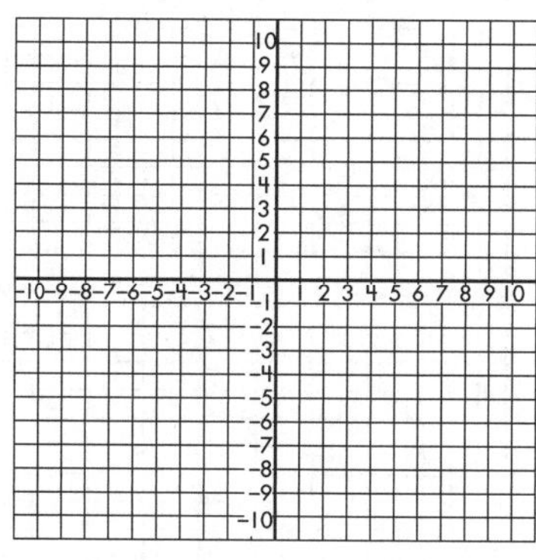

b $y = 2x + 2$

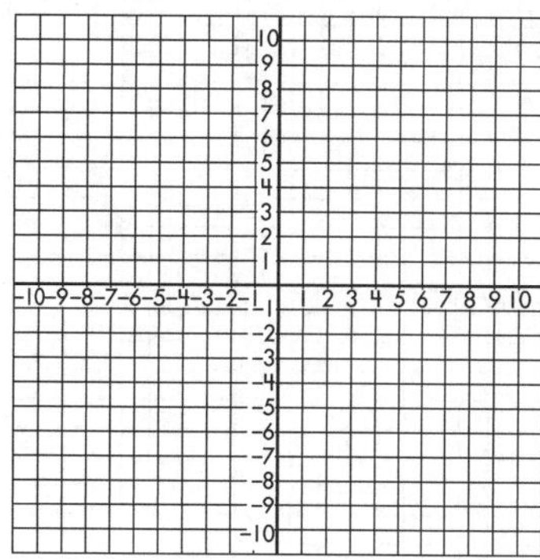

NAME ______________________________

Lesson 4.9 Graphing Functions

Sketch each linear function shown.

a **b**

1. $y = 2x - 1$

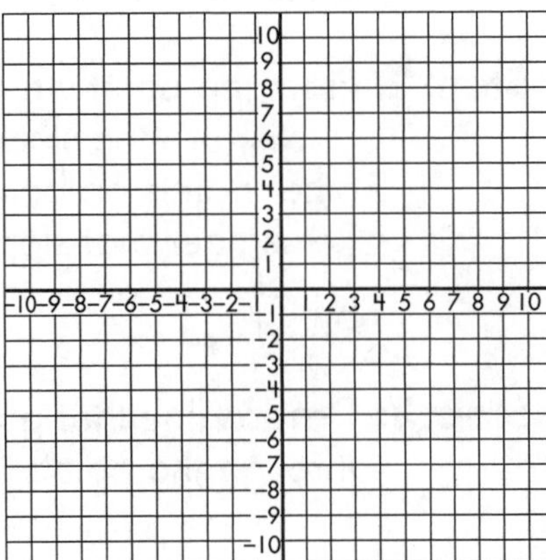

$y = -\frac{1}{2}x - 3$

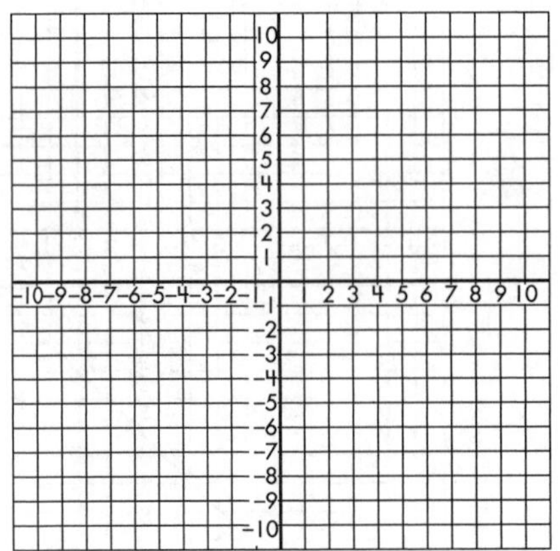

2. $y = 3x - 6$

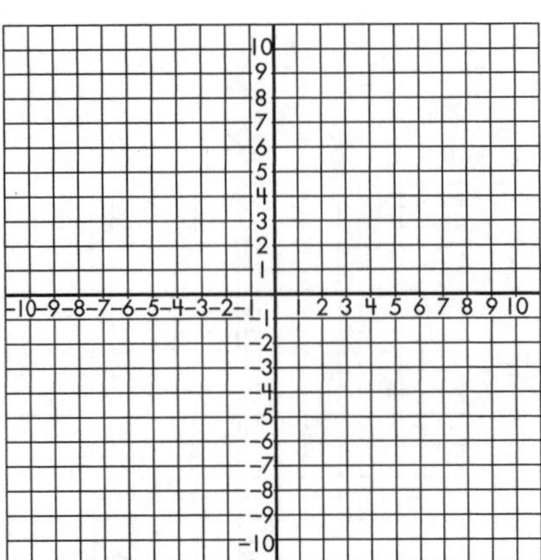

$y = -\frac{2}{3}x + 4$

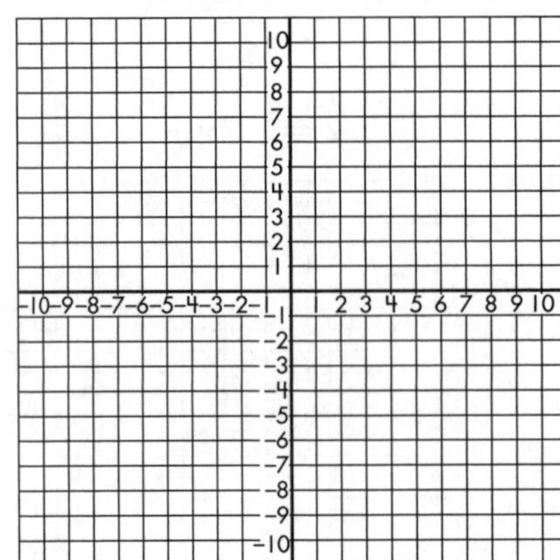

3. $y = 4x + 3$

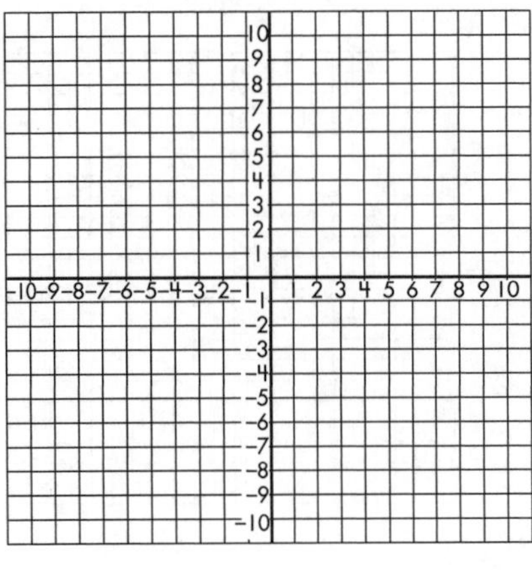

$y = -\frac{1}{3}x + 2$

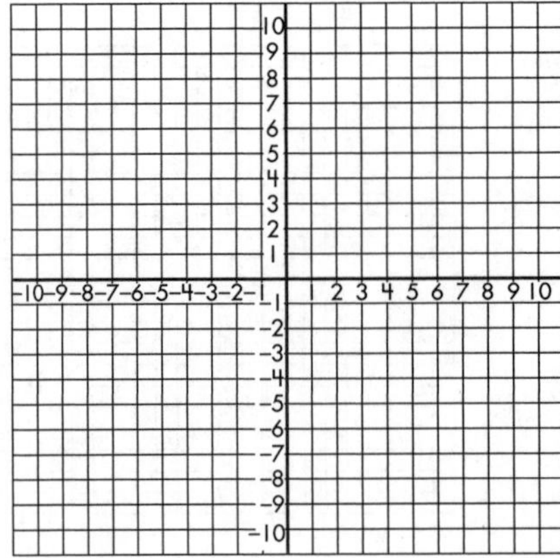

NAME ____________________

Lesson 4.9 Graphing Functions

Sketch each linear function shown.

	a	b
1.	$y = 3x + 9$	$y = 2x - 5$

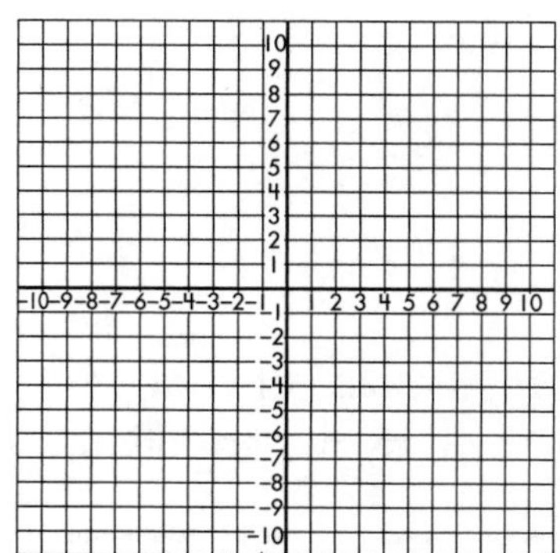

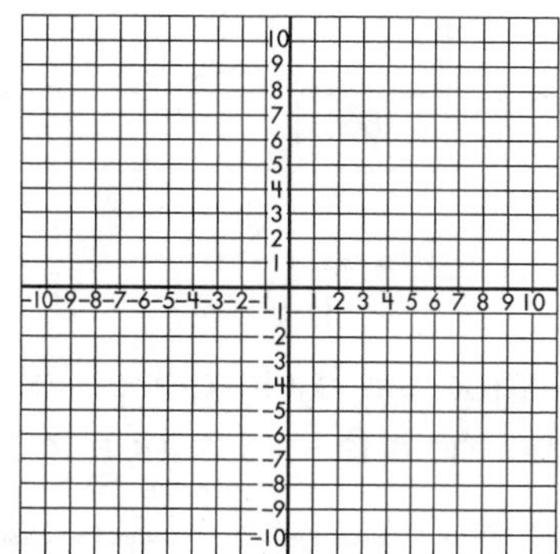

	a	b
2.	$y = -3x + 4$	$y = 5$

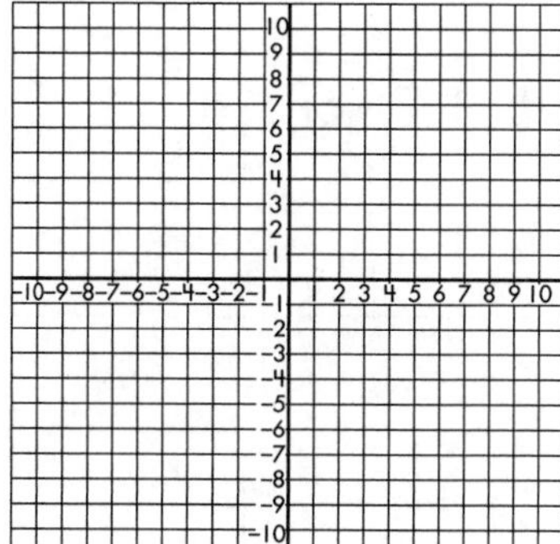

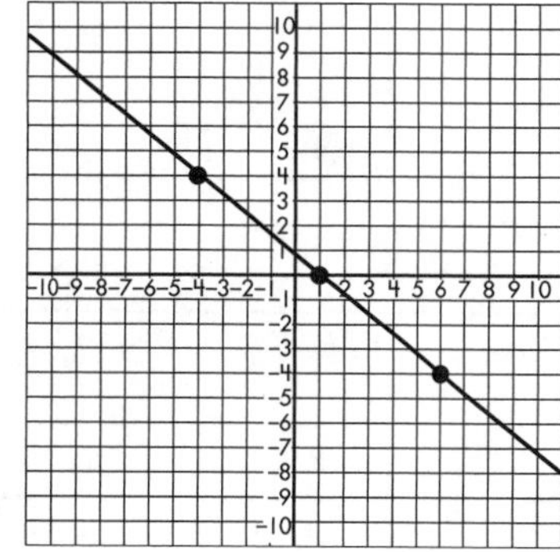

	a	b
3.	$y = \frac{1}{2}x + 4$	$y = -\frac{4}{5}x + 1$

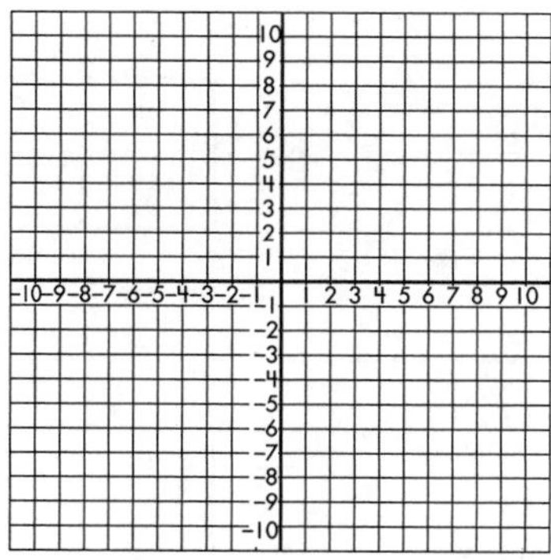

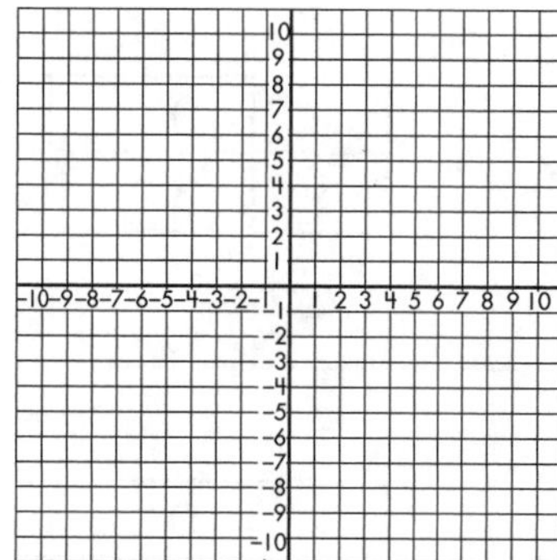

NAME ____________________

Lesson 4.10 Comparing Functions

Functions that are represented in different ways can be compared by their rate of change or by specific values at a certain point. The functions do not have to be in the same format in order to compare them.

Which function has a greater rate of change?

$y = -\frac{16}{5}x + 6$ or

x	0	1	2
y	1	–3	–7

Rate of change for table $= \frac{-7 - 1}{2 - 0} = -\frac{8}{2} = -4$

Rate of change is judged by larger absolute value, therefore, the rate of change for the function represented in the table is larger than the rate of change shown by the equation.

Compare the rate of change for the equations and tables shown below and decide which has a greater rate of change by writing *equation* or *table*.

a

1. $y = 2x + 6$ or

x	0	1	2
y	10	16	26

____

b

$y = 4x + 7$ or

x	0	1	2
y	9	12	15

____

2. $y = 7x + 4$ or

x	0	1	2
y	8	10	12

____

$y = 3x + 4$ or

x	0	1	2
y	7	12	17

____

3. $y = 5x + 2$ or

x	0	1	2
y	3	10	17

____

$y = \frac{3}{2}x - 2$ or

x	0	1	2
y	–2	–1	0

____

4. $y = 7x + 4$ or

x	0	1	2
y	1	–3	–7

____

$y = \frac{3}{2}x + 2$ or

x	0	1	2
y	1	$\frac{7}{3}$	$\frac{11}{3}$

____

NAME ____________________

Lesson 4.10 Comparing Functions

Functions represented in a table and an equation can be compared when the value of x is provided. In the example below, you are given the value of x, which can be substituted into each equation to determine which function has the greater value.

$y = -\frac{16}{5}x + 6$

or

x	0	1	2
y	1	−3	−7

when $x = 2$

Step 1: Substitute 2 for x in the equation and solve the first function.

$y = -\frac{16}{5}(2) + 6 \quad y = -6\frac{2}{5} + 6$

$y = -\frac{2}{5}$

Step 2: Find the rate of change for the table.

$\frac{\text{change in } y}{\text{change in } x} = -\frac{-1}{2} - 0 = \frac{-8}{2} = -4$

Step 3: Find the y-intercept of the table. This is found on the table where $x = 0$.

$x = 0$ where $y = 1$

Step 4: Substitute the rate of change, the given value of x, and the y-intercept into the equation $y = mx + b$.

$y = mx + b$

$y = (-4)(2) + 1$

$y = -7$

Step 5: Compare the value of y in the formula to the value of y in the table to determine which function has the greater value.

Equation: $y = \frac{-2}{5}$ Table: $y = -7$

Therefore, the function shown in the equation has a greater value.

Which function has a greater value for the given value of x? Write *equation*, *table*, or *equal*.

a

1. $y = 2x + 6$ or
when $x = 1$

x	0	1	2
y	10	16	26

____

b

$y = 4x + 7$ or
when $x = 2$

x	0	1	2
y	9	12	15

____

2. $y = 7x + 4$ or
when $x = 3$

x	0	1	2
y	8	10	12

____

$y = 3x + 4$ or
when $x = 0$

x	0	1	2
y	7	12	17

____

3. $y = 5x + 2$ or
when $x = -3$

x	0	1	2
y	3	10	17

____

$y = x - 2$ or
when $x = 4$

x	0	1	2
y	−2	−1	0

____

NAME ______________________________

Lesson 4.10 Comparing Functions

Functions represented on a graph can be compared to functions represented by an equation.

Which function has a greater rate of change?

$y = -2x + 3$ or

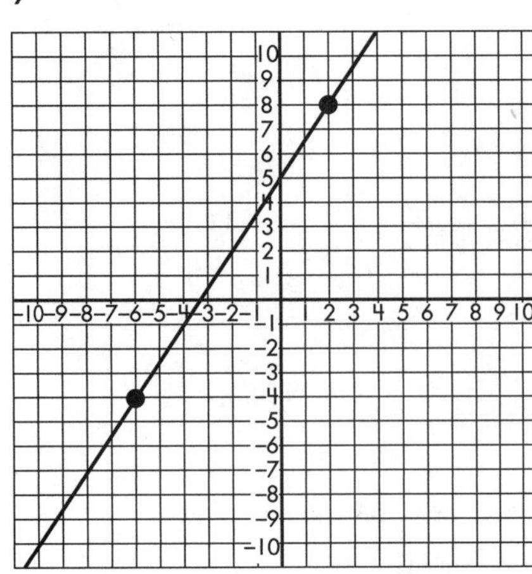

Step 1: Identify the slope, or rate of change, for the function represented by the equation. In this case, the rate of change is –2.

Step 2: Identify two points on the line and calculate the rate of change, or slope, for the function represented by the graph. In this case: $\frac{8 - (-4)}{2 - (-6)} = \frac{12}{8} = \frac{3}{2}$

Step 3: Compare the rates of change to see which is greater. The absolute value of –2 is greater than $\frac{3}{2}$, therefore the function represented by the equation has a greater rate of change.

Which function has a greater rate of change? Write *equation*, *graph*, or *equal*.

	a	b	c
1.	$y = \frac{1}{2}x - 2$ or 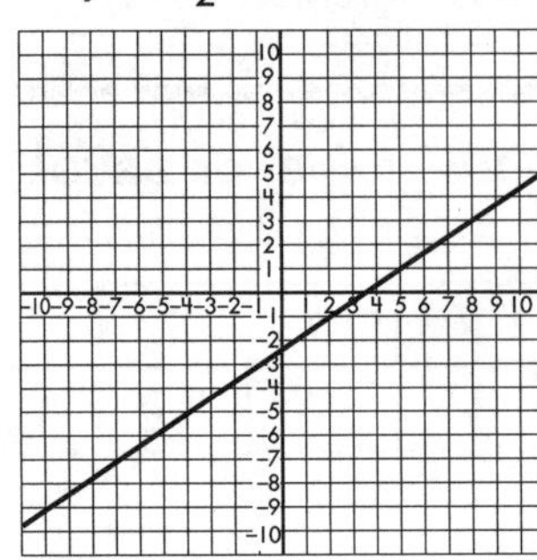 ______________	$y = -6x + 1$ or 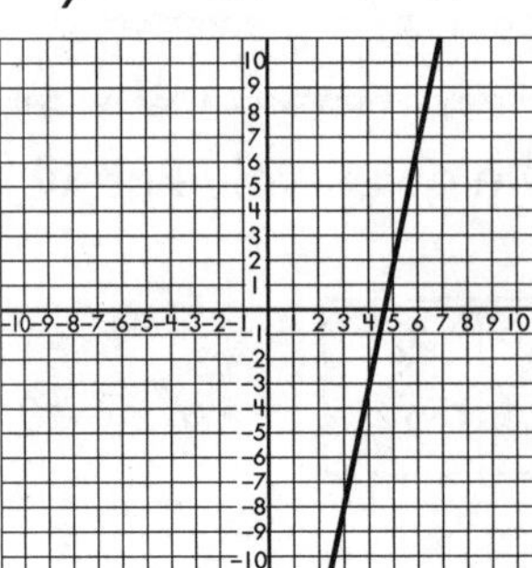 ______________	$y = 3x - 2$ or 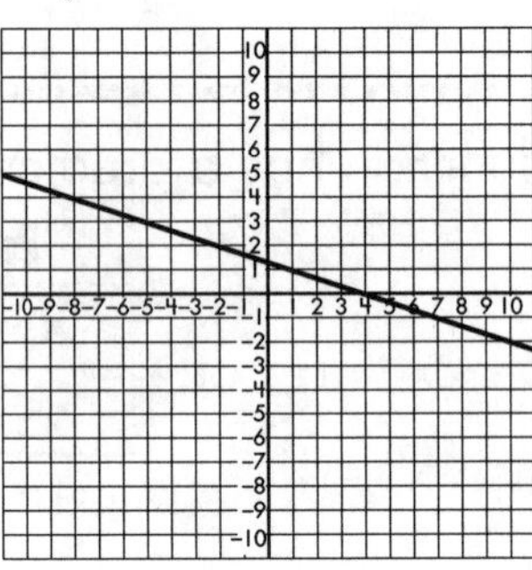 ______________
2.	$y = 4x + 3$ or 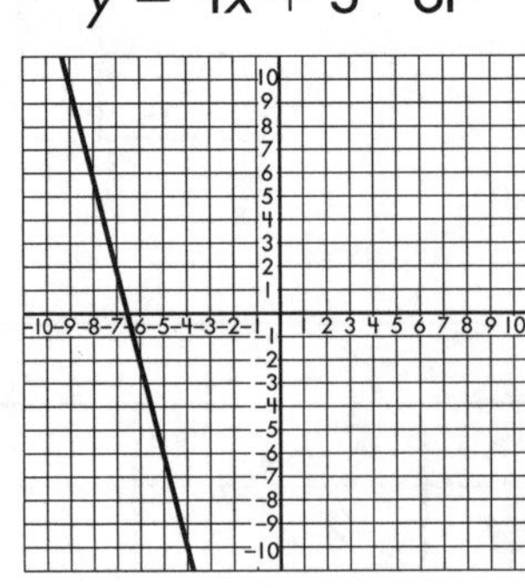 ______________	$y = -\frac{2}{3}x + 2$ or 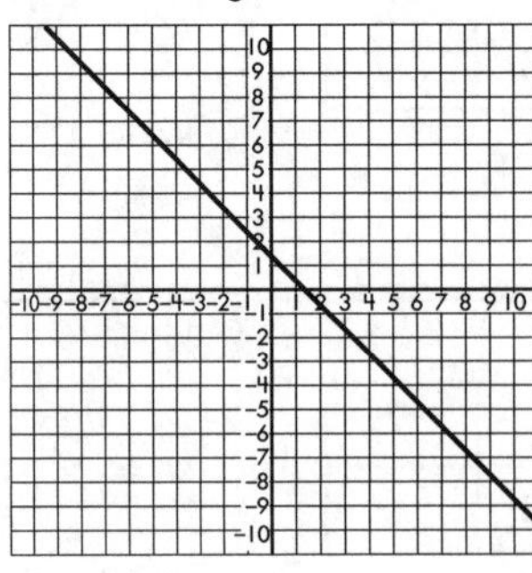 ______________	$y = 2x - 5$ or 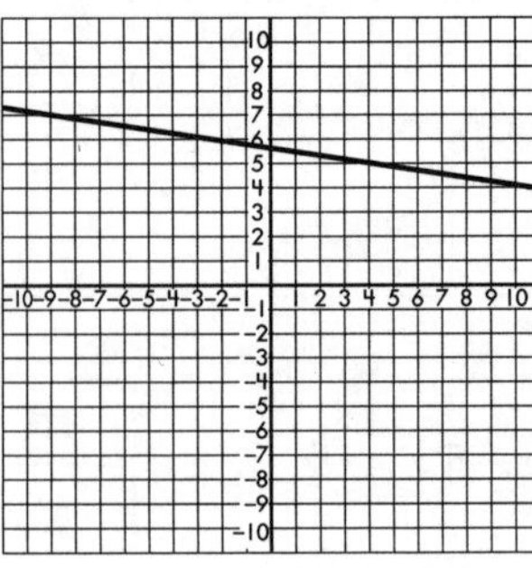 ______________

NAME ______________________

Check What You Learned

Functions

Decide if each table represents a function by stating *yes* or *no*.

1.

a

input	output
0	−2, 1
1	2
2	1
3	4

____

b

input	output
−1	2
0	2
1	−3
2	−2

____

c

input	output
−3	4
−2	4
−1	−1
3	−1

____

Complete each function table for the given function.

2. $y = 3x + 24$

x	y
10	
14	
19	
25	
29	

$y = 2x - 13$

x	y
15	
29	
37	
59	
73	

$y = \frac{1}{19}x + 3$

x	y
38	
76	
171	
228	
285	

Find the relationship for each function table and then complete the table.

3.

a

x	y
6	
7	1
8	2
12	

Function: ______________

b

x	y
1	6
7	
9	
11	−4

Function: ______________

Find the rate of change, or slope, for points on the function table and decide if it represents a *linear* or *nonlinear* relationship.

4.

x	y	Rate
−2	−7	
−1	−3	
0	1	
1	5	

Relationship: ______________

x	y	Rate
0	0	
1	2	
2	8	
3	26	

Relationship: ______________

CHAPTER 4 POSTTEST

NAME ______________________

Check What You Learned

Functions

CHAPTER 4 POSTTEST

Find the rate of change for each function table. Write fractions in simplest form.

5.

a

input	output
2	3
4	11
6	19

rate of change: ____________

b

input	output
2	10
4	18
6	26

rate of change: ____________

c

input	output
3	0
7	2
11	4

rate of change: ____________

Find the initial value of the function represented below.

6. Jacob is filling a flower bed with dirt. It already has 5 cubic ft. of dirt in it. After 30 minutes of shoveling, the flower bed has 20 cubic ft. in it. How much dirt will be in the flower bed after 1 hour?

Initial Value: ____________

Use the given information to find the function models for the linear functions shown.

7.

a

(4, 5) and (5, 8)

$y =$ ____________

b

input	output
0	6
1	16
2	26

$y =$ ____________

c

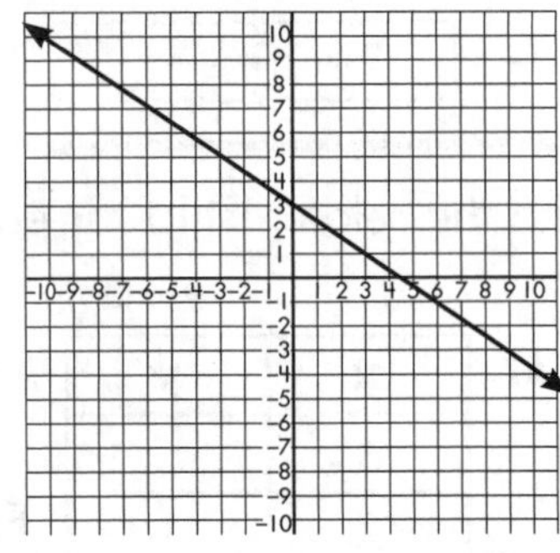

$y =$ ____________

Sketch the linear function shown below.

8. $y = \frac{1}{2}x - 2$

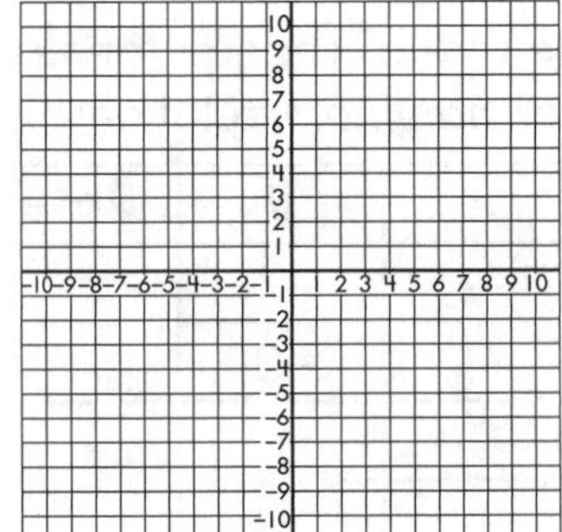

NAME ____________________

Check What You Know

Geometry

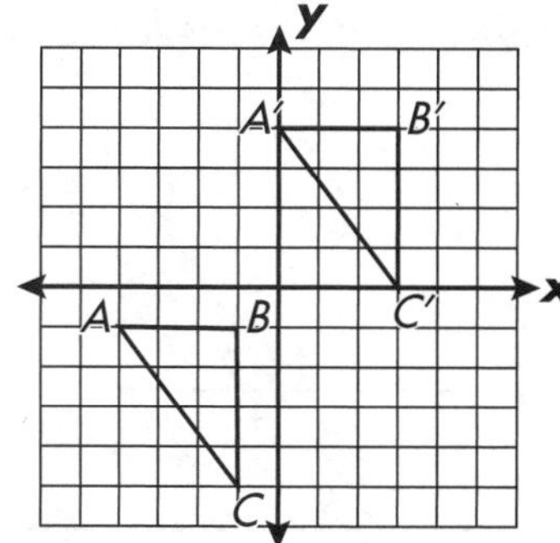

1. What are the coordinates of the preimage?

   A (__________), B (__________), C (__________)

2. What are the coordinates of the image?

   A′ (__________), B′ (__________), C′ (__________)

3. What transformation was performed on the figure? __________

Determine if a set of translations exist between figures 1 and 2 to determine if the figures are *similar*, *congruent*, or *not*.

4.

a

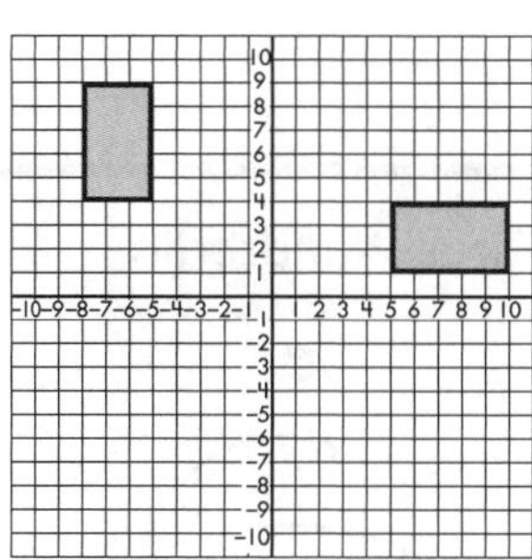

____

b

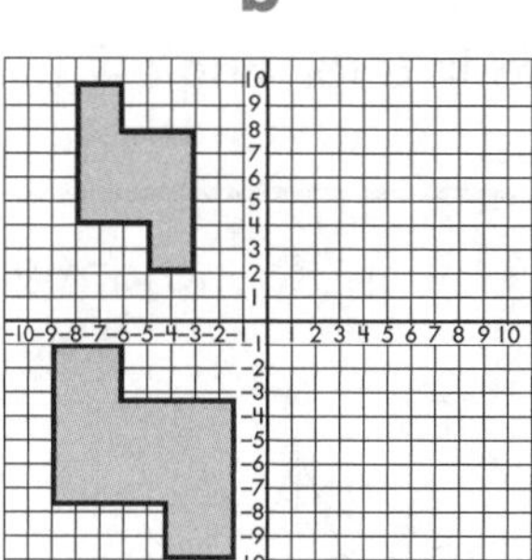

____

c

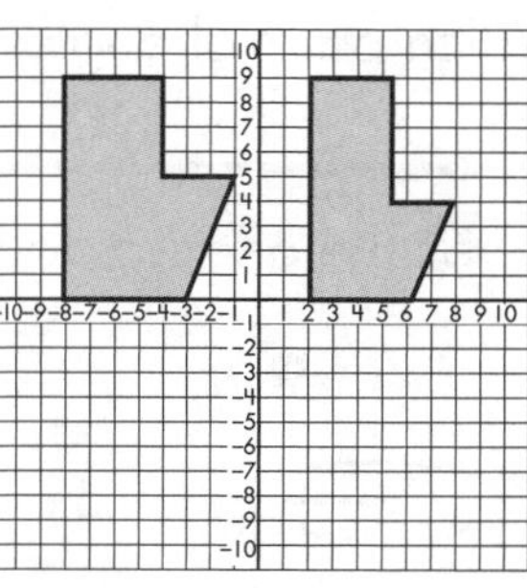

____

Draw similar right triangles to show that each line has a constant slope.

5.

a

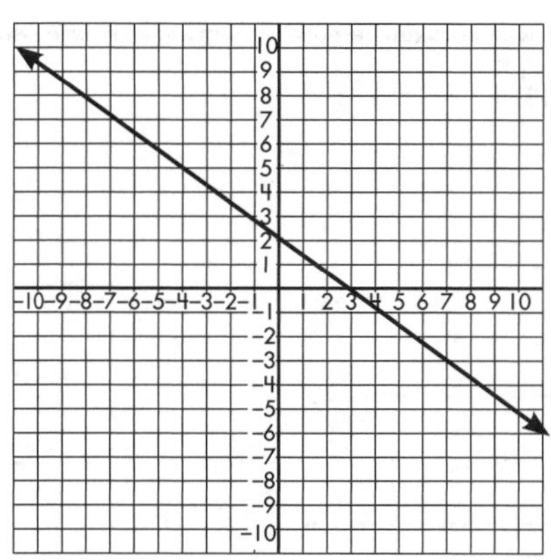

Triangle 1 Legs: ______ & ______

Triangle 2 Legs: ______ & ______

b

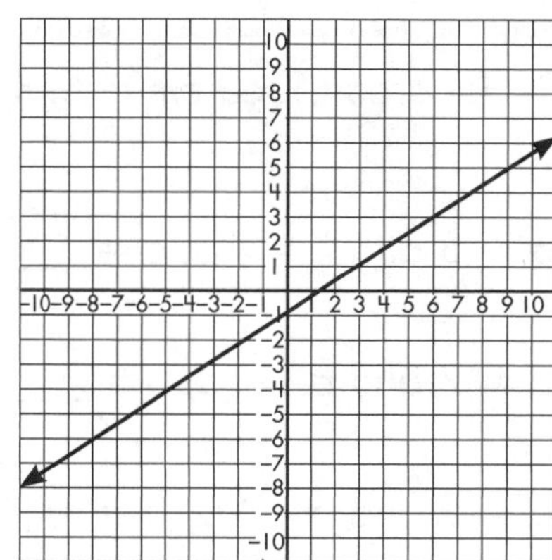

Triangle 1 Legs: ______ & ______

Triangle 2 Legs: ______ & ______

NAME ______________________

Check What You Know

Geometry

Answer each question using letters to name each line and numbers to name each angle.

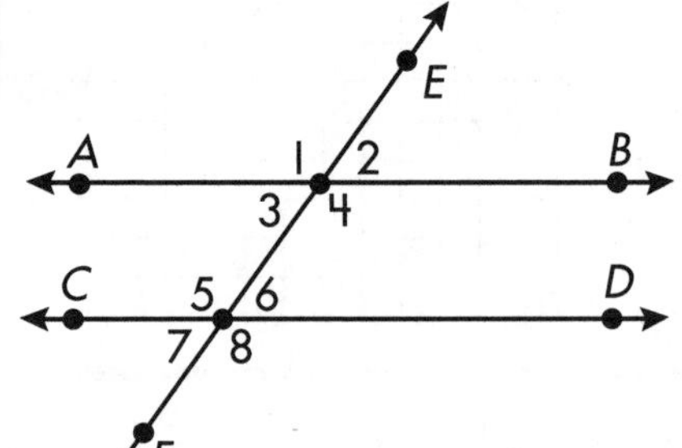

6. What is the name of the transversal? ______________

7. Which angles are acute? ______________

8. Which angles are obtuse? ______________

9. Which pairs of angles are vertical angles? ______________

10. Which pairs of angles are alternate exterior angles?

____

11. Which pairs of angles are alternate interior angles? ______________

Find the volume of each figure. Use 3.14 for π. Round answers to the nearest hundredth.

	a	b	c
12.	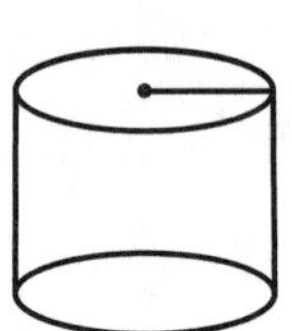 $r = 4.5$ cm, $h = 7$ cm	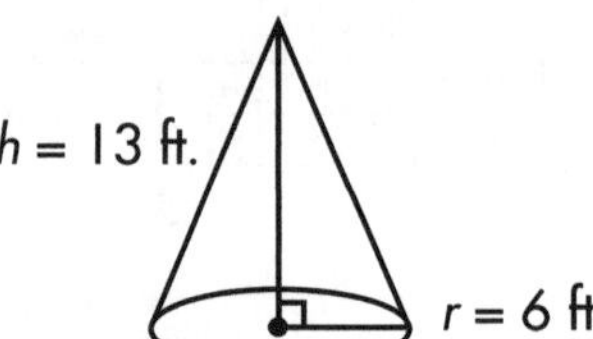 $h = 13$ ft., $r = 6$ ft.	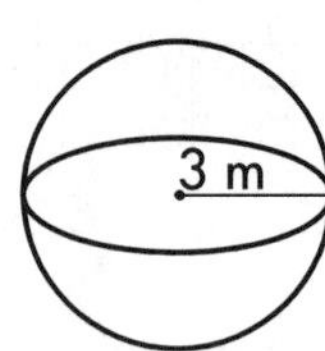 3 m
	$V =$ ______________ cm^3	$V =$ ______________ ft.^{3}	$V =$ ______________ m^3

Use the Pythagorean Theorem to find the unknown lengths.

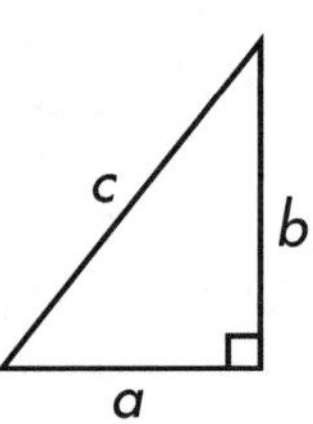

13. If $a = 8$ and $b = 15$, $c = \sqrt{}$ ______ or ______.

14. If $b = 7$ and $c = 13$, $a = \sqrt{}$ ______ or about ______.

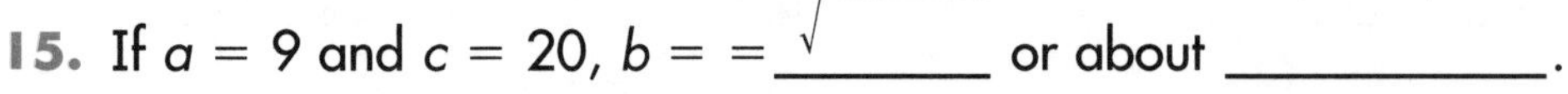

15. If $a = 9$ and $c = 20$, $b = = \sqrt{}$ ______ or about ______.

NAME ______________________________

Lesson 5.1 Transformations: Translations

A **transformation** is a type of function that describes a change in the position, size, or shape of a figure.

A **translation** is a slide of a figure. The figure can be slid up, down, or sideways. However, the size, shape, and orientation of the figure remain the same.

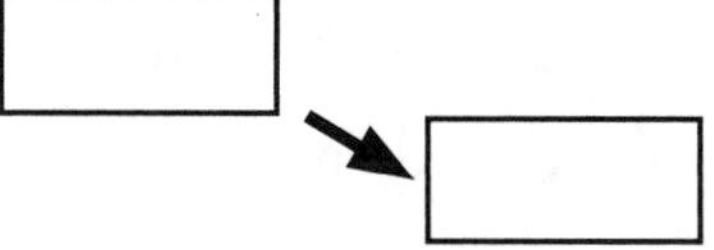

This figure has been translated down and to the right.

State if the figures below represent a translation by writing *yes* or *no*.

	a	b	c
1.	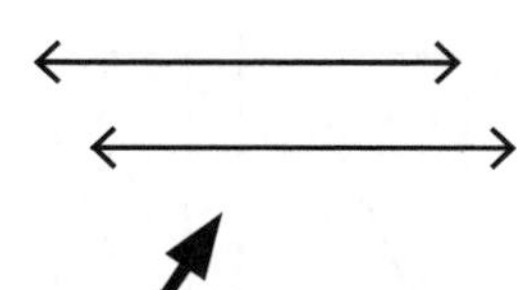	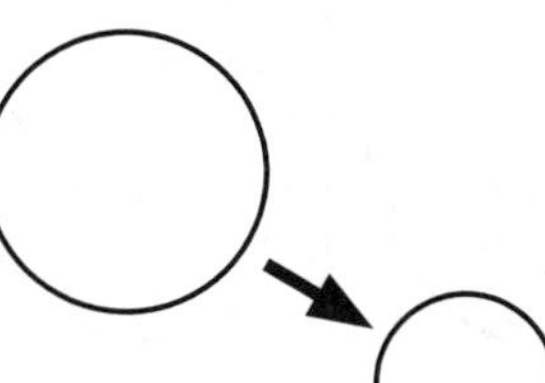	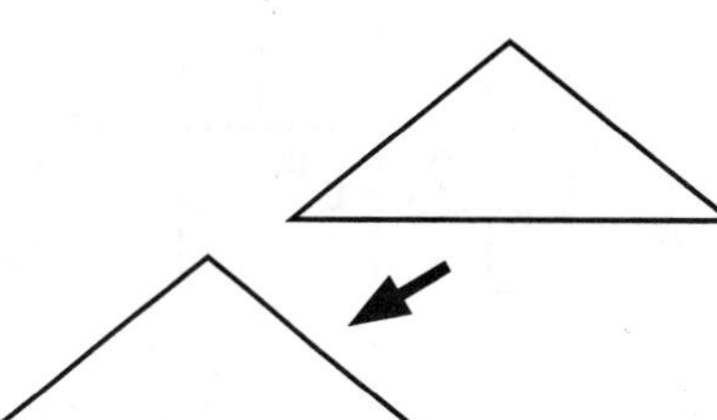
	____________	____________	____________
2.	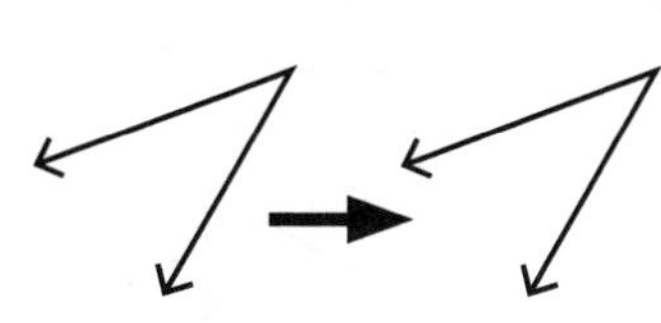		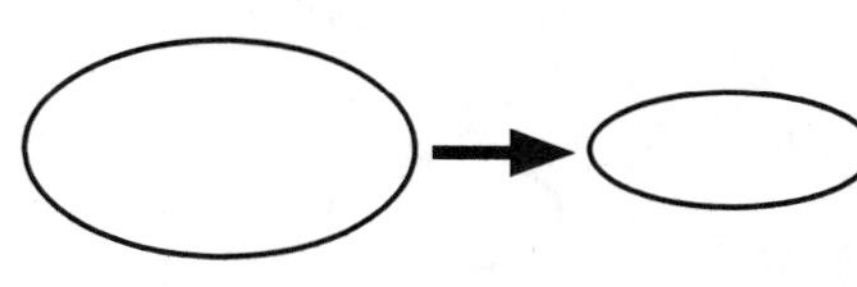
	____________	____________	____________
3.	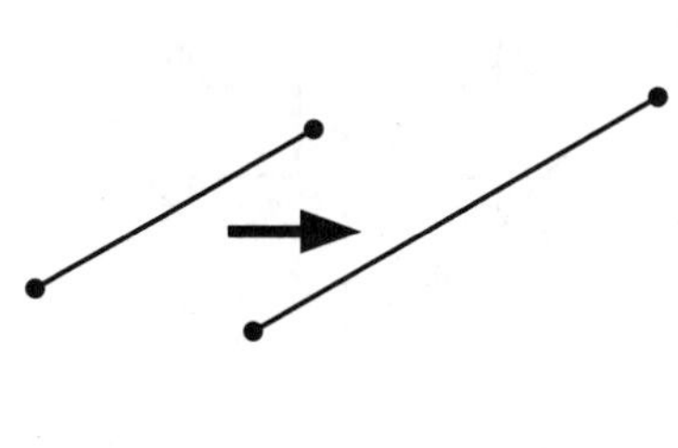	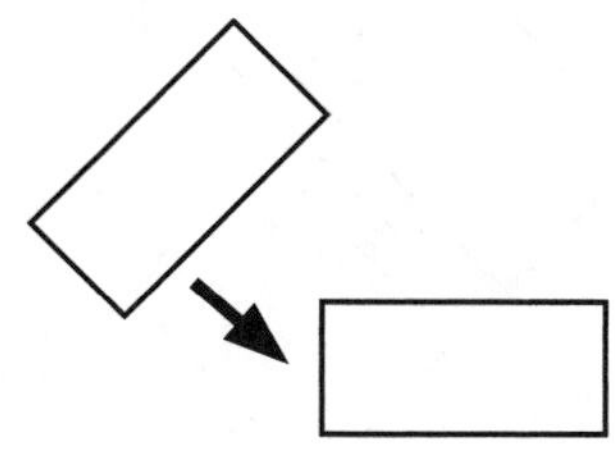	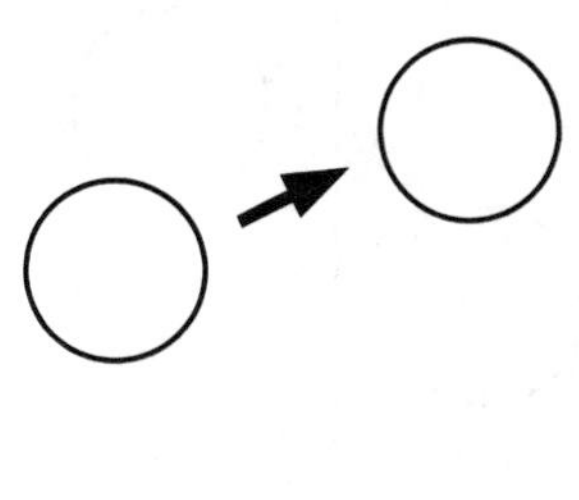
	____________	____________	____________

NAME ______________________________

Lesson 5.1 Transformations: Reflections

A **transformation** is a type of function that describes a change in the position, size, or shape of a figure.

A **reflection** is a flip of a figure. It can be flipped to the side, up, or down.

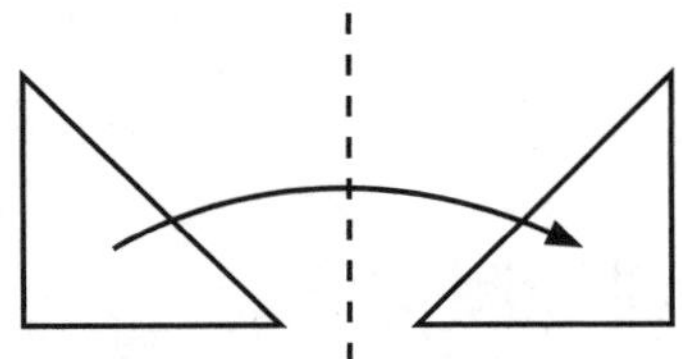

This figure has been flipped horizontally over the dotted line.

State if the figures below represent a reflection by writing *yes* or *no*.

	a	b	c
1.	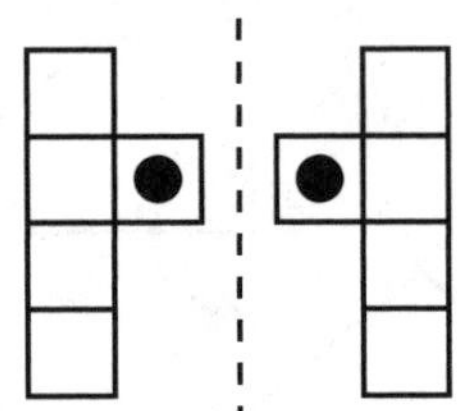 ______	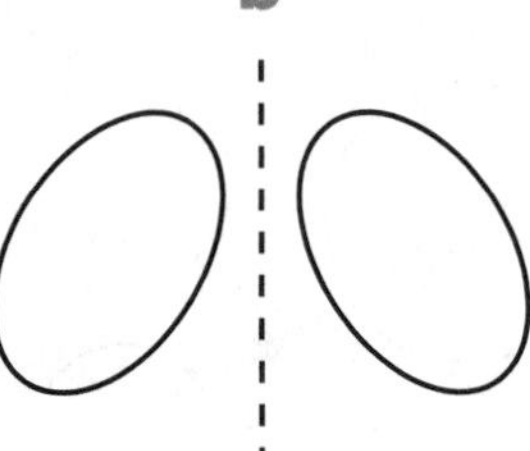 ______	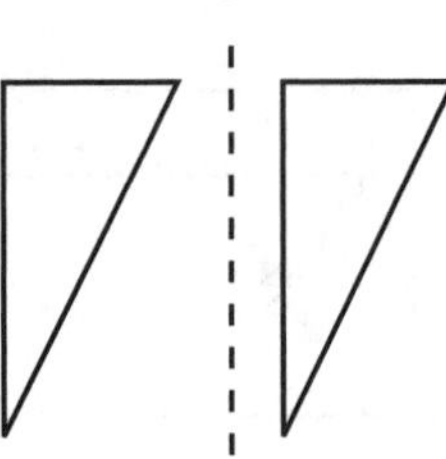 ______
2.	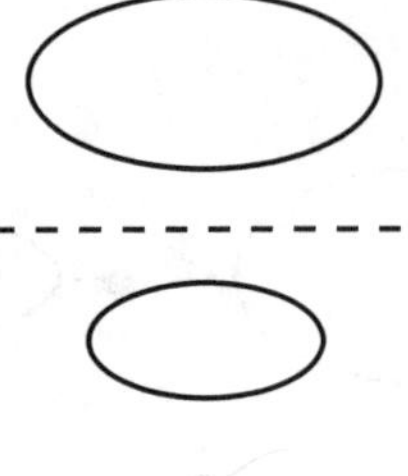 ______	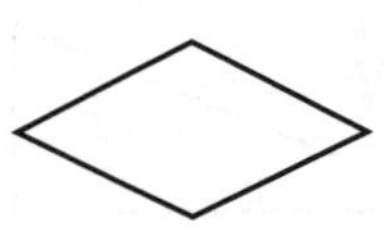 ______	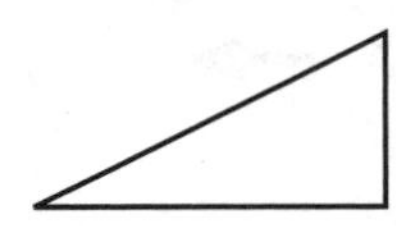 ______
3.	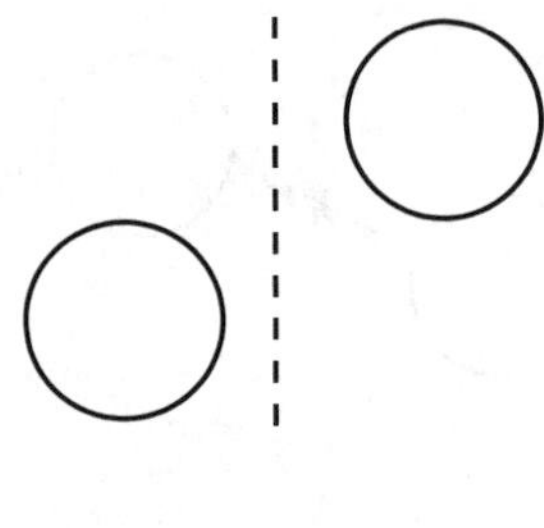 ______	______	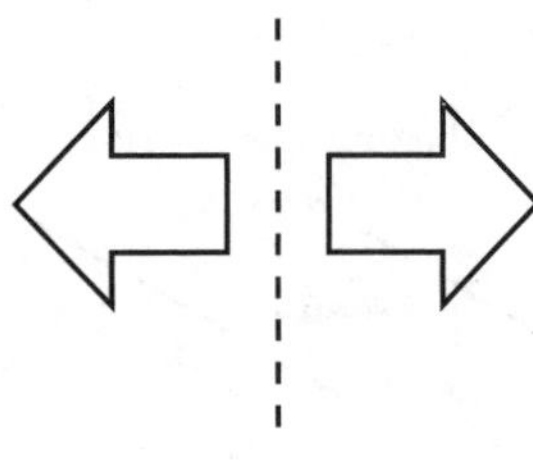 ______

NAME ____________________

Lesson 5.1 Transformations: Rotations

A **transformation** is a type of function that describes a change in the position, size, or shape of a figure.

A **rotation** is a turn of a figure. The figure can be rotated any number of degrees.

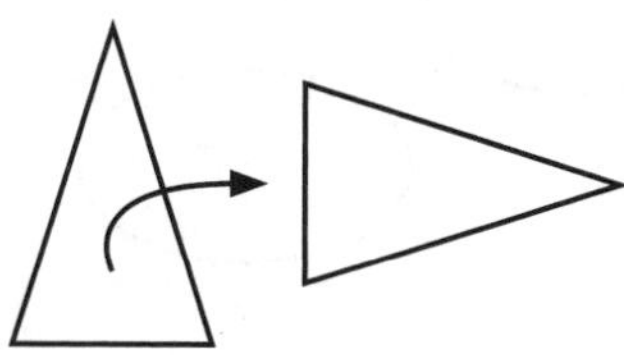

This figure has been rotated 90° clockwise about the point. This point is called the **center of rotation**.

State if the figures below represent a rotation by writing *yes* or *no*.

	a	b	c
1.	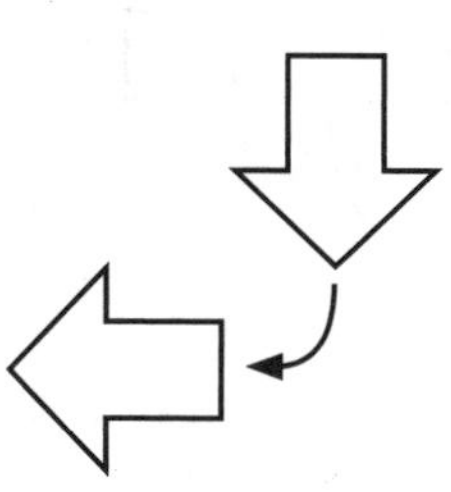 ____________	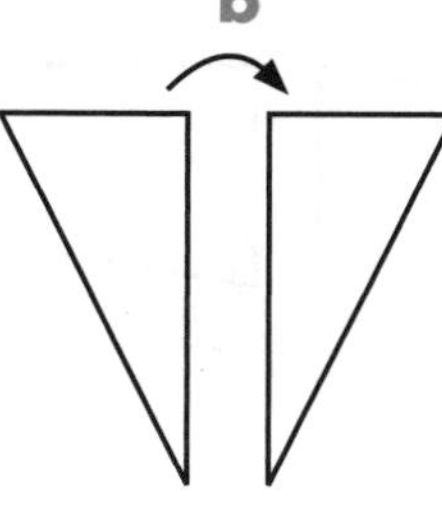 ____________	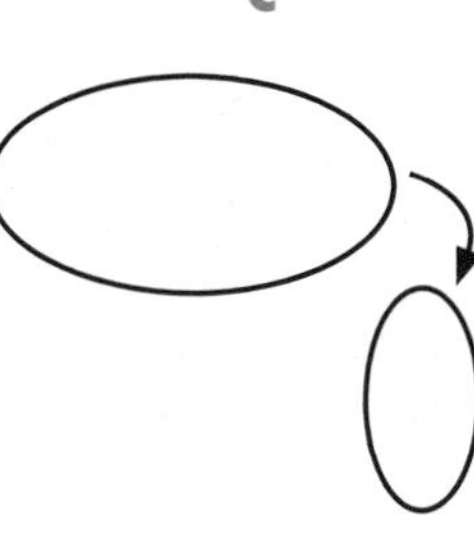 ____________
2.	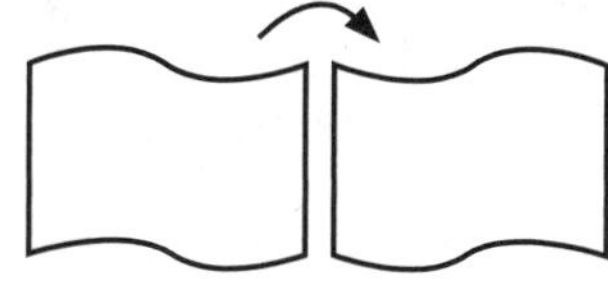 ____________	____________	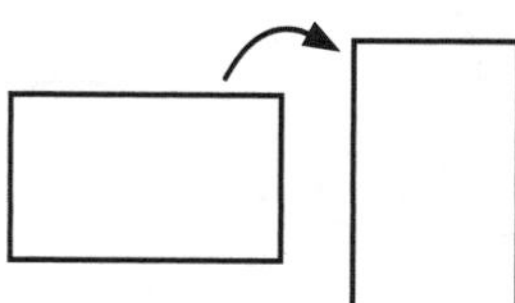 ____________
3.	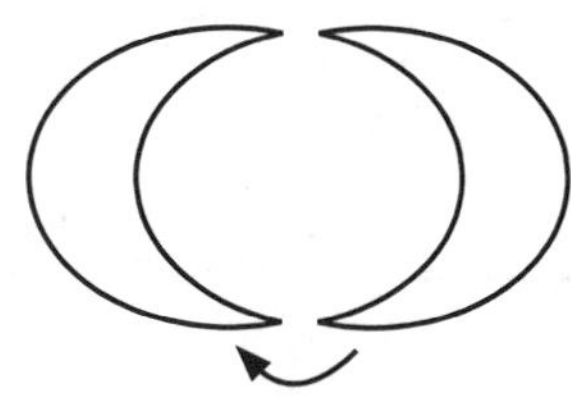 ____________	____________	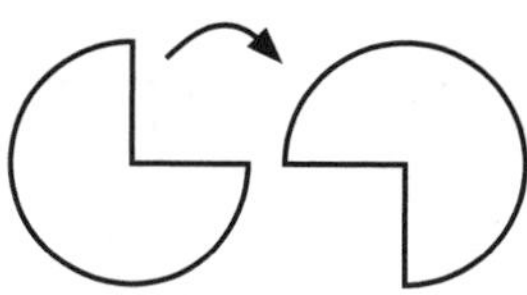 ____________

NAME ______________________

Lesson 5.1 Transformations: Rotations, Reflections, and Translations

State if the figures below represent a *rotation*, *reflection*, or *translation*.

1.

a 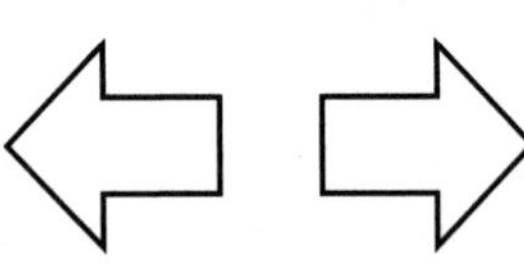 ______________

b 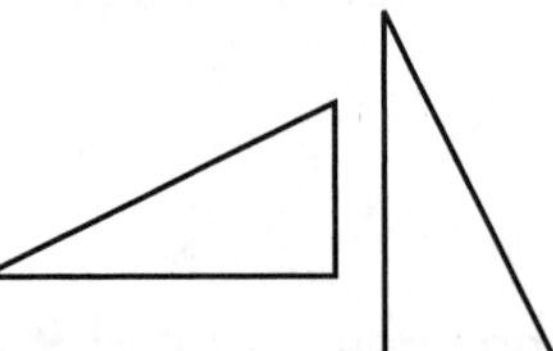 ______________

c 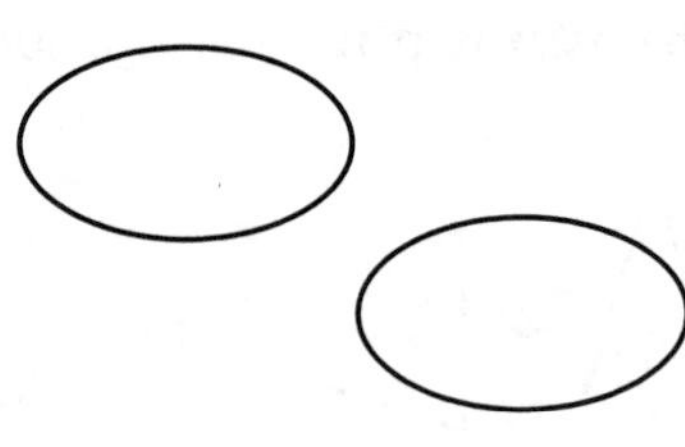 ______________

2.

a 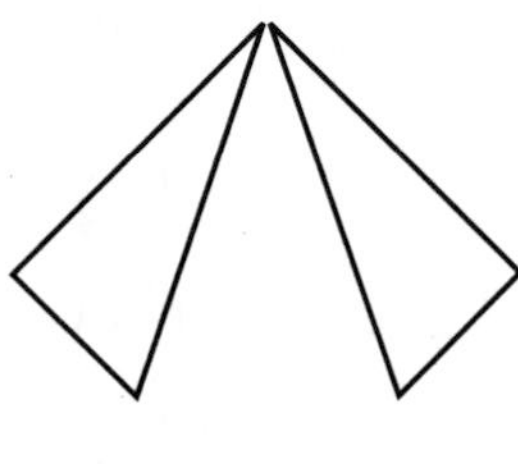 ______________

b ______________

c 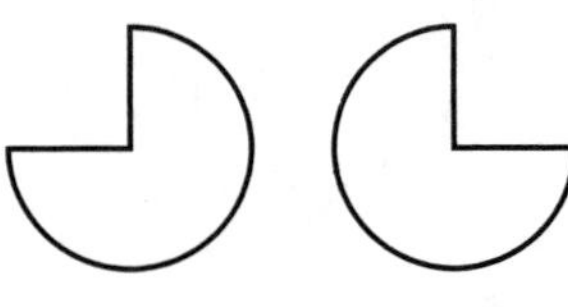 ______________

3.

a 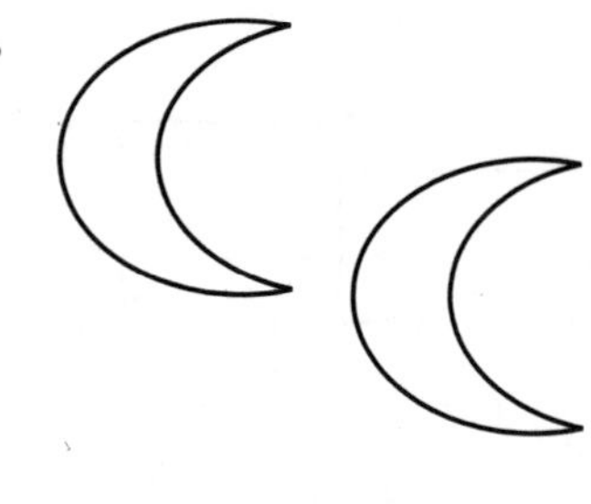 ______________

b ______________

c 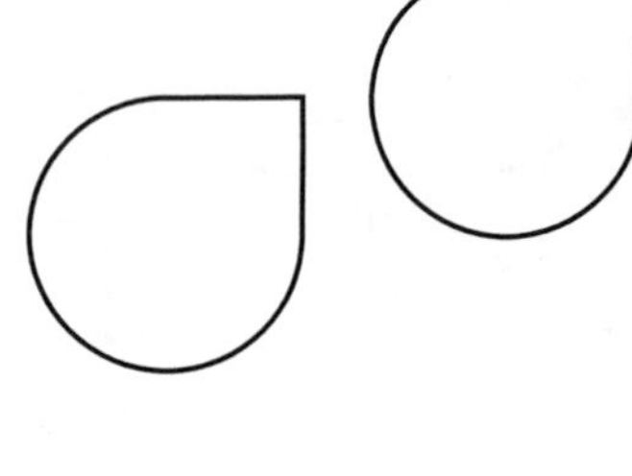 ______________

4.

a 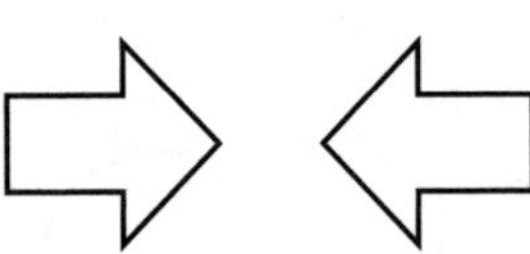 ______________

b ______________

c 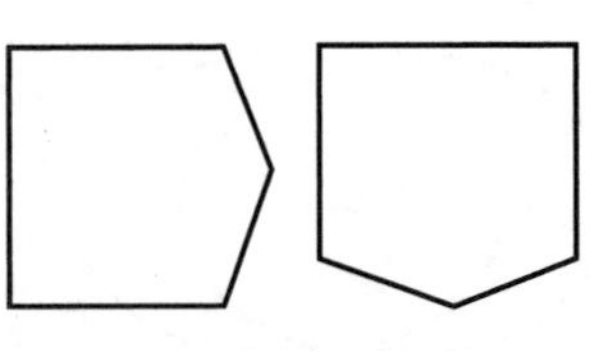 ______________

NAME ______________________

Lesson 5.2 Congruence

Two shapes are said to be **congruent** if they are the same size and shape regardless of orientation. If a figure is **rotated**, **translated**, or **reflected** over a line, the two resulting shapes are congruent.

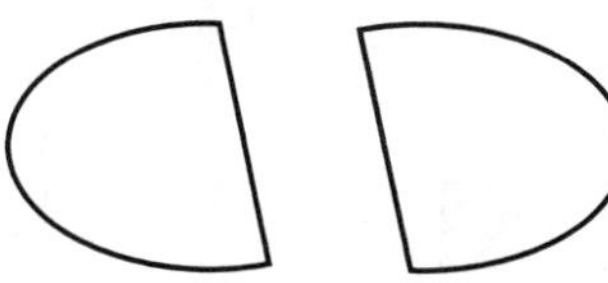

congruent

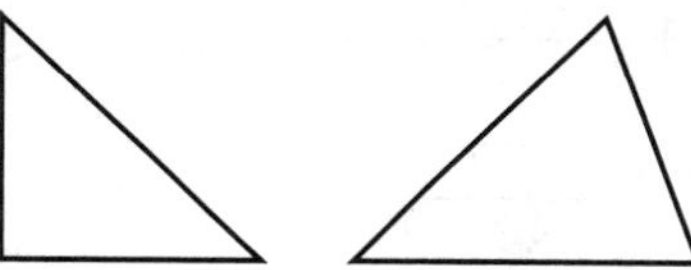

not congruent

Decide if the figures below are congruent. Write *yes* or *no*.

	a	b	c
1.	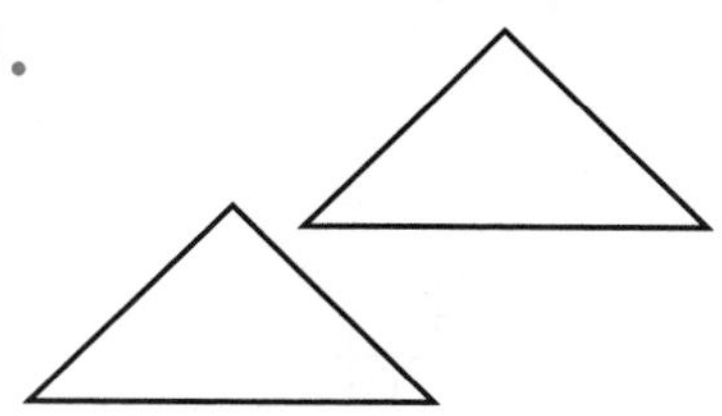 ________	 ________	 ________
2.	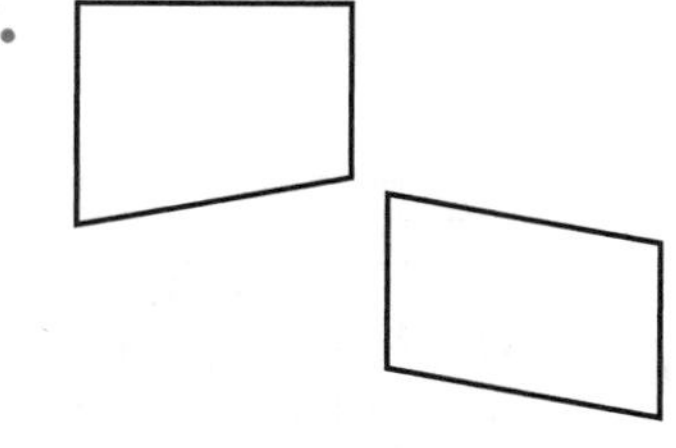 ________	 ________	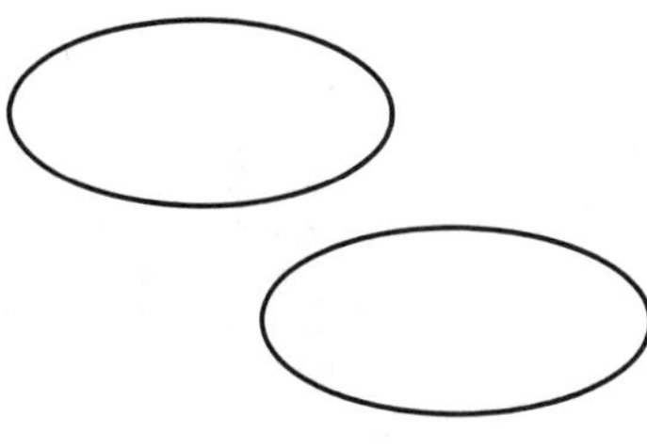 ________
3.	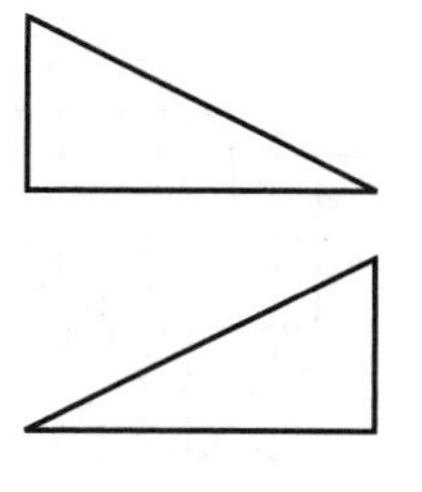 ________	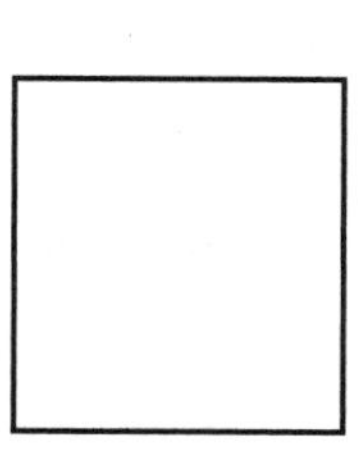 ________	________

NAME ______________________

Lesson 5.3 Rotations, Reflections, and Translations in the Coordinate Plane

A **transformation** is a change of the position or size of an image. In a **translation**, an image slides in any direction. In a **reflection**, an image is flipped over a line. In a **rotation**, an image is turned about a point. In a **dilation**, an image is enlarged or reduced. One way to view an image and its transformation is to graph it on a coordinate plane.

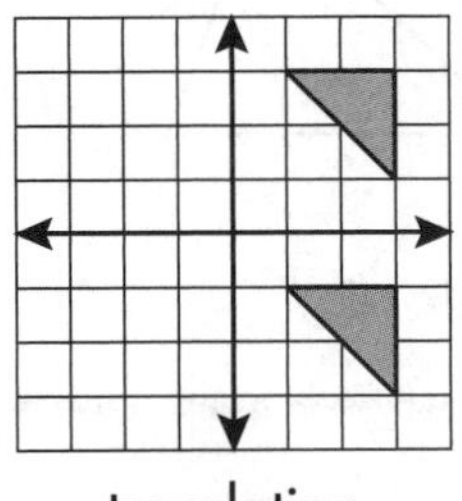
translation

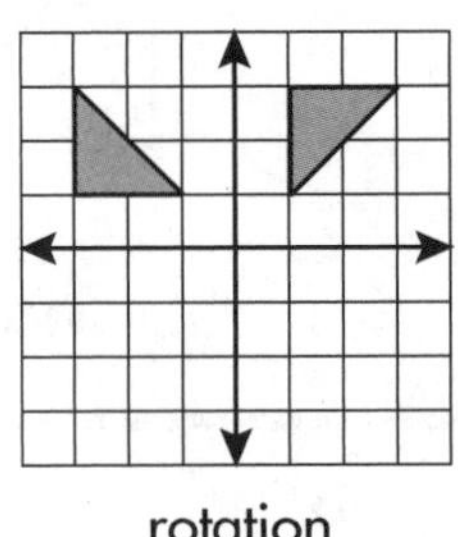
rotation

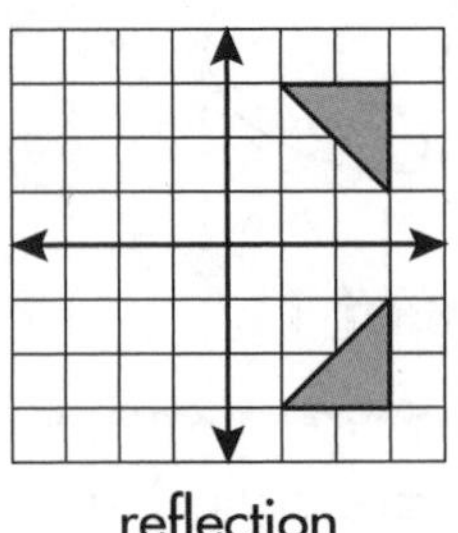
reflection

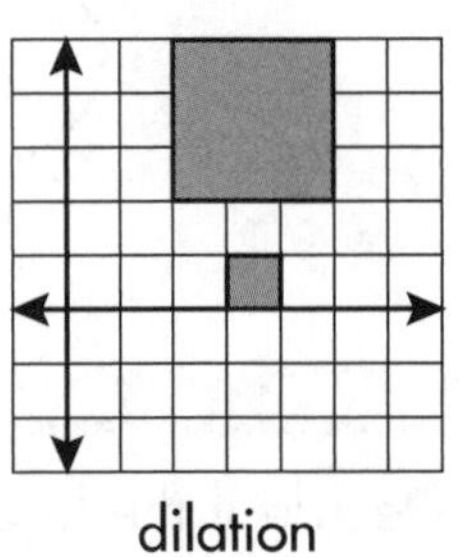
dilation

Write whether each transformation is a *translation, rotation, reflection,* or *dilation.*

	a	b	c
1.	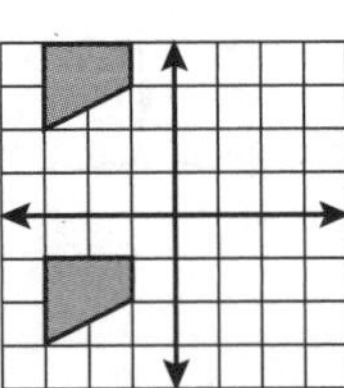 ________	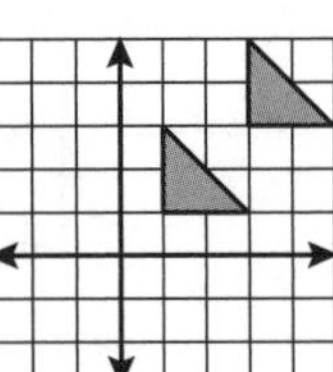 ________	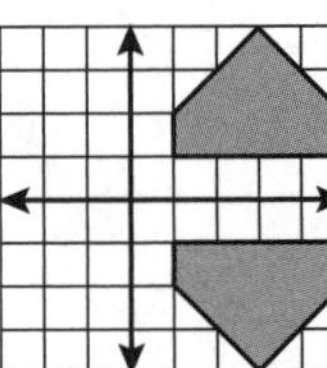 ________
2.	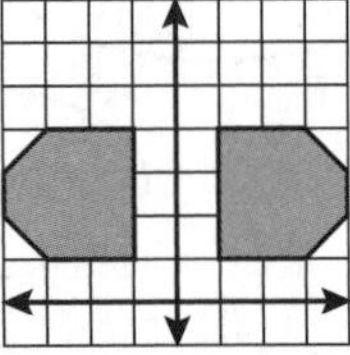 ________	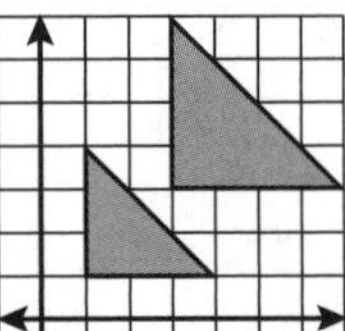 ________	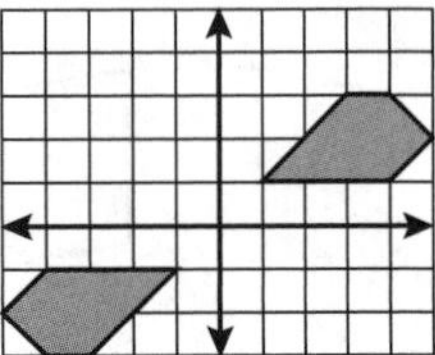 ________
3.	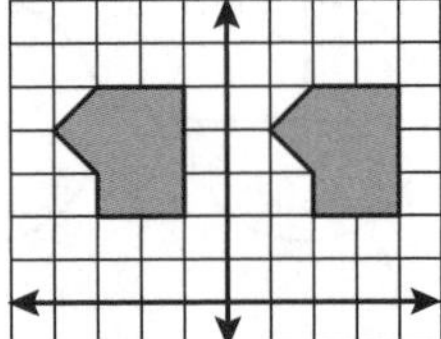 ________	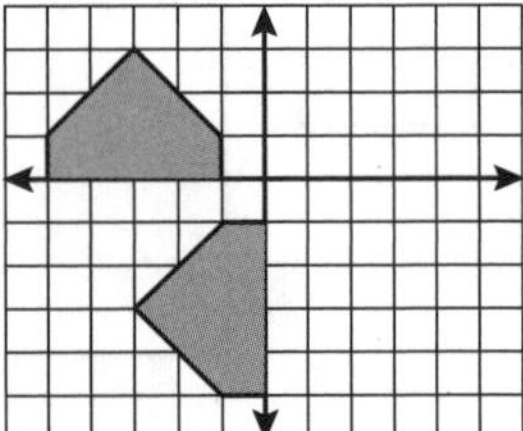 ________	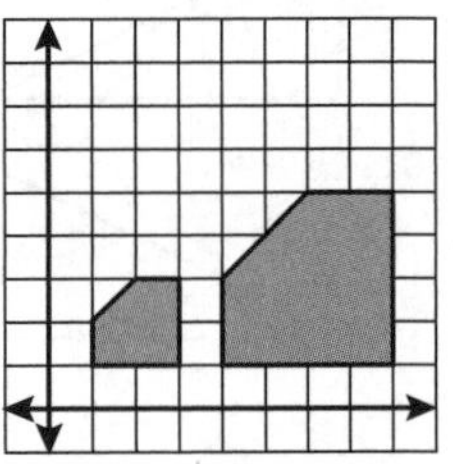 ________

NAME ____________________

Lesson 5.3 Rotations, Reflections, and Translations in the Coordinate Plane

Graphing figures on a coordinate plane helps show how they are transformed. The original figure is called a **preimage.** The transformed figure is called the **image.** Read the numbers on the *x*-axis and *y*-axis to determine the location of the figure.

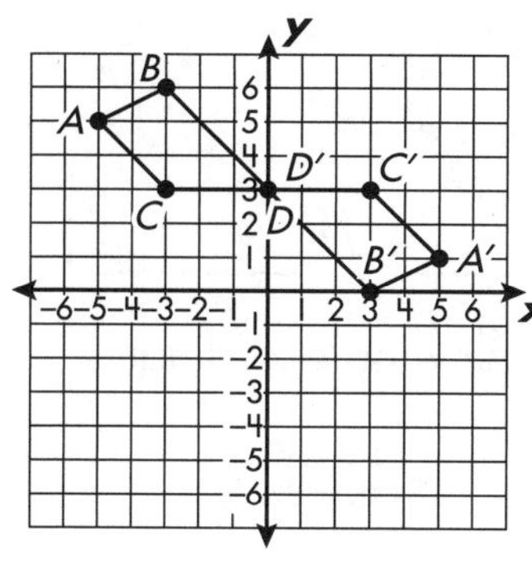

This figure has been rotated 180° about one point of the figure. As a result, the preimage and the image share a point. The 4 corners of the preimage are points A, B, C, and D. The four corners of the image are also labeled A′, B′, C′, and D′, but note the prime symbol (′) after each.

The coordinates of the preimage are: *A* (−5, 5), *B* (−3, 6) *C* (−3, 3), *D* (0, 3).
The coordinates of the image are: *A*′(5, 1), *B*′(3, 0), *C*′(3, 3), *D*′(0, 3).

The location of each figure is identified by the coordinates of its corners. The first figure, or preimage, has coordinate points labeled *A*, *B*, etc. The transformed figure, or image, has coordinate points labeled *A*′, *B*′, etc.

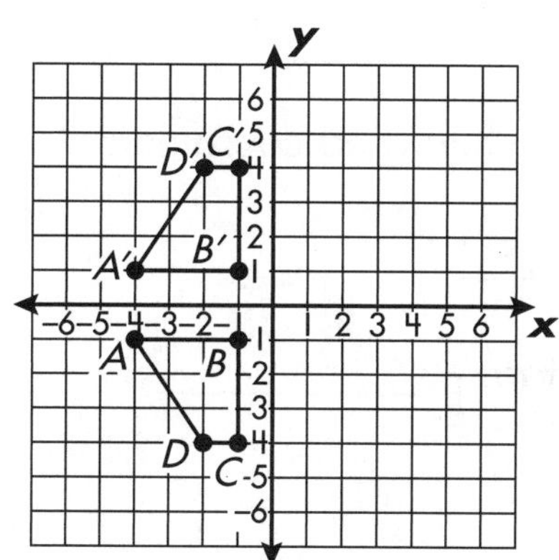

1. What are the coordinates of the preimage?

A (__________), *B* (__________), *C* (__________), *D* (__________)

2. What are the coordinates of the image?

A′(__________), *B*′(__________), *C*′(__________), *D*′(__________)

3. What transformation was performed on the figure? __________

4. What are the coordinates of the preimage?

A (__________), *B* (__________), *C* (__________)

5. What are the coordinates of the image?

A′(__________), *B*′(__________), *C*′(__________),

6. What transformation was performed on the figure? __________

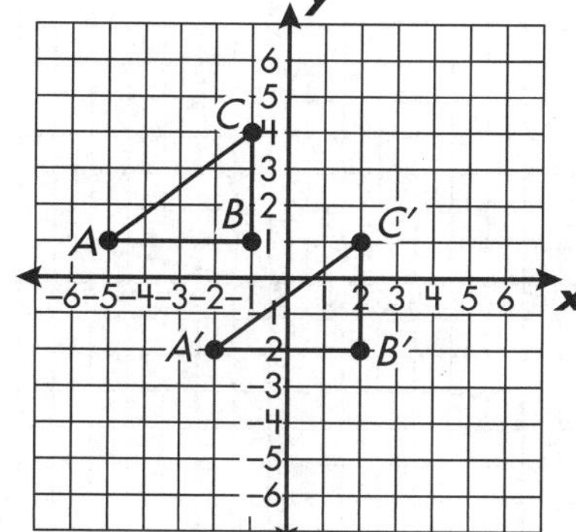

NAME ______________________________

Lesson 5.3 Rotations, Reflections, and Translations in the Coordinate Plane

The location of each figure is identified by the coordinates of its corners. The first figure, or preimage, has coordinate points labeled *A*, *B*, etc. The transformed figure, or image, has coordinate points labeled *A*′, *B*′, etc.

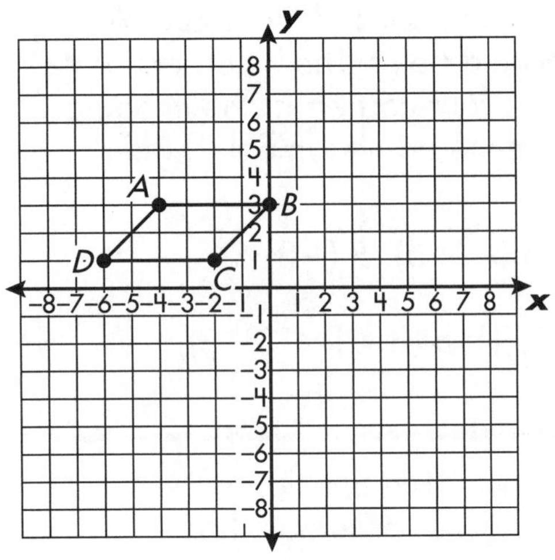

1. What are the coordinates of the preimage?

A(________) *B*(________), *C*(________), *D*(________)

2. Draw a transformed image with the following coordinates:

A′(−1, 4), *B*′(5, 4), *C*′(2, 1), *D*′(−4, 1)

3. What transformation did you perform? ____________

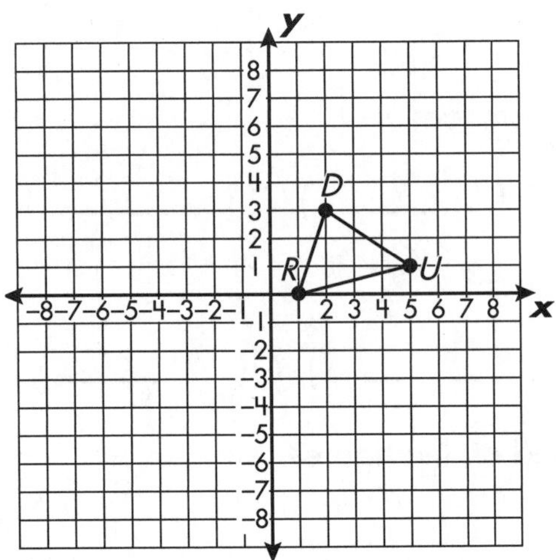

4. What are the coordinates of the preimage?

D (________), *U* (________), *R* (________)

5. Draw a transformed image with the following coordinates:

D′(4, −1), *U*′(2, −4), *R*′(1, 0)

6. What transformation did you perform? ____________

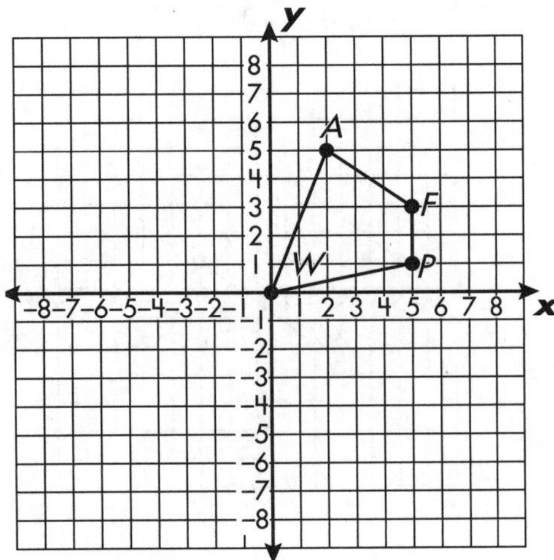

7. What are the coordinates of the preimage?

A (________), *W* (________), *F* (________), *P* (________)

8. Draw a transformed image with the following coordinates:

A′(−2, 5), *W*′(0, 0), *F*′(−5, −3), *P*′(−5, 1)

9. What transformation did you perform? ____________

NAME ______________________

Lesson 5.4 Transformation Sequences

If there exists a sequence of translations, reflections, rotations, and/or dilations that will transform one figure into the other, the two figures are either **similar** or **congruent**. Similar figures are the same shape but not the same size while congruent shapes are both the same shape and the same size. Follow the sequence of transformations to determine if two figures are similar or congruent.

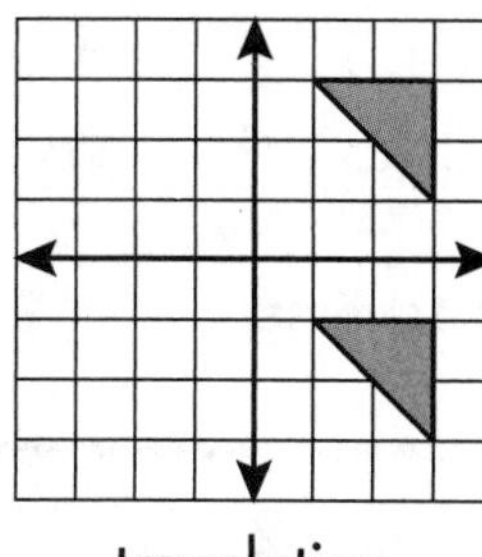
translation

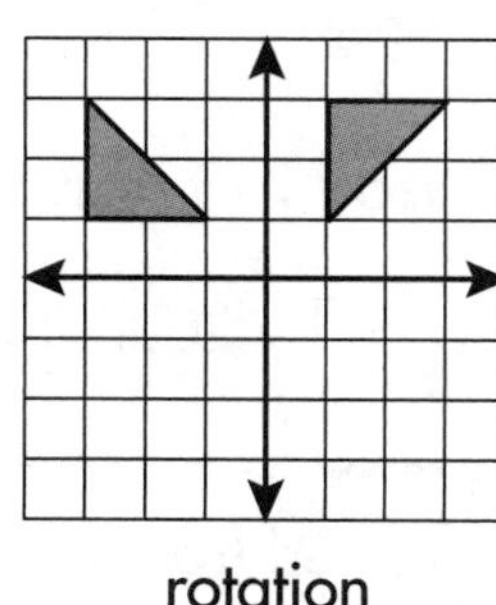
rotation

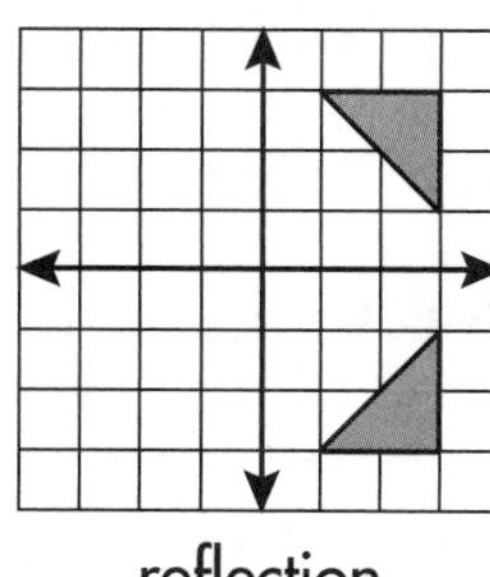
reflection

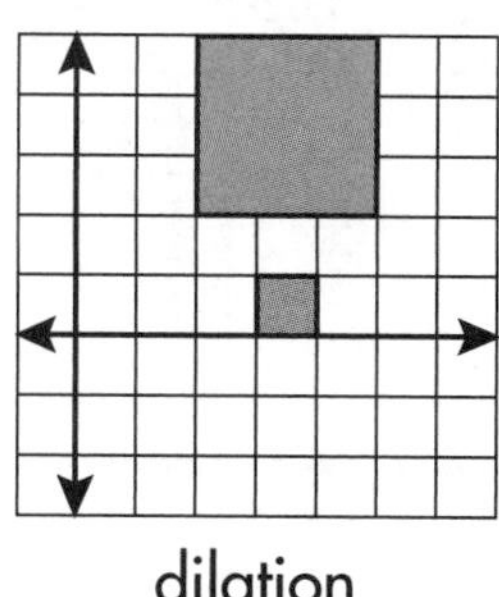
dilation

Determine if a set of transformations exist between figures 1 and 2. Then, write *similar, congruent,* or *neither.*

1.

a

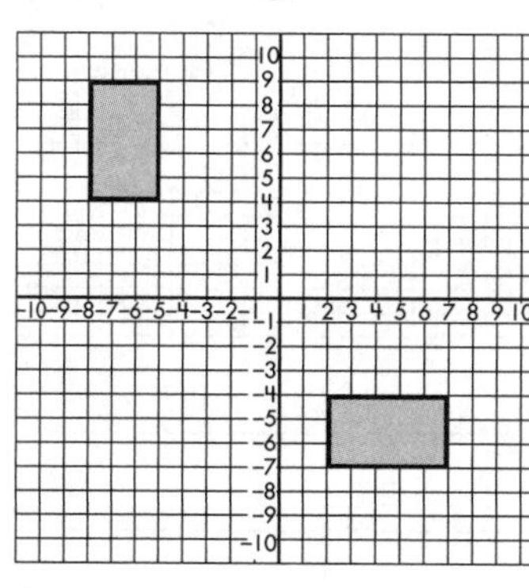

____

b

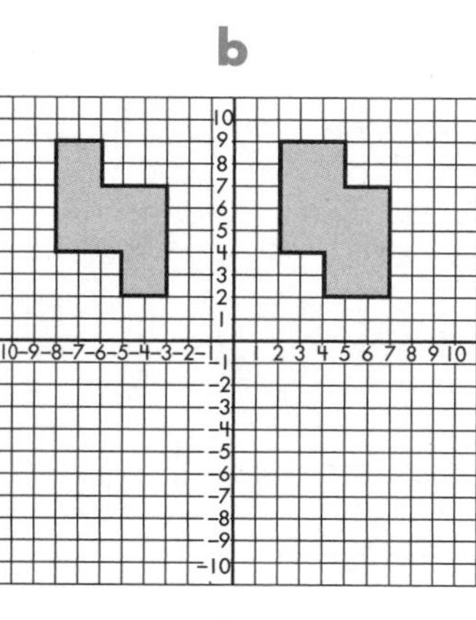

____

c

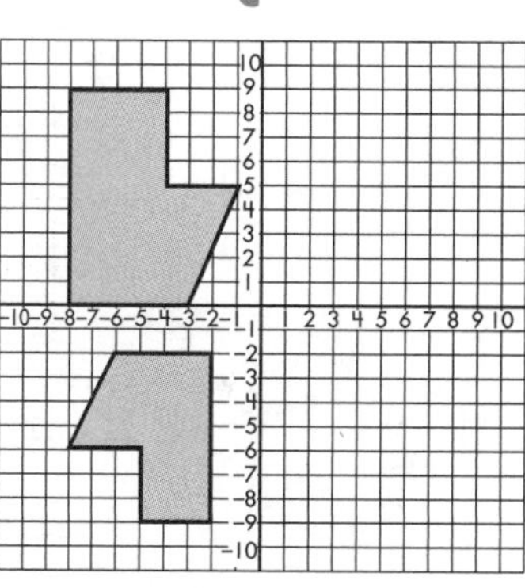

____

2.

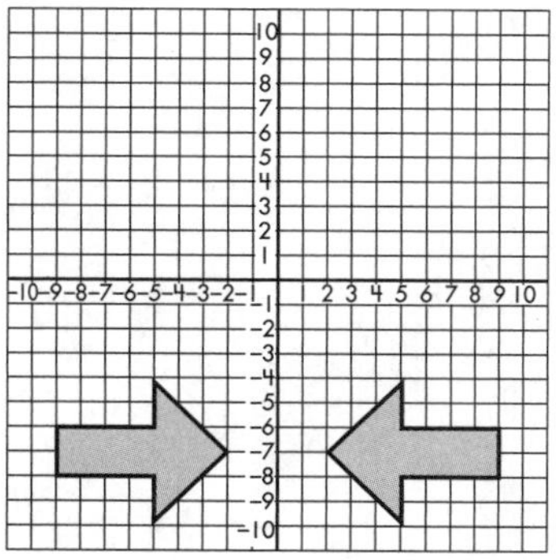

a

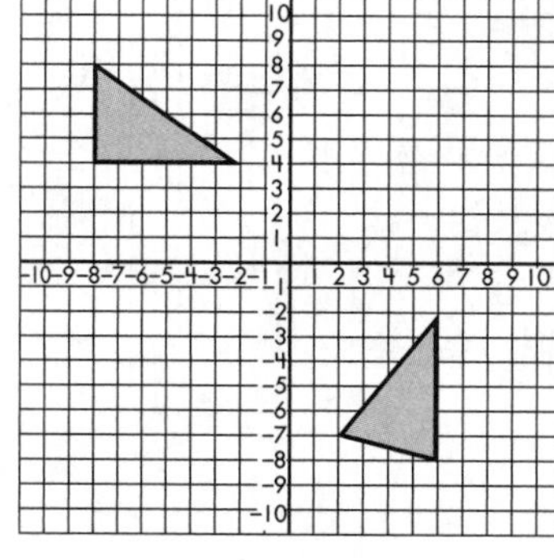

____

b

____

c

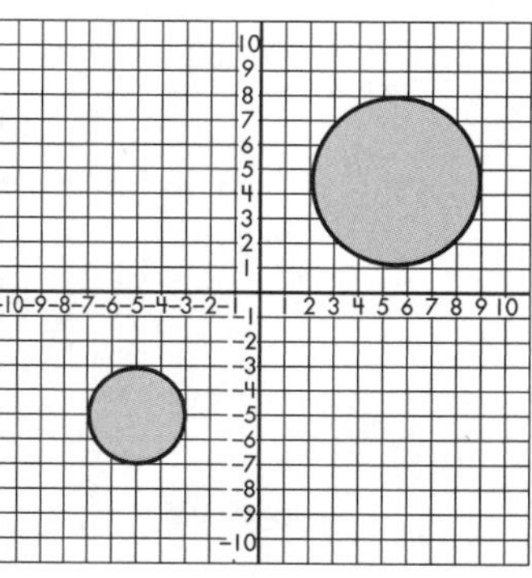

____

NAME ______________________

Lesson 5.4 Transformation Sequences

Sometimes the order of the steps in a transformation sequence will vary, but every shape has a specific sequence it must go through in order to be transformed.

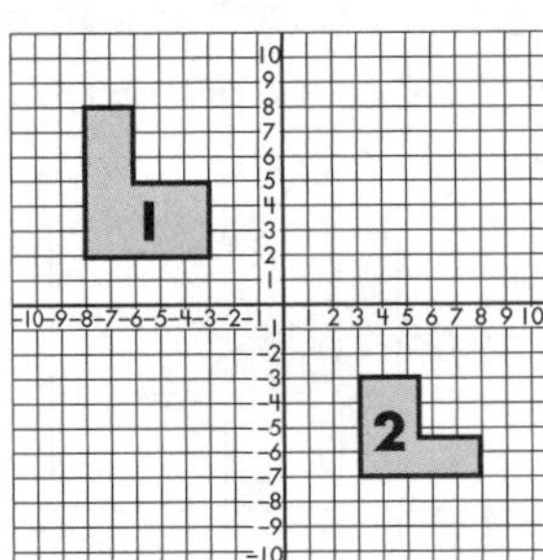

Step 1: The figure is reflected across the y-axis.

Step 2: The figure is rotated 90°.

Step 3: The figure is translated by -8 along the y-axis.

Step 4: The figure is decreased by 20% (dilation in reverse).

Write the steps each figure must go through to be transformed from figure 1 to figure 2.

	a	b
1.	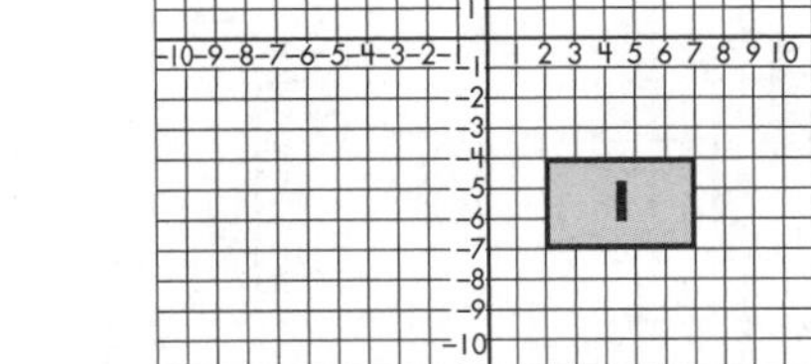 Step 1: ______________ Step 2: ______________ Step 3: ______________	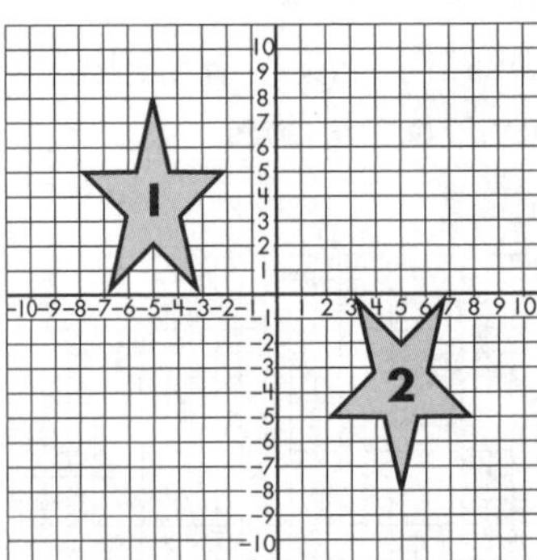 Step 1: ______________ Step 2: ______________
2.	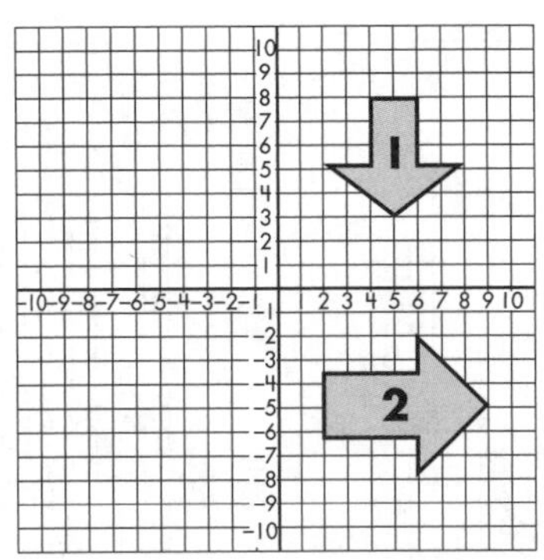 Step 1: ______________ Step 2: ______________ Step 3: ______________	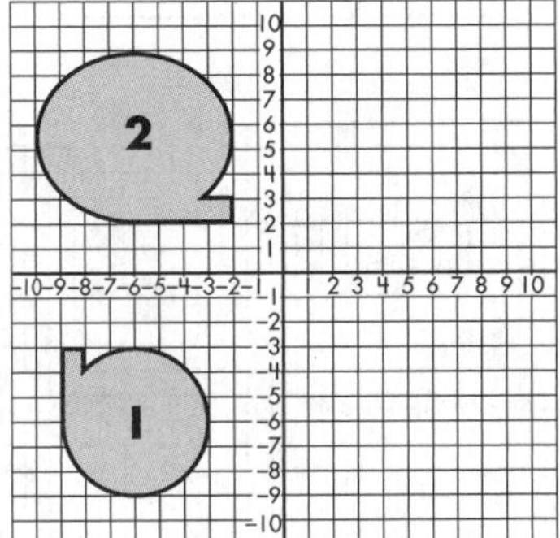 Step 1: ______________ Step 2: ______________ Step 3: ______________

NAME ___________________________

Lesson 5.5 Slope and Similar Triangles

The rate of change, or slope, of a line can be tested for constancy by using similar triangles.

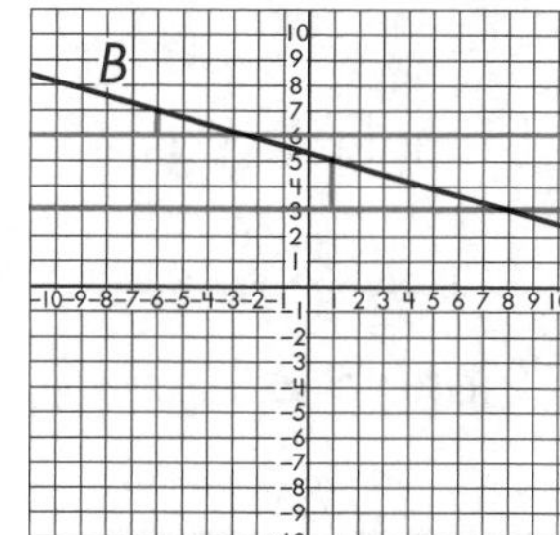

To test if the slope of the line *B* is constant, draw a set of parallel lines that intersect the line.

Then, draw a line segment from each of the parallel lines to line *B* to create a set of right triangles.

Find the length of the legs for each set of triangles. 3 & 1 and 6 & 2

Test the leg lengths for proportionality. $\frac{3}{1} = \frac{6}{2}$

$3 \times 2 = 6$ and $6 \times 1 = 6$

These leg lengths are proportional, so the line has a constant slope.

Use similar right triangles to prove that each line has a constant slope.

	a	b
1.	Triangle 1 Legs: ______ & ______ Triangle 2 Legs: ______ & ______ Proportionality Test: ___ = ___	Triangle 1 Legs: ______ & ______ Triangle 2 Legs: ______ & ______ Proportionality Test: ___ = ___
2.	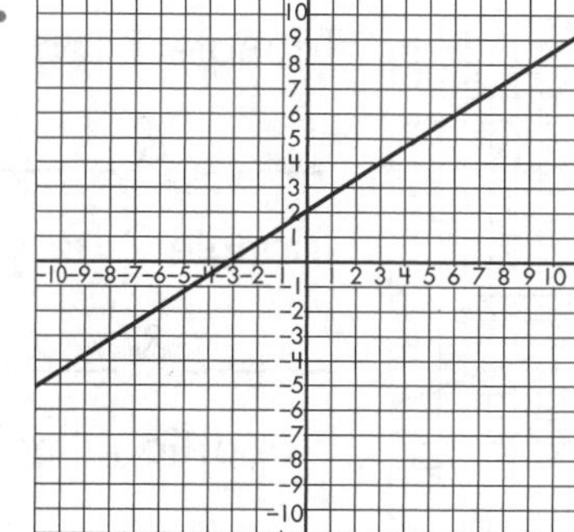 Triangle 1 Legs: ______ & ______ Triangle 2 Legs: ______ & ______ Proportionality Test: ___ = ___	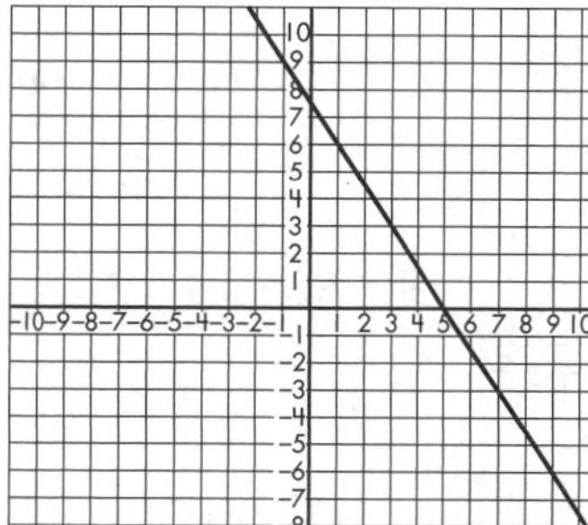 Triangle 1 Legs: ______ & ______ Triangle 2 Legs: ______ & ______ Proportionality Test: ___ = ___

NAME ____________________

Lesson 5.5 Slope and Similar Triangles

Use similar right triangles to prove that each line has a constant slope.

a

1.

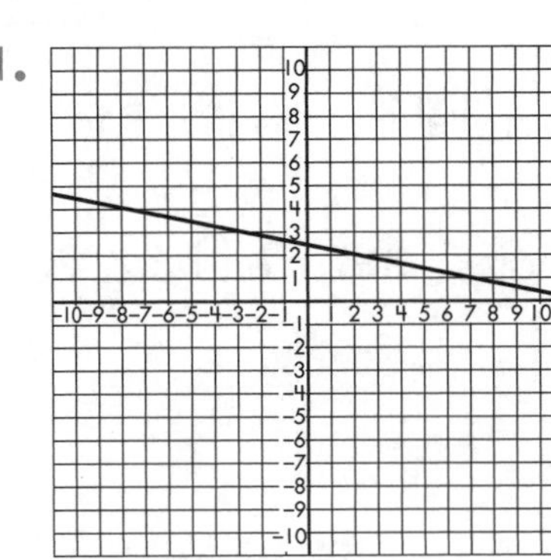

Triangle 1 Legs:

______ & ______

Triangle 2 Legs:

______ & ______

Proportionality Test:

—— = ——

b

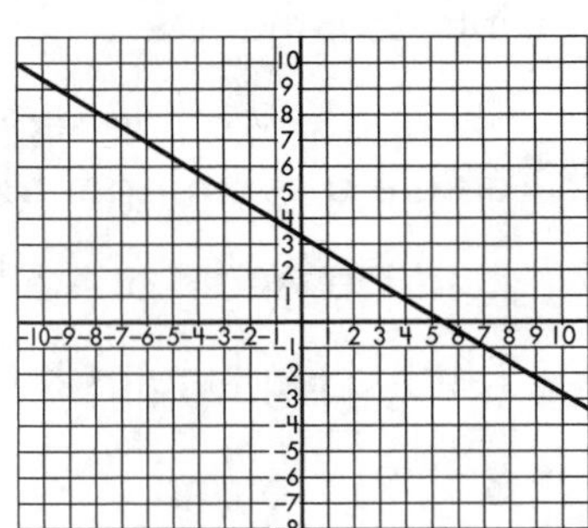

Triangle 1 Legs:

______ & ______

Triangle 2 Legs:

______ & ______

Proportionality Test:

—— = ——

2.

Triangle 1 Legs:

______ & ______

Triangle 2 Legs:

______ & ______

Proportionality Test:

—— = ——

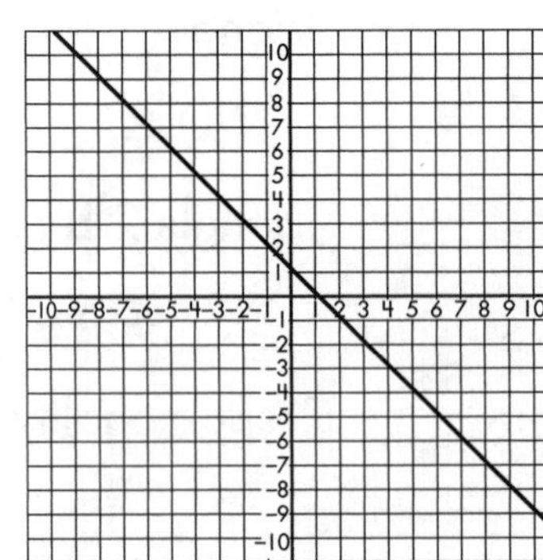

Triangle 1 Legs:

______ & ______

Triangle 2 Legs:

______ & ______

Proportionality Test:

—— = ——

3.

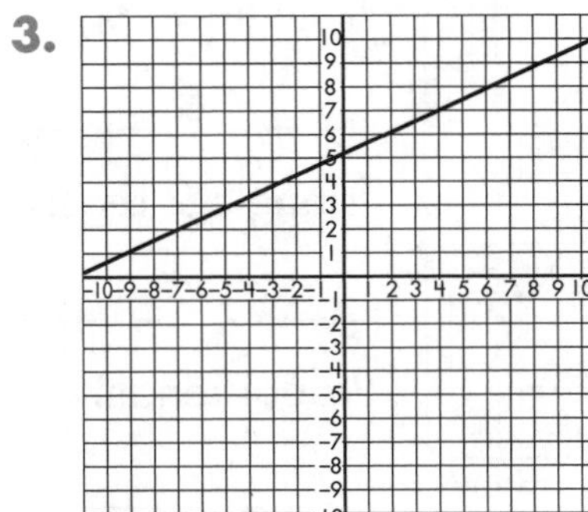

Triangle 1 Legs:

______ & ______

Triangle 2 Legs:

______ & ______

Proportionality Test:

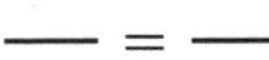

—— = ——

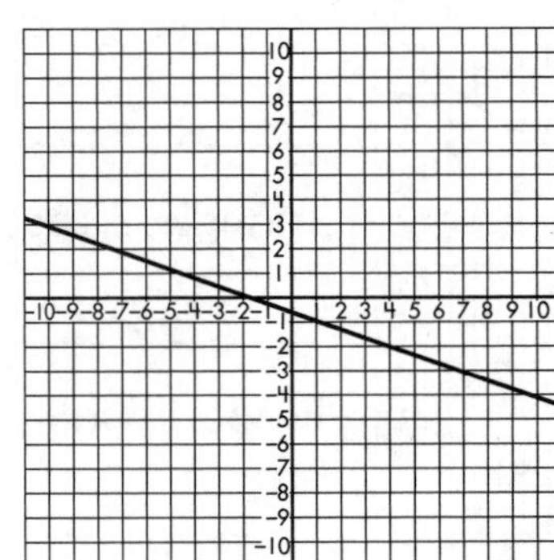

Triangle 1 Legs:

______ & ______

Triangle 2 Legs:

______ & ______

Proportionality Test:

—— = ——

NAME ______________________________

Lesson 5.6 Transversals and Calculating Angles

A **transversal** is a line that intersects two or more lines at different points. The angles that are formed are called **alternate interior angles** and **alternate exterior angles**. When a transversal intersects parallel lines, **corresponding angles** are formed.

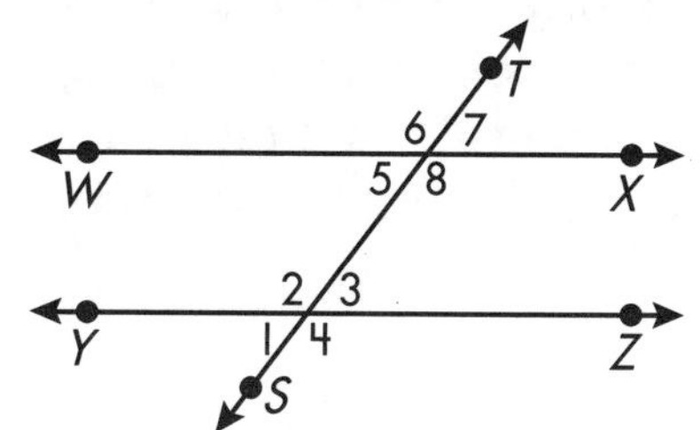

In the figure, $\overleftrightarrow{ST}$ is a transversal. $\overleftrightarrow{WX}$ and $\overleftrightarrow{YZ}$ are parallel.

The alternate interior angles are ∠2 and ∠8, and ∠3 and ∠5.

The alternate exterior angles are ∠4 and ∠6, and ∠1 and ∠7.

The corresponding angles are ∠1 and ∠5, ∠2 and ∠6, ∠3 and ∠7, and ∠4 and ∠8.

Use the figure to the right. Name the transversal that forms each pair of angles. Write whether the angles are *alternate interior, alternate exterior,* or *corresponding*.

1. ∠1 and ∠9 ____________ ________________________
2. ∠5 and ∠4 ____________ ________________________
3. ∠11 and ∠3 ____________ ________________________
4. ∠5 and ∠16 ____________ ________________________
5. ∠13 and ∠8 ____________ ________________________
6. ∠15 and ∠10 ____________ ________________________
7. ∠7 and ∠14 ____________ ________________________
8. ∠8 and ∠16 ____________ ________________________
9. ∠6 and ∠3 ____________ ________________________
10. ∠12 and ∠13 ____________ ________________________
11. ∠10 and ∠2 ____________ ________________________
12. ∠5 and ∠13 ____________ ________________________

NAME ______________________

Lesson 5.6 Transversals and Calculating Angles

Adjacent angles are any 2 angles that are next to one another. In the figure, ∠1 and ∠2 are adjacent. ∠2 and ∠4 are also adjacent. Adjacent angles share a ray. They also form supplementary angles (180°).

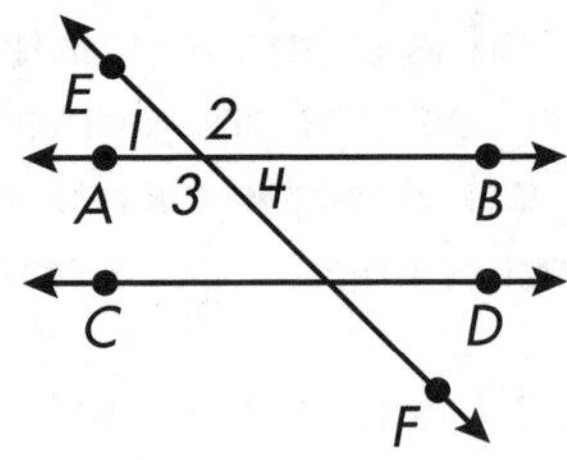

1. Name the pairs of adjacent angles in the figure.

∠ ___/∠ ___, ∠ ___/∠ ___, ∠ ___/∠ ___, ∠ ___/∠ ___,
∠ ___/∠ ___, ∠ ___/∠ ___, ∠ ___/∠ ___, ∠ ___/∠ ___

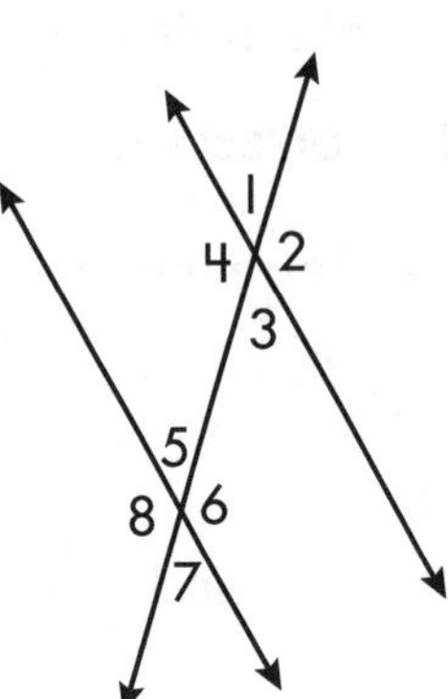

Alternate interior angles are those that are inside the parallel lines and opposite one another. ∠3 and ∠5 are alternate interior angles. Alternate interior angles are congruent.

2. Name another pair of alternate interior angles in the figure. ∠ ___/∠ ___

Alternate exterior angles are those that are outside the parallel lines and opposite one another. ∠1 and ∠7 are alternate exterior angles. Alternate exterior angles are also congruent.

3. Name another pair of alternate exterior angles in the figure. ∠ ___/∠ ___

Look at the figure. List the following pairs of angles.

4. Adjacent: ∠ ___/∠ ___, ∠ ___/∠ ___, ∠ ___/∠ ___, ∠ ___/∠ ___,
∠ ___/∠ ___, ∠ ___/∠ ___, ∠ ___/∠ ___, ∠ ___/∠ ___

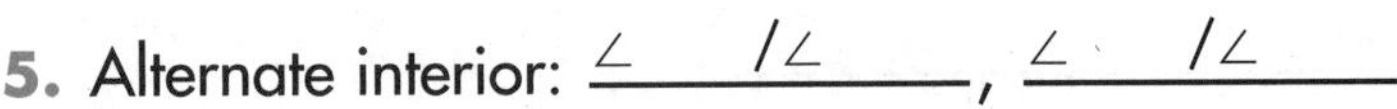

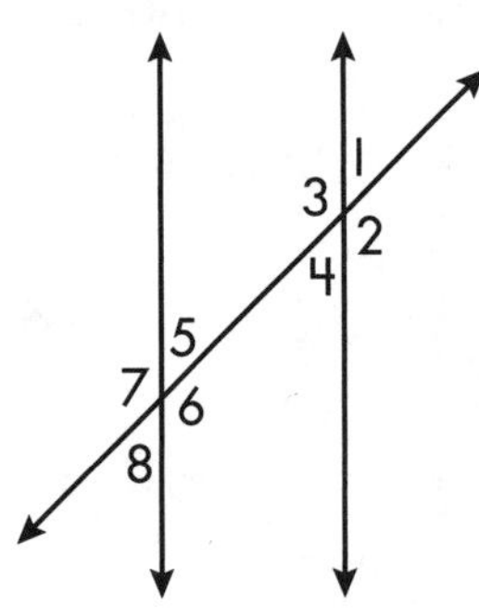

5. Alternate interior: ∠ ___/∠ ___, ∠ ___/∠ ___

6. Alternate exterior: ∠ ___/∠ ___, ∠ ___/∠ ___

7. Vertical: ∠ ___/∠ ___, ∠ ___/∠ ___,
∠ ___/∠ ___, ∠ ___/∠ ___

NAME ______________________________

Lesson 5.6 Transversals and Calculating Angles

Use the figures below to answer the questions.

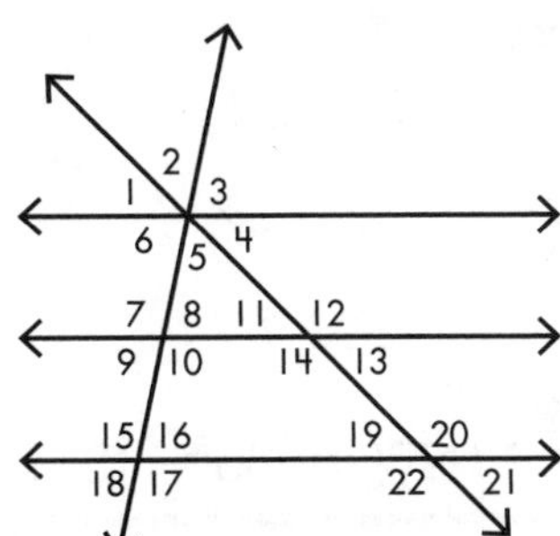

1. If the measure of $\angle 1$ is 45°, what is the measure of $\angle 4$? __________

2. If the measure of $\angle 12$ is 102°, what is the measure of $\angle 11$? __________

3. If the measure of $\angle 18$ is 76°, what is the measure of $\angle 8$? __________

4. If the measure of $\angle 9$ is 97°, what is the measure of $\angle 10$? __________

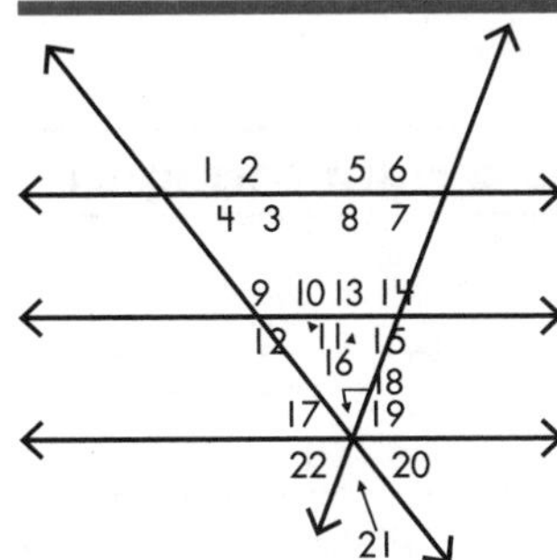

5. If the measure of $\angle 2$ is 115°, what is the measure of $\angle 12$? __________

6. If the measure of $\angle 6$ is 84°, what is the measure of $\angle 13$? __________

7. If the measure of $\angle 18$ is 35°, what is the measure of $\angle 21$? __________

8. If the measure of $\angle 15$ is 102 °, what is the measure of $\angle 5$? __________

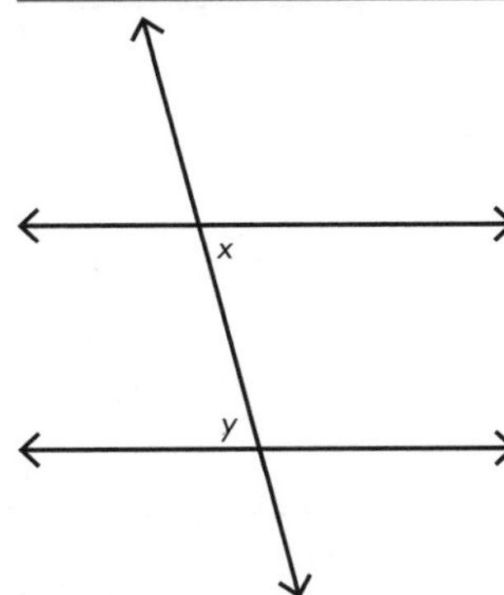

9. If $\angle x = 70°$, what is the measure of $\angle y$? __________

10. If $\angle x = 80°$, what is the measure of $\angle y$? __________

11. If $\angle y = 75°$, what is the measure of $\angle x$? __________

12. If $\angle y = 85°$, what is the measure of $\angle x$? __________

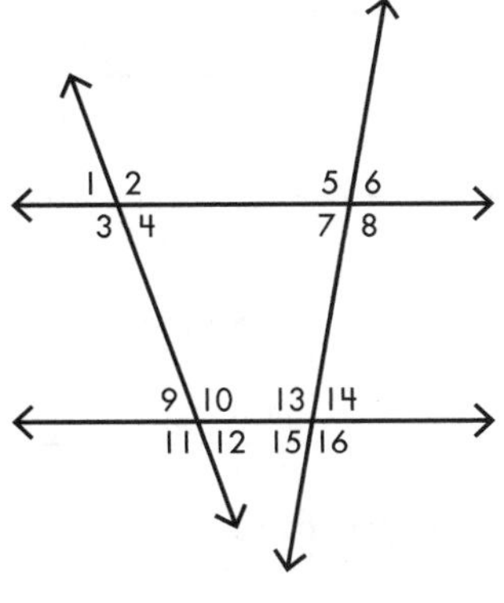

13. If $\angle 5 = 100°$, what is the measure of $\angle 15$? __________

14. If $\angle 6 = 70°$, what is the measure of $\angle 13$? __________

15. If $\angle 2 = 110°$, what is the measure of $\angle 9$? __________

16. If $\angle 4 = 85°$, what is the measure of $\angle 11$? __________

17. Can you determine the measure of $\angle 11$ if you know the measure of $\angle 6$? Why or why not?

____

____

NAME ______________________

Lesson 5.7 Defining Pythagorean Theorem

The **Pythagorean Theorem** states that if a triangle is a right triangle, then $a^2 + b^2 = c^2$, when a and b represent the legs of the triangle and c represents the hypotenuse.

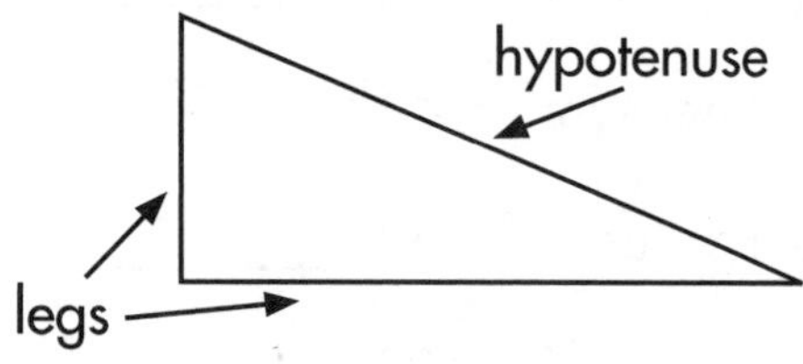

The Pythagorean Theorem:
If a triangle is a right triangle, then $a^2 + b^2 = c^2$.

Converse of Pythagorean Theorem:
If $a^2 + b^2 = c^2$, then the triangle is a right triangle.

Complete the table below to prove if each set of sides creates a right triangle.

	a	b	c	Is $a^2 + b^2 = c^2$ true?	Makes a right triangle?
1.	3	4	5		
2.	3	4	6		
3.	4	6	9		
4.	5	12	13		
5.	6	8	13		
6.	7	24	25		
7.	7	13	15		
8.	8	20	25		
9.	8	15	17		
10.	10	27	30		
11.	13	20	30		
12.	13	21	29		

13. Based on the true results in the table above, what pattern can be inferred about the Pythagorean Theorem?

____

____

NAME ____________________

Lesson 5.8 Using Pythagorean Theorem

If a, b, and c are the lengths of the sides of this triangle, $a^2 + b^2 = c^2$.

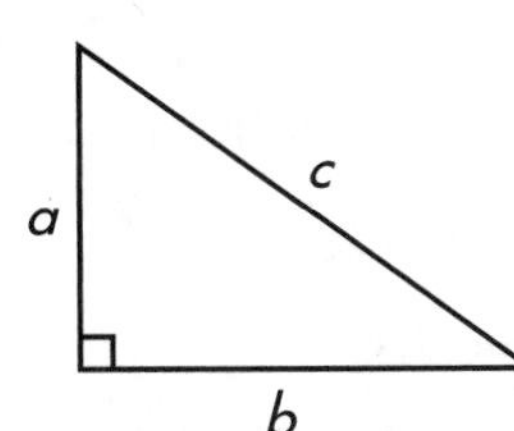

If $a = 3$ and $b = 4$, what is c?

$a^2 + b^2 = c^2$

$3^2 + 4^2 = c^2$

$9 + 16 = c^2$

$25 = c^2$

$\sqrt{25} = c$

$5 = c$

If $a = 4$ and $b = 6$, what is b?

$a^2 + b^2 = c^2$

$4^2 + 6^2 = c^2$

$16 + 36 = c^2$

$52 = c^2$

$\sqrt{52} = c$

$c =$ *about* 7.21

Use the Pythagorean Theorem to determine the length of c. Assume that each problem describes a right triangle. Sides a and b are the legs and the hypotenuse is c.

1. If $a = 9$ and $b = 4$, $c = \sqrt{\_\_\_\_}$ or about ________.

2. If $a = 5$ and $b = 7$, $c = \sqrt{\_\_\_\_}$ or about ________.

3. If $a = 3$ and $b = 6$, $c = \sqrt{\_\_\_\_}$ or about ________.

4. If $a = 2$ and $b = 9$, $c = \sqrt{\_\_\_\_}$ or ________.

5. If $a = 5$ and $b = 6$, $c = \sqrt{\_\_\_\_}$ or about ________.

6. If $a = 3$ and $b = 5$, $c = \sqrt{\_\_\_\_}$ or about ________.

7. If $a = 7$ and $b = 6$, $c = \sqrt{\_\_\_\_}$ or about ________.

8. If $a = 8$ and $b = 6$, $c = \sqrt{\_\_\_\_}$ or ________.

9. If $a = 7$ and $b = 2$, $c = \sqrt{\_\_\_\_}$ or about ________.

10. If $a = 8$ and $b = 5$, $c = \sqrt{\_\_\_\_}$ or about ________.

NAME ____________________

Lesson 5.8 Using the Pythagorean Theorem

You can use the Pythagorean Theorem to find the unknown length of a side of a right triangle as long as the other two lengths are known.

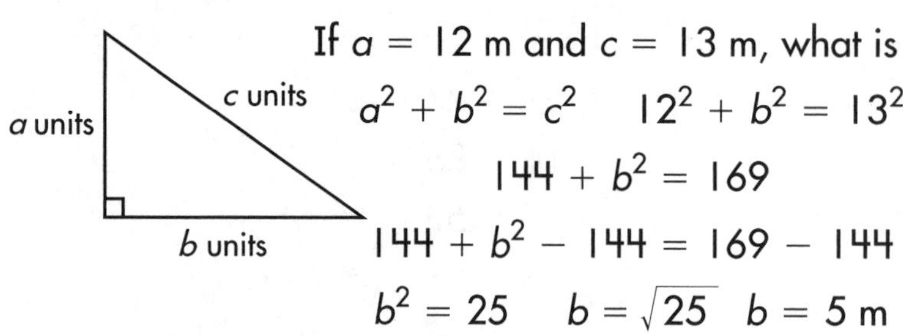

If $a = 12$ m and $c = 13$ m, what is b?

$a^2 + b^2 = c^2$ $\quad 12^2 + b^2 = 13^2$

$144 + b^2 = 169$

$144 + b^2 - 144 = 169 - 144$

$b^2 = 25 \quad b = \sqrt{25} \quad b = 5$ m

If $b = 15$ ft. and $c = 17$ ft., what is a?

$a^2 + b^2 = c^2$ $\quad a^2 + 15^2 = 17^2$

$a^2 + 225 = 289$

$a^2 + 225 - 225 = 289 - 225$

$a^2 = 64 \quad a = \sqrt{64} \quad a = 8$ ft.

Assume that each problem describes a right triangle. Use the Pythagorean Theorem to find the unknown lengths.

1. If $a = 12$ and $c = 20$, $b = \sqrt{}$ __________ or __________.
2. If $b = 24$ and $c = 26$, $a = \sqrt{}$ __________ or __________.
3. If $c = 8$ and $a = 5$, $b = \sqrt{}$ __________ or about __________.
4. If $b = 13$ and $c = 17$, $a = \sqrt{}$ __________ or about __________.
5. If $a = 20$ and $c = 32$, $b = \sqrt{}$ __________ or about __________.
6. If $c = 15$ and $b = 12$, $a = \sqrt{}$ __________ or __________.
7. If $c = 41$ and $b = 40$, $a = \sqrt{}$ __________ or __________.
8. If $a = 36$ and $c = 85$, $b = \sqrt{}$ __________ or __________.
9. If $c = 73$ and $b = 48$, $a = \sqrt{}$ __________ or __________.
10. If $a = 14$ and $c = 22$, $b = \sqrt{}$ __________ or about __________.

NAME ____________________

Lesson 5.8 Using the Pythagorean Theorem

SHOW YOUR WORK

Use the Pythagorean Theorem to solve each problem.

1. A boat has a sail with measures as shown. How tall is the sail?

The sail is _______ feet tall.

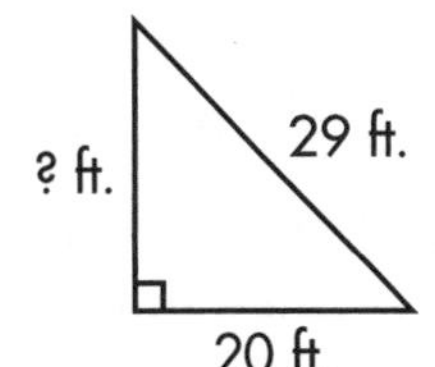

2. Kelsey drove on a back road for 15 miles from Benton to a lake. Her friend Paul drove 12 miles on the highway from Middleville to the lake. This area is shown at the right. How long is the road from Benton to Middleville?

The road is _______ miles long.

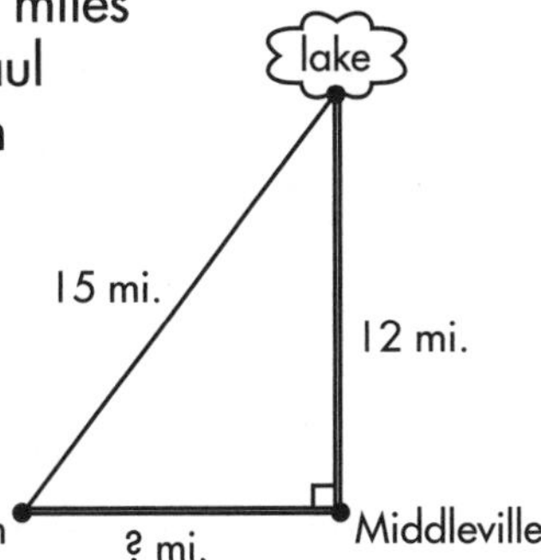

3. A 14-foot ladder is leaning against a building as shown. It touches a point 11 feet up on the building. How far away from the base of the building does the ladder stand?

The ladder stands about

_______ feet from the building.

14 ft.

11 ft.

? ft.

4. This gangway connects a dock to a ship, as shown. How long is the gangway?

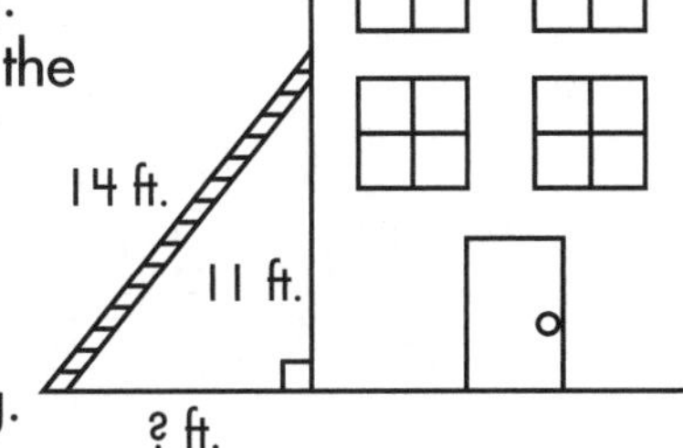

The gangway is _______ feet long.

5. About how long is the lake shown at right?

The lake is about

_______ km long.

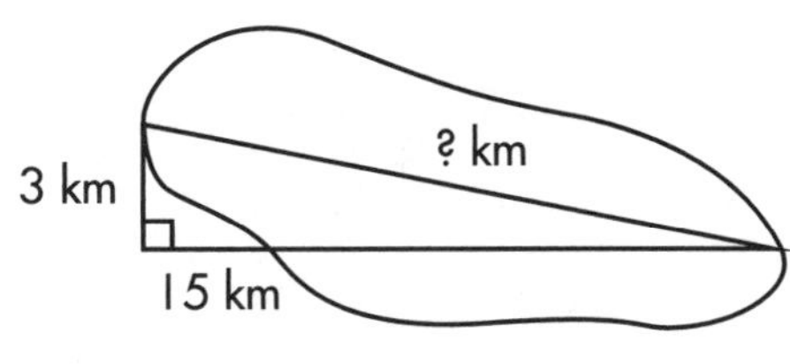

1.

2.

3.

4.

5.

NAME ______________________________

Lesson 5.9 Pythagorean Theorem in the Coordinate Plane

The Pythagorean Theorem can be used to find an unknown distance between two points on a coordinate plane.

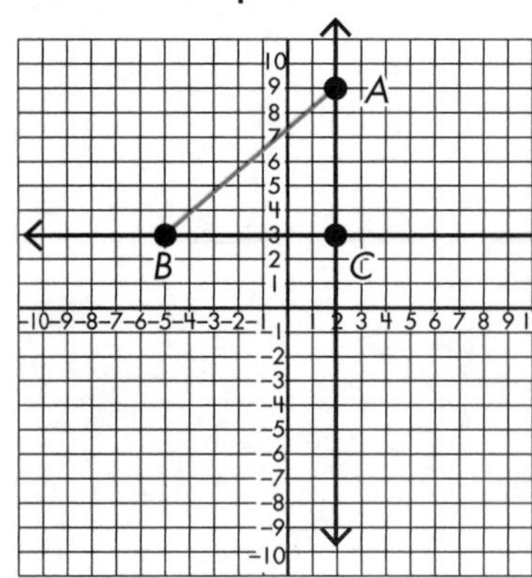

Find the distance between points A and B.

Step 1: Draw lines extending from points A and B so that when they intersect they create a right angle. Label the point at which they meet, point C.

Step 2: Find the distance of segment $\overline{AC}$ (7), and segment $\overline{BC}$ (6).

Step 3: Use Pythagorean Theorem to find the length of segment $\overline{AB}$.

$$7^2 + 6^2 = 85$$

$$(\overline{AB})^2 = 85$$

$$\overline{AB} = \sqrt{85} = 9.22$$

Find the distance between each of the points given below using the Pythagorean Theorem. Round answers to the nearest hundredth.

	a	b	c
1.	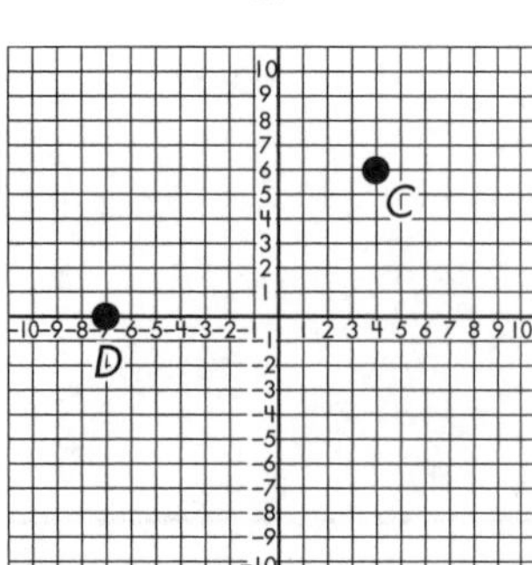	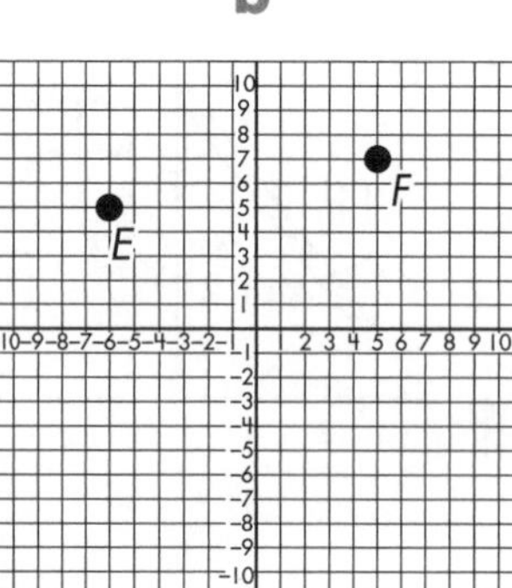	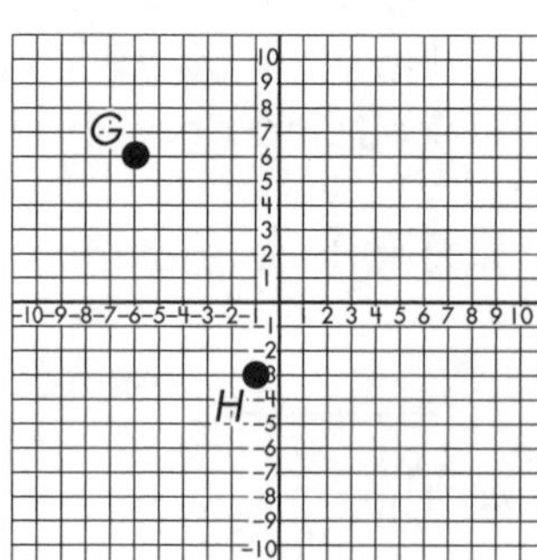
	$\overline{CD}$ = ____________	$\overline{EF}$ = ____________	$\overline{GH}$ = ____________
2.	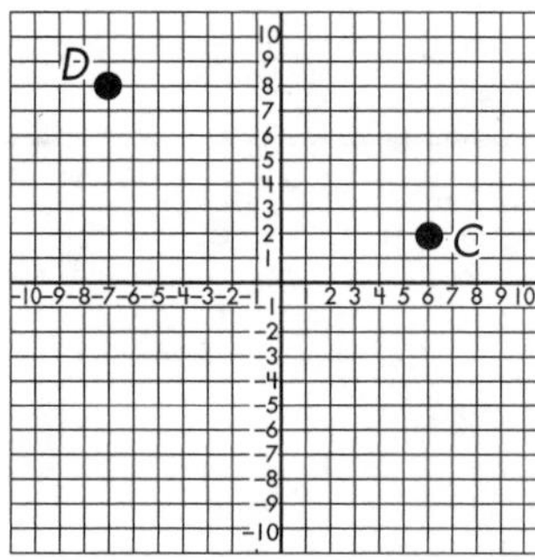	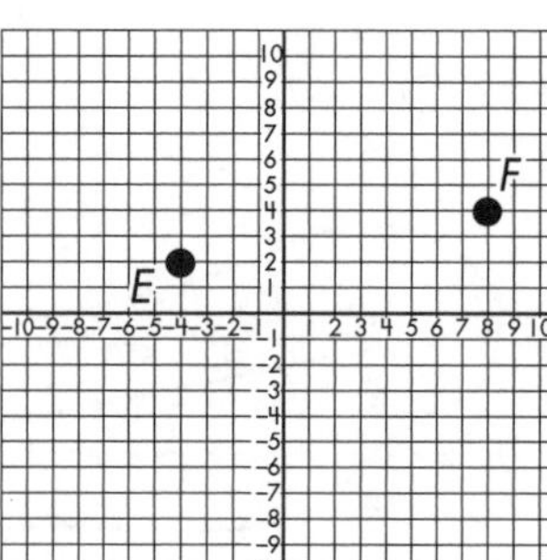	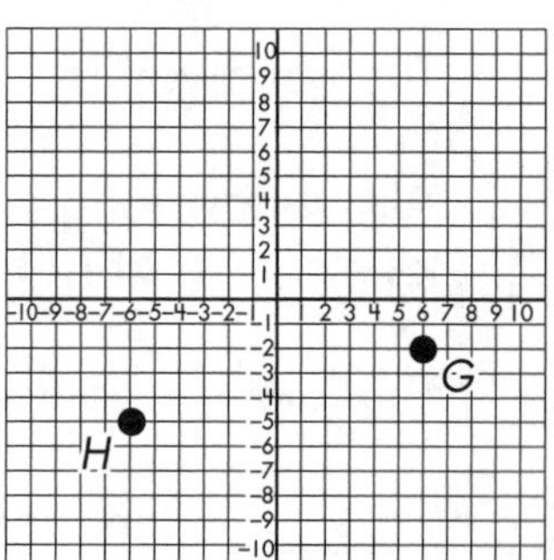
	$\overline{CD}$ = ____________	$\overline{EF}$ = ____________	$\overline{GH}$ = ____________

Lesson 5.9 Pythagorean Theorem in the Coordinate Plane

Find the distance between each of the points given below using the Pythagorean Theorem. Round answers to the nearest hundredth.

	a	b	c
1.	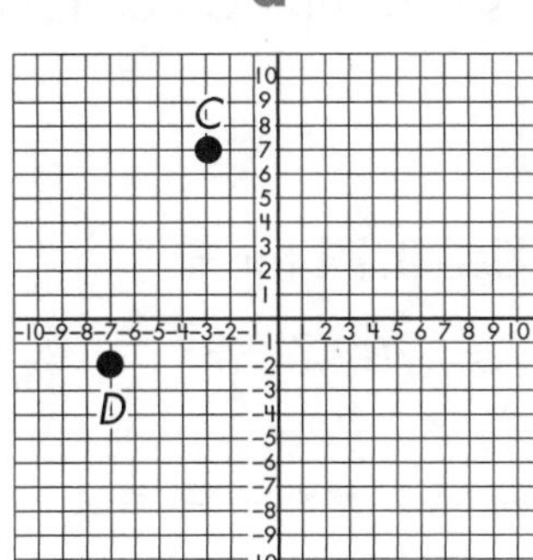 $\overline{CD}$ = ____________	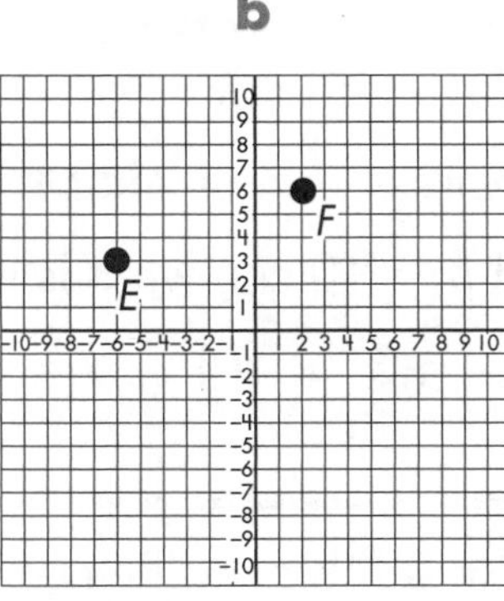 $\overline{EF}$ = ____________	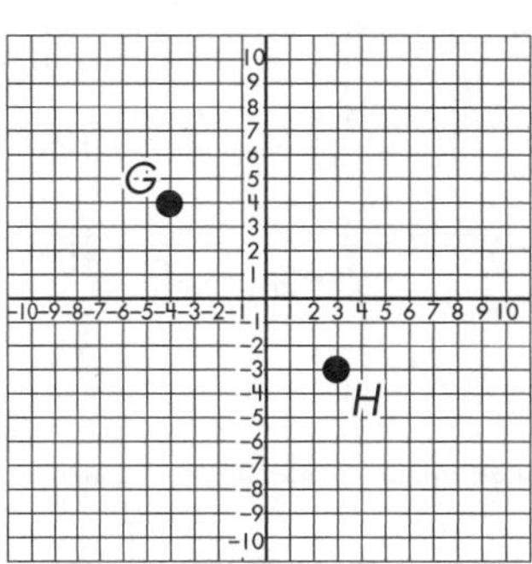 $\overline{GH}$ = ____________
2.	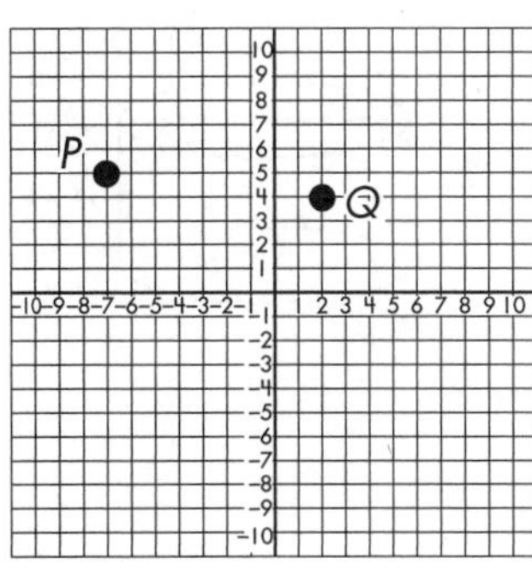 $\overline{PQ}$ = ____________	$\overline{AB}$ = ____________	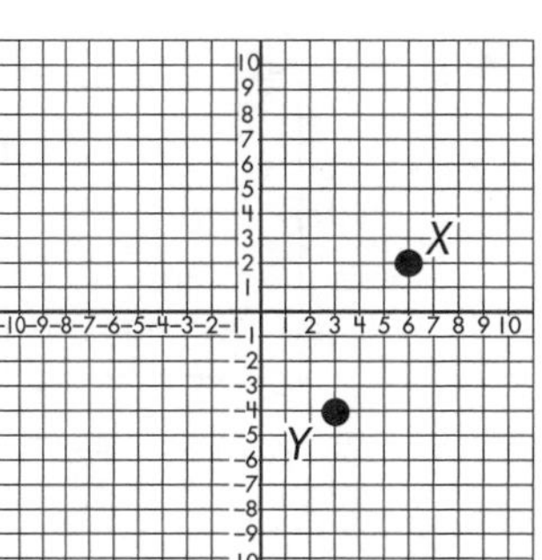 $\overline{XY}$ = ____________
3.	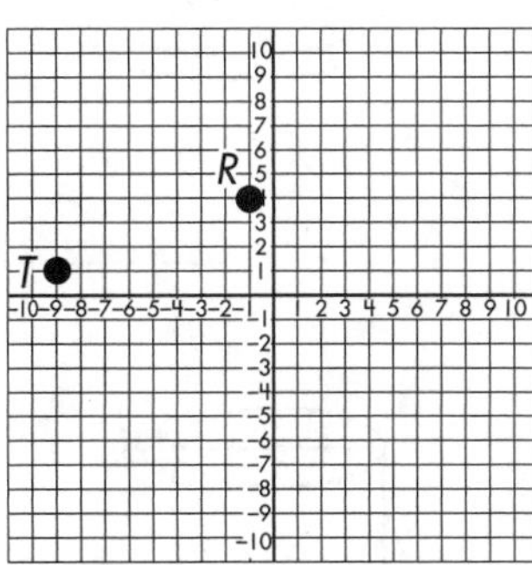 $\overline{TR}$ = ____________	$\overline{BK}$ = ____________	$\overline{JE}$ = ____________

NAME ______________________________

Lesson 5.10 Volume: Cylinders

Volume is the amount of space a three-dimensional figure occupies. You can calculate the **volume of a cylinder** by multiplying the area of the base by the height (Bh).

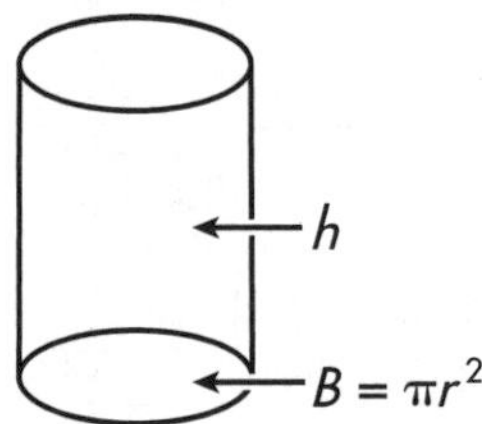

The area of the base is the area of the circle, πr^2, so volume can be found using the formula: $V = \pi r^2 h$

The volume is expressed in **cubic units**, or **units³**.

If $r = 3$ cm and $h = 10$ cm, what is the volume? Use 3.14 for π.

$V = \pi r^2 h$ $\quad V = \pi(3^2 \times 10)$ $\quad V = \pi \times 90$ $\quad V = 282.6\text{ cm}^3$

Find the volume of each cylinder. Use 3.14 for π. Remember that $d = 2r$. Round answers to the nearest hundredth.

	a	b	c

1.

a $r = 5$ in. $h = 12$ in.

$V =$ ________ in.³

b $r = 4$ ft. $h = 10$ ft.

$V =$ ________ ft.³

c

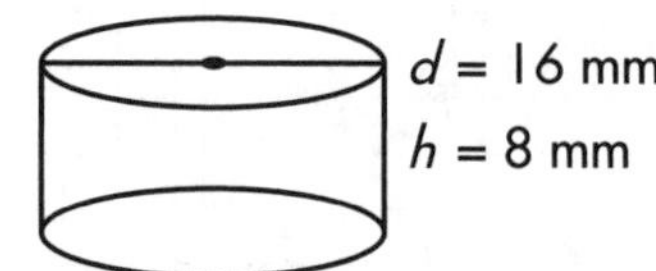

$V =$ ________ mm³

2.

a

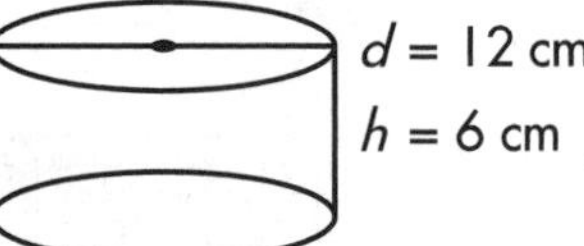

$V =$ ________ cm³

b $r = 5$ in. $h = 7$ in.

$V =$ ________ in.³

c $r = 0.6$ m $h = 1$ m

$V =$ ________ m³

3.

a

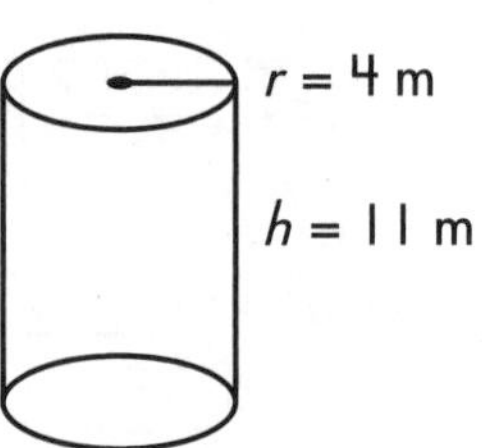

$V =$ ________ m³

b

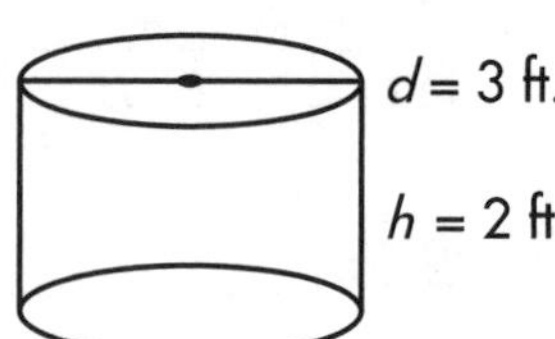

$V =$ ________ ft.³

c

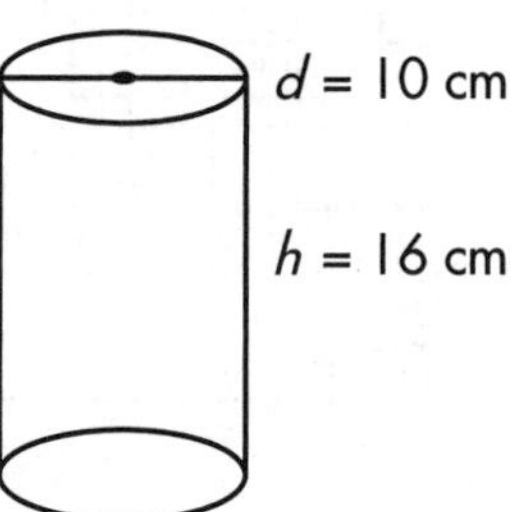

$V =$ ________ cm³

NAME ______________________

Lesson 5.10 Volume: Cylinders

Find the volume of each cylinder. Use 3.14 for π. Round answers to the nearest hundredth.

	a	b	c
1.	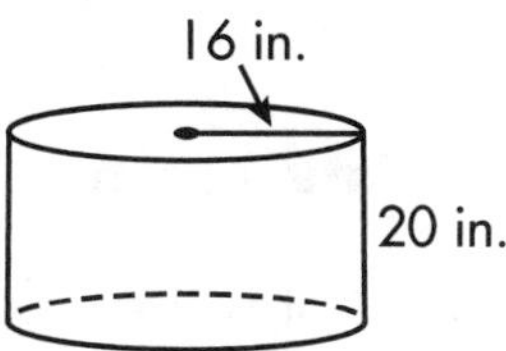	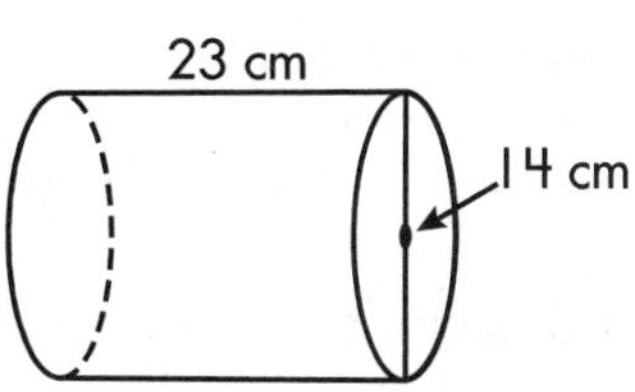	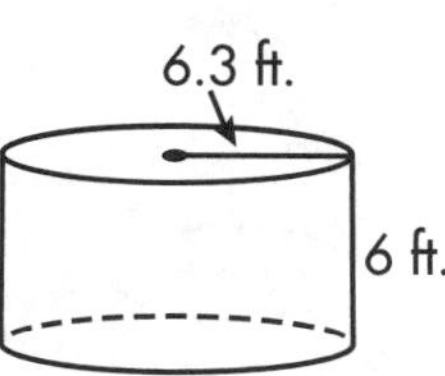
	$V =$ ________ in.^{3}	$V =$ ________ cm^3	$V =$ ________ ft.^{3}
2.	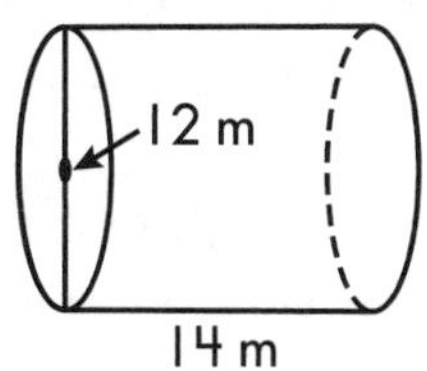	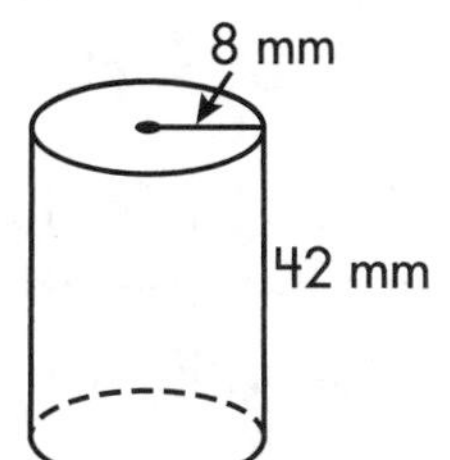	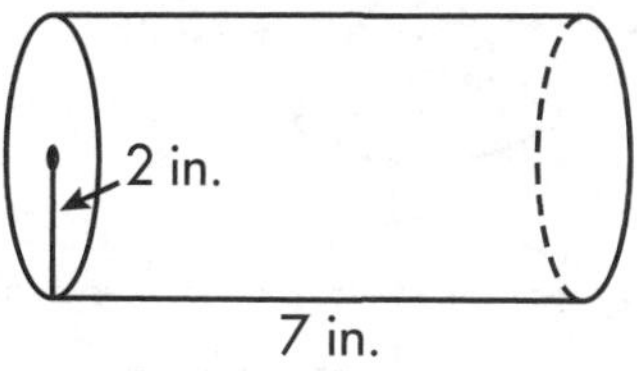
	$V =$ ________ m^3	$V =$ ________ mm^3	$V =$ ________ in.^{3}
3.	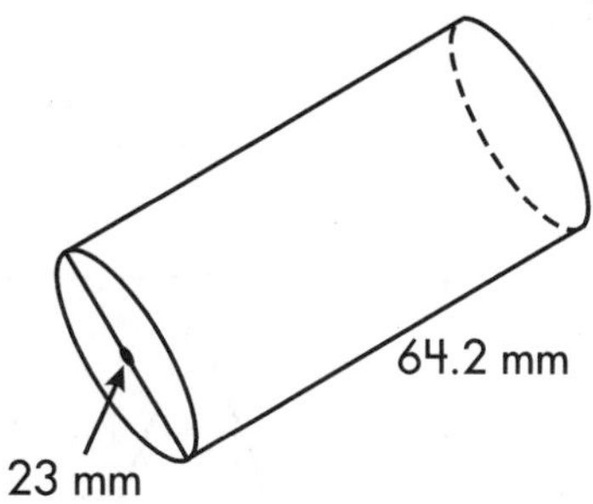	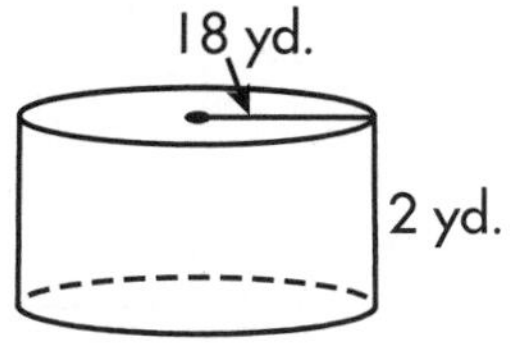	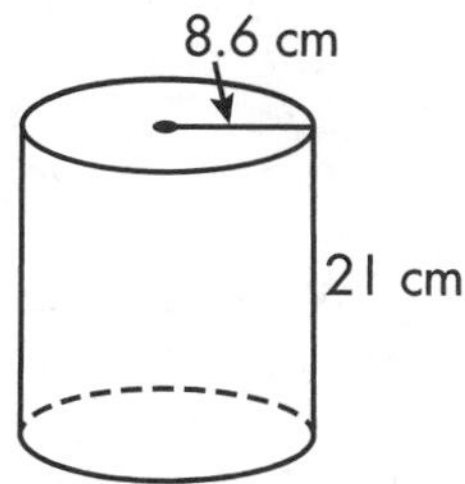
	$V =$ ________ mm^3	$V =$ ________ yd.^{3}	$V =$ ________ cm^3
4.	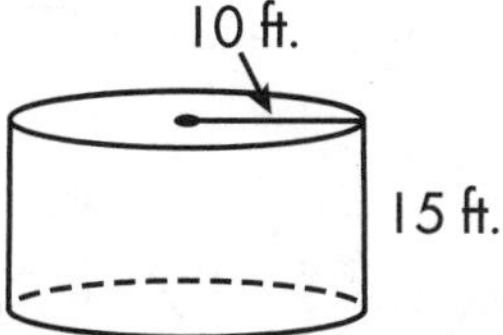	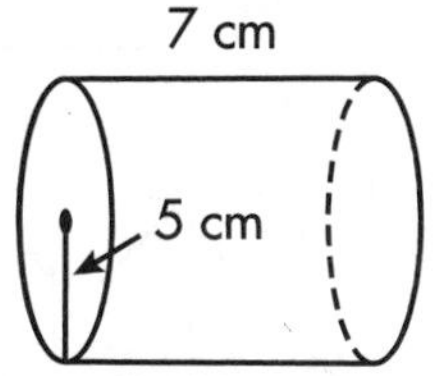	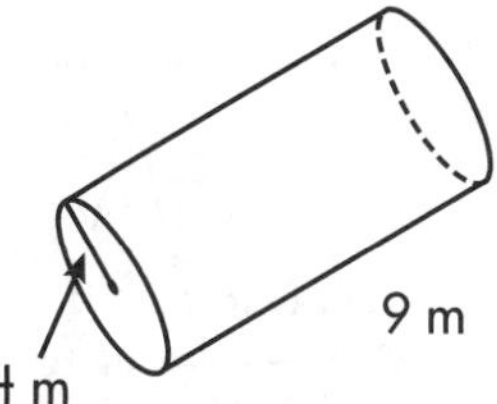
	$V =$ ________ ft.^{3}	$V =$ ________ cm^3	$V =$ ________ m^3

NAME ___________________________

Lesson 5.11 Volume: Cones

Volume is the amount of space a three-dimensional figure occupies. The **volume of a cone** is calculated as $\frac{1}{3}$ base $\times$ height.

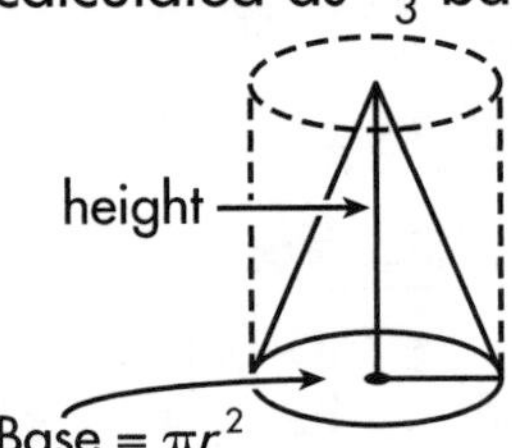

This is because a cone occupies $\frac{1}{3}$ of the volume of a cylinder of the same height. Base is the area of the circle, πr^2.

$V = \frac{1}{3}\pi r^2 h$ Volume is given in **cubic units**, or **units³**.

If the height of a cone is 7 cm and radius is 3 cm, what is the volume?

Use 3.14 for π. $V = \frac{1}{3}\pi 3^2 7$ $V = \frac{\pi 63}{3}$ $V = \pi 21$ $V = 65.94$ cm^3

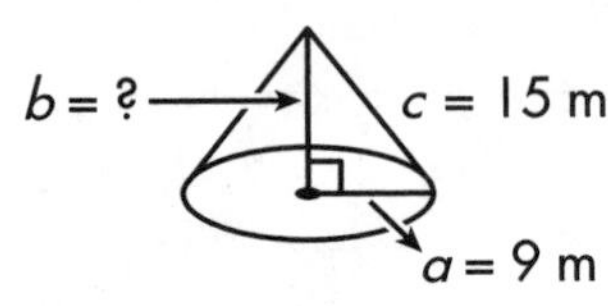

If you do not know the height but you do know the radius and the length of the side, you can use the Pythagorean Theorem to find the height.
What is b? $a^2 + b^2 = c^2$ $81 + b^2 = 225$ $b^2 = 144$ $b = 12$ m

$V = \frac{1}{3}\pi r^2 h = \frac{1}{3}\pi\ 9^2\ 12 = \frac{972\pi}{3} = 324\pi = 1{,}017.36$ m^3

Find the volume of each cone. Use 3.14 for π. Remember that $d = 2r$. Round answers to the nearest hundredth.

a **b** **c**

1.

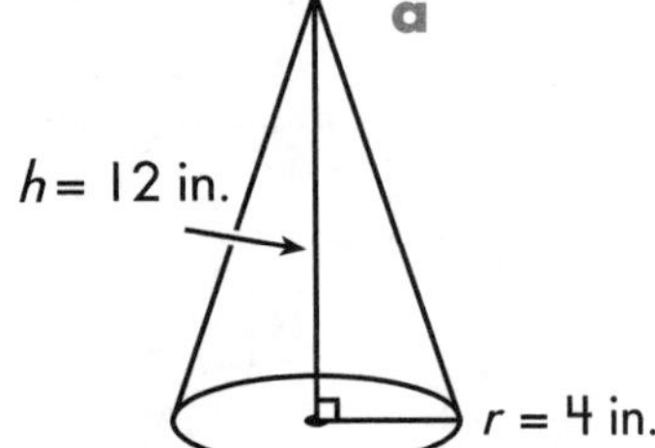

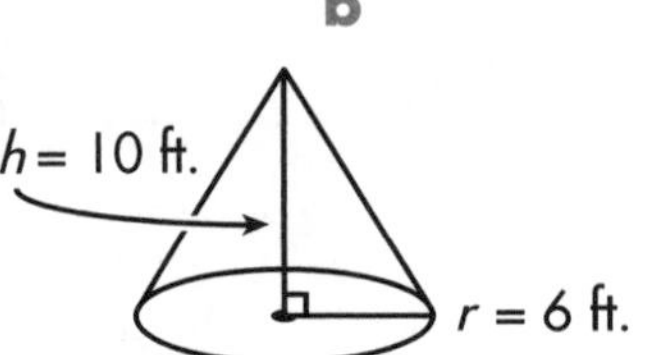

h = 6 cm
d = 5 cm

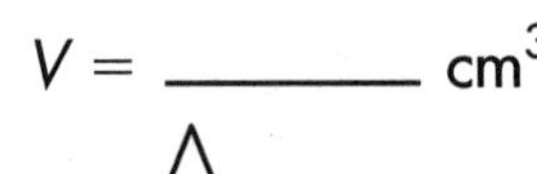

V = ________ in.^{3} V = ________ ft.^{3} V = ________ cm^3

2.

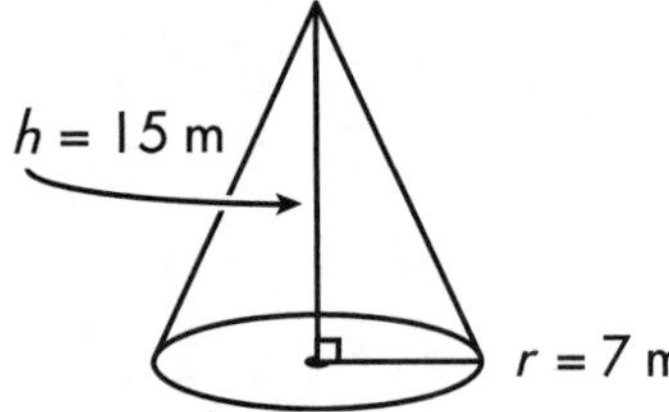

ℓ = 5 in.
r = 4 in.

ℓ = 13 m
r = 5 m

V = ________ m^3 V = ________ in.^{3} V = ________ m^3

3.

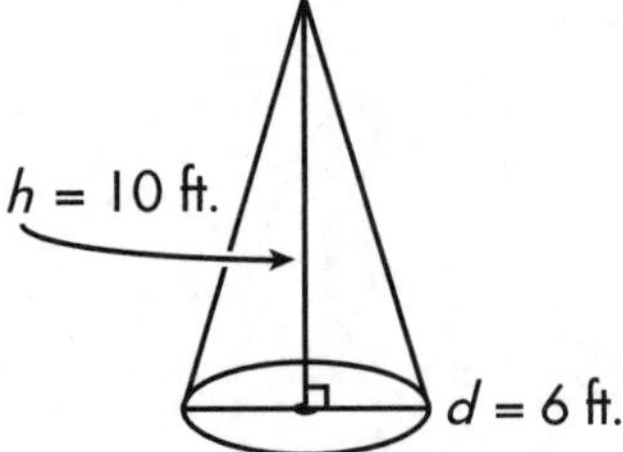

ℓ = 29 cm
r = 21 cm

h = 5 in.
r = 3 in.

V = ________ ft.^{3} V = ________ cm^3 V = ________ in.^{3}

NAME ____________________

Lesson 5.11 Volume: Cones

Find the volume of each cone. Use 3.14 for π. Round answers to the nearest hundredth.

	a	b	c
1.	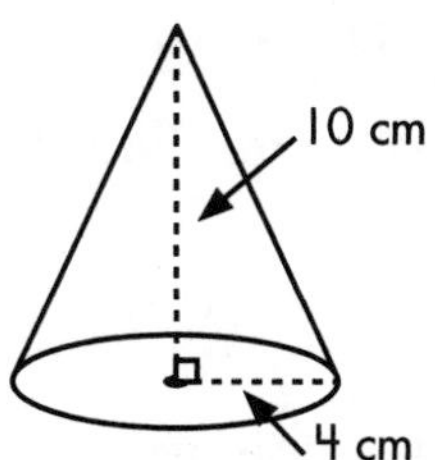 $V =$ ______ cm^3	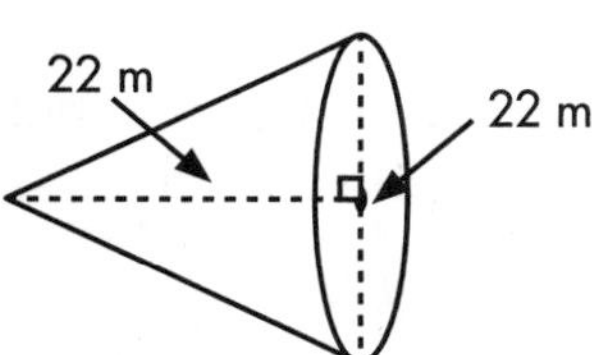 $V =$ ______ m^3	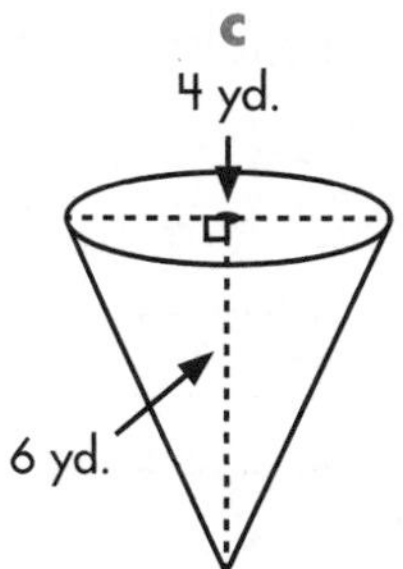 $V =$ ______ yd.^{3}
2.	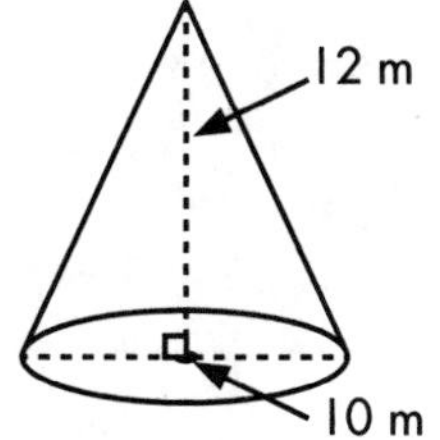 $V =$ ______ m^3	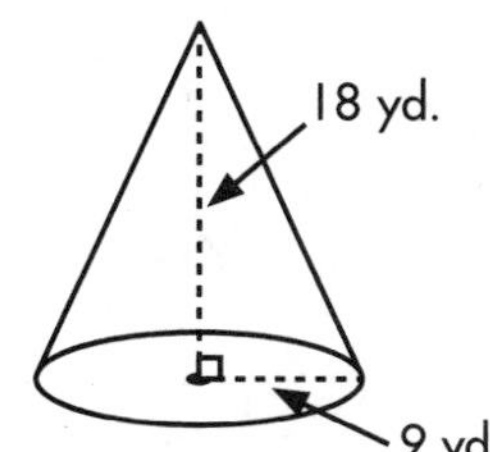 $V =$ ______ yd.^{3}	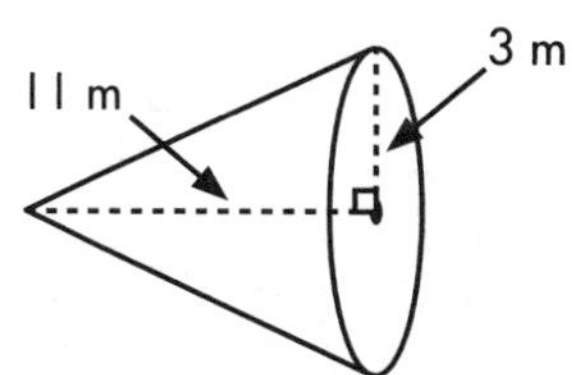 $V =$ ______ m^3
3.	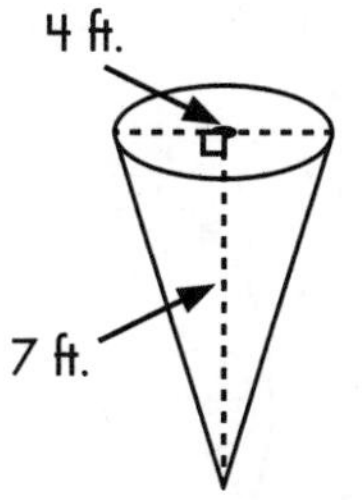 $V =$ ______ ft.^{3}	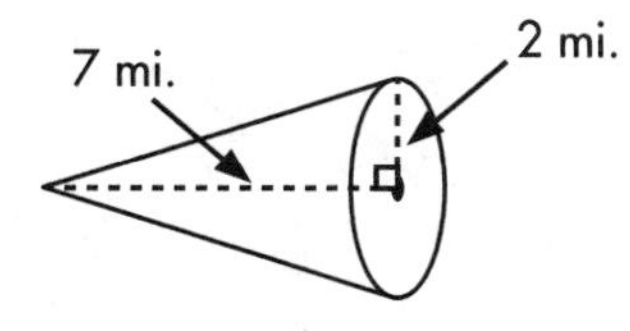 $V =$ ______ mi.^{3}	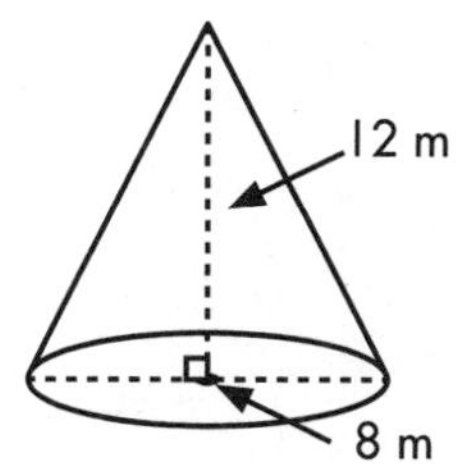 $V =$ ______ m^3
4.	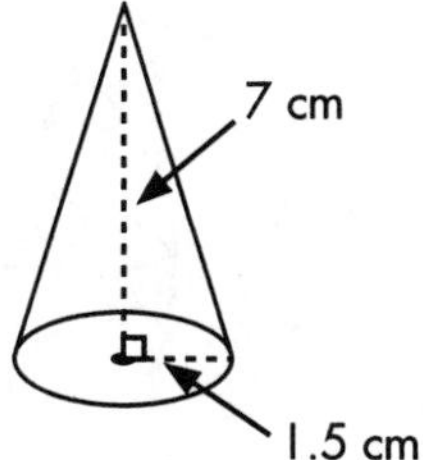 $V =$ ______ cm^3	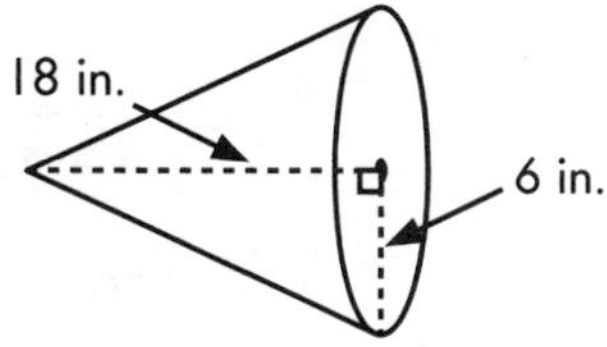 $V =$ ______ in.^{3}	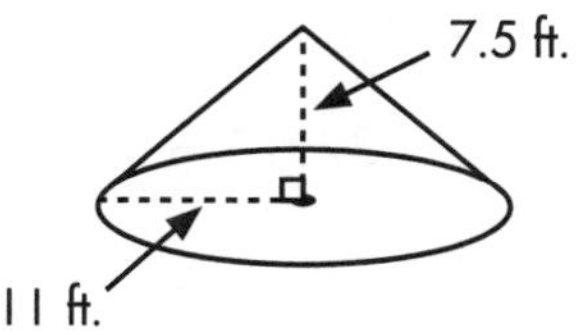 $V =$ ______ ft.^{3}

NAME ______________________

Lesson 5.12 Volume: Spheres

Volume is the amount of space a three-dimensional figure occupies. The **volume of a sphere** is calculated as $V = \frac{4}{3}\pi r^3$. When the diameter of a sphere is known, it can be divided by 2 and then the formula for the volume of a sphere can be used.

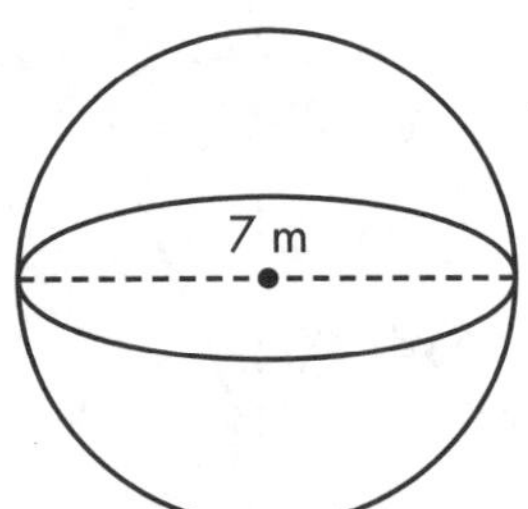

$V = \frac{4}{3}\pi r^3$ Volume is given in **cubic units** or **units^3**.

The radius of a sphere is half of its diameter. Find the radius, then calculate the volume.

$r = \frac{1}{2}d = \frac{1}{2}(7) = \frac{7}{2} = 3.5$

$V = \frac{4}{3}\pi(3.5)^3 = \frac{4}{3}\pi(42.875) = 179.5$ cubic meters

Find the volume of each sphere. Use 3.14 to represent π. Round answers to the nearest hundredth.

	a	b	c
1.	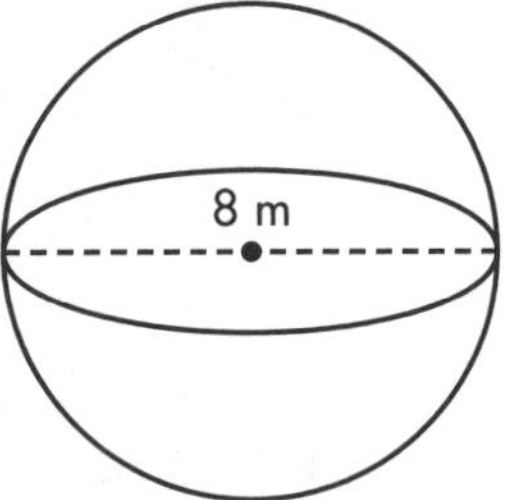 $V =$ ________ m^3	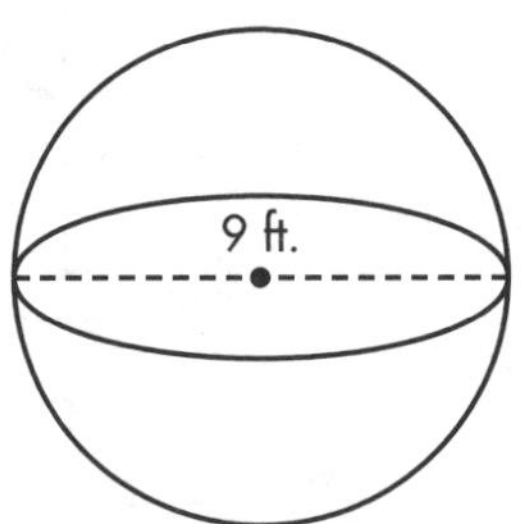 $V =$ ________ $ft.^3$	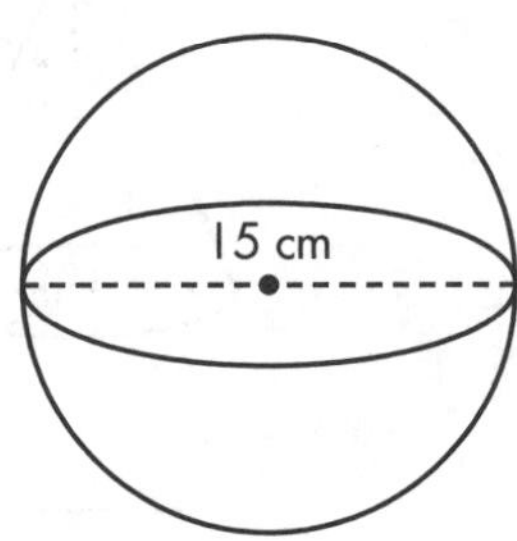 $V =$ ________ cm^3
2.	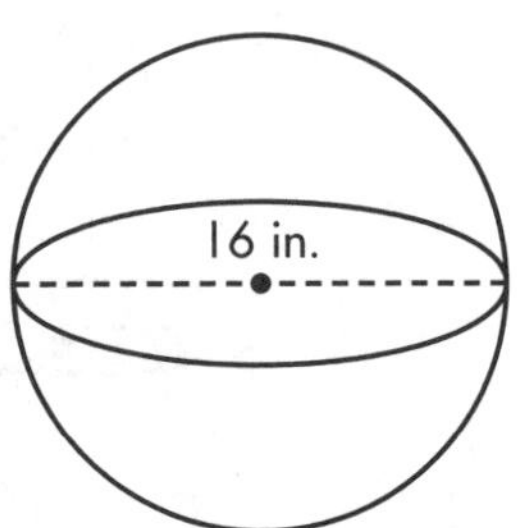 $V =$ ________ $in.^3$	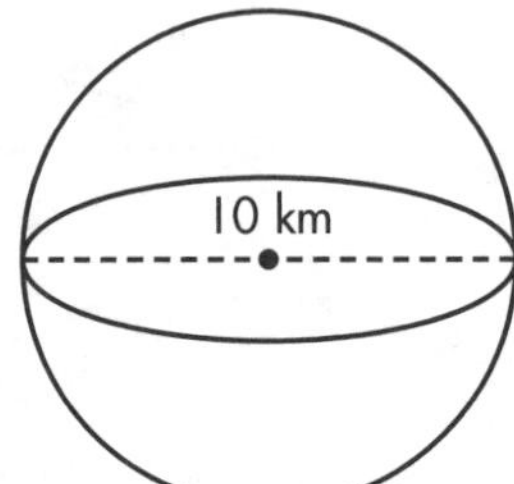 $V =$ ________ km^3	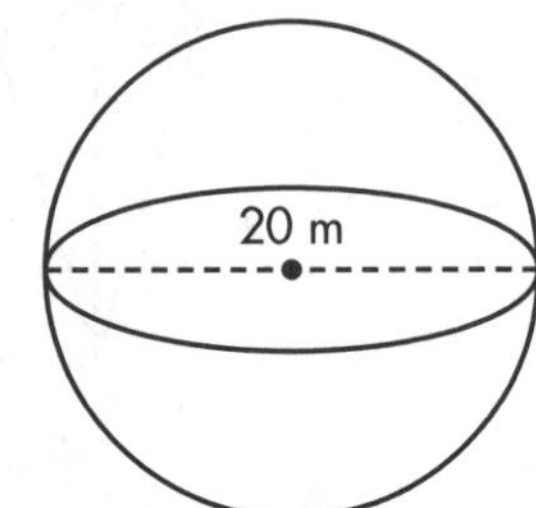 $V =$ ________ m^3
3.	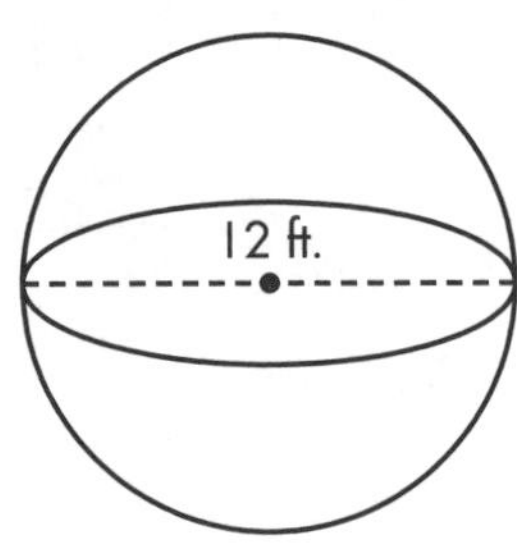 $V =$ ________ $ft.^3$	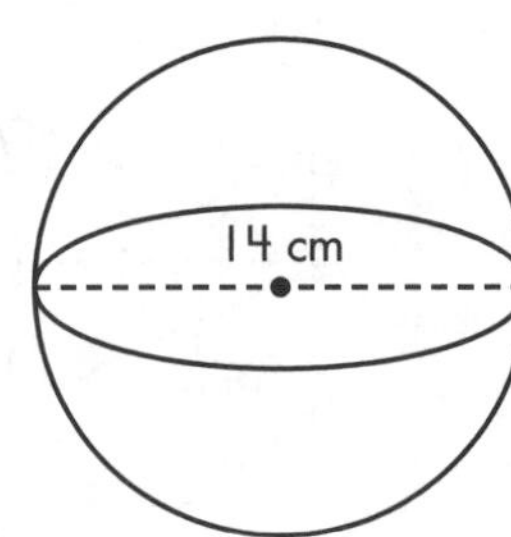 $V =$ ________ cm^3	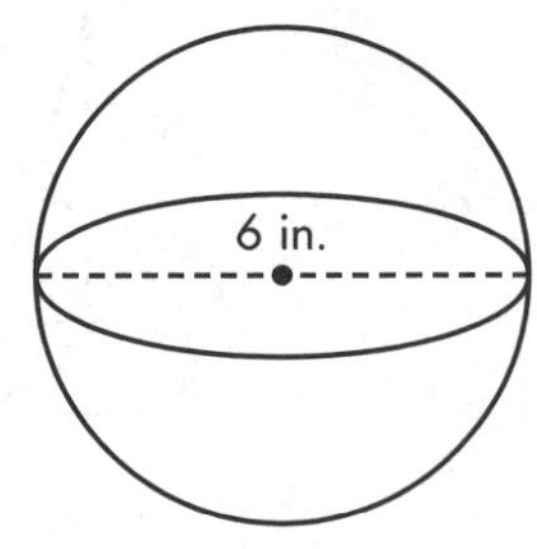 $V =$ ________ $in.^3$

NAME ______________________

Lesson 5.12 Volume: Spheres

Find the volume of each sphere. Use 3.14 to represent π. Round answers to the nearest hundredth.

	a	b	c
1.	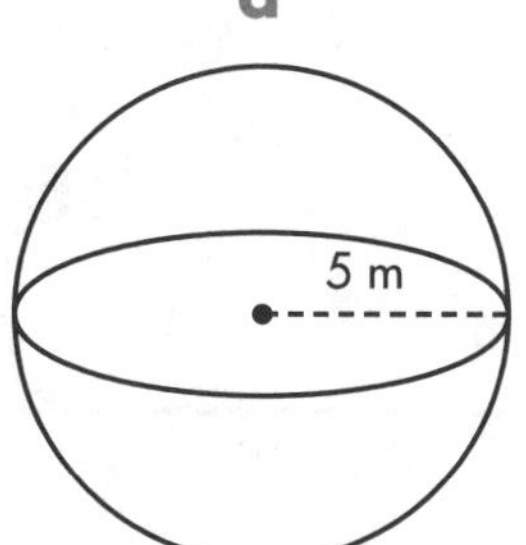 $V =$ ______ m^3	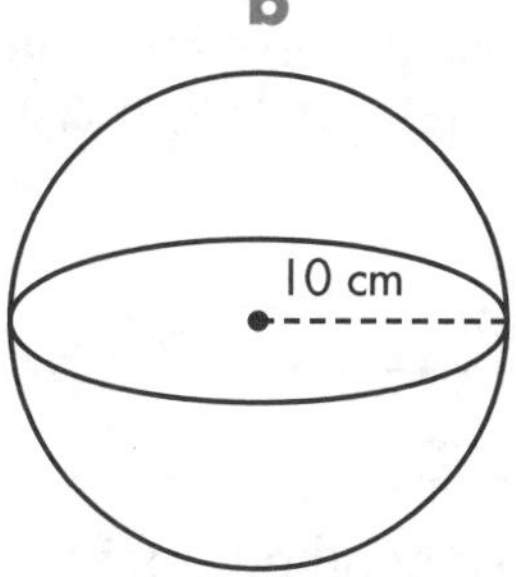 $V =$ ______ cm^3	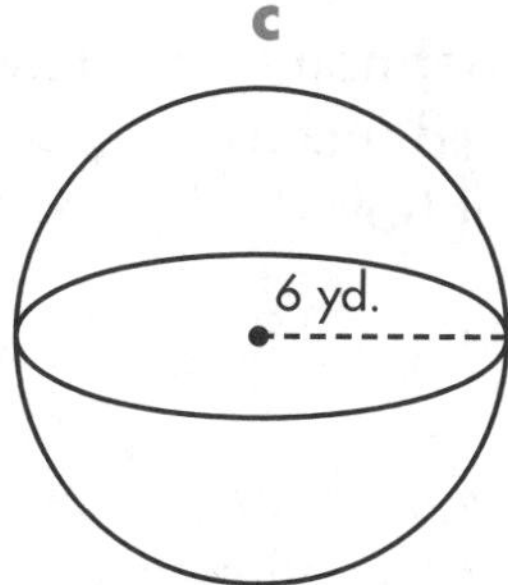 $V =$ ______ $yd.^3$
2.	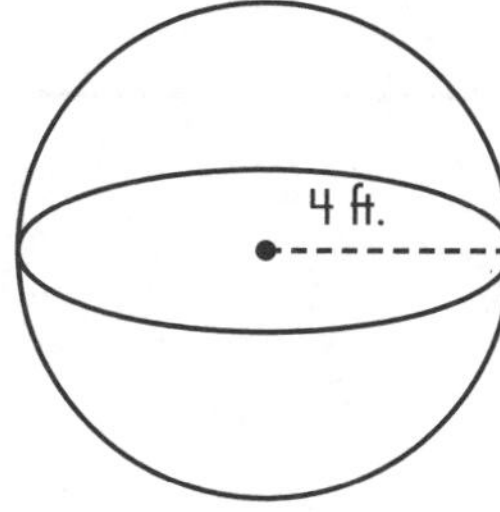 $V =$ ______ $ft.^3$	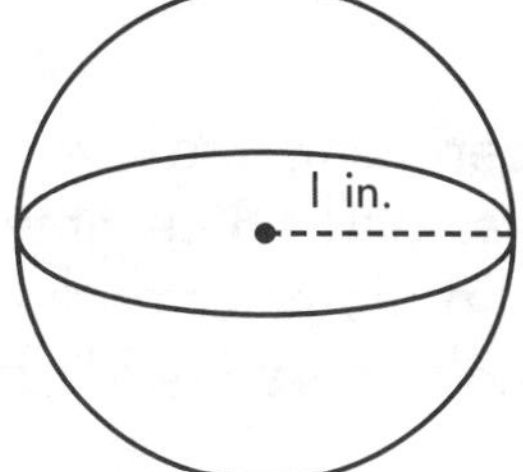 $V =$ ______ $in.^3$	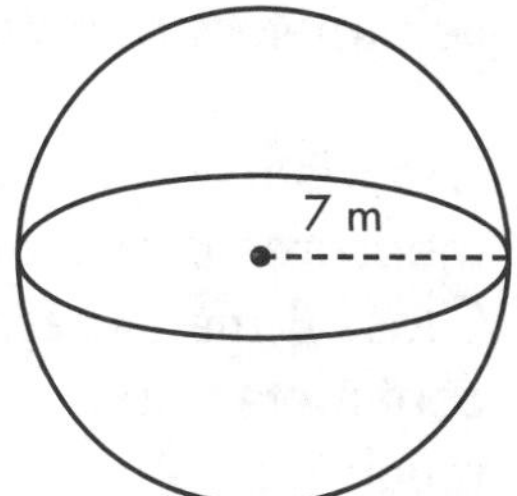 $V =$ ______ m^3
3.	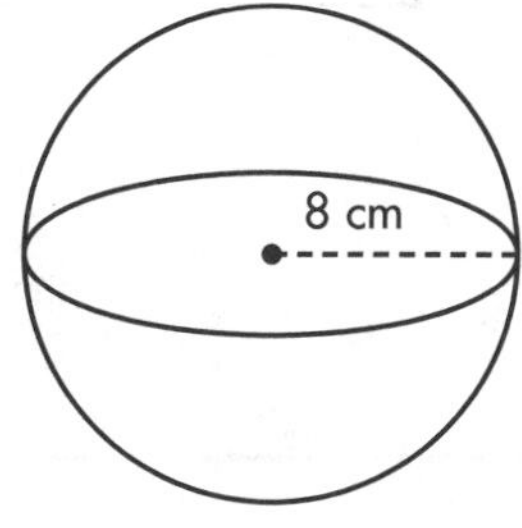 $V =$ ______ cm^3	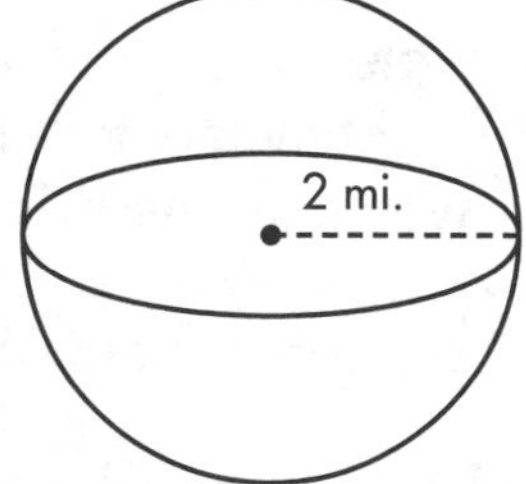 $V =$ ______ $mi.^3$	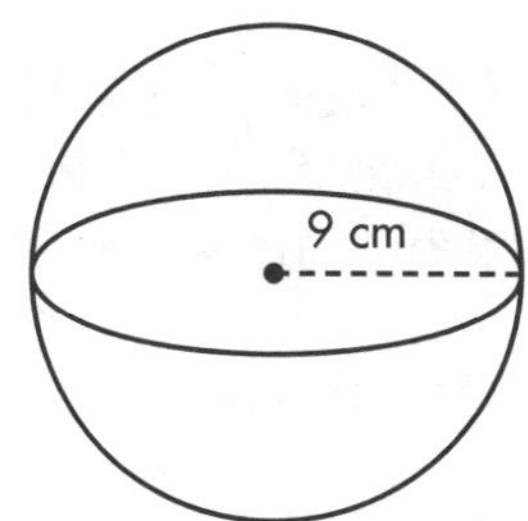 $V =$ ______ cm^3
4.	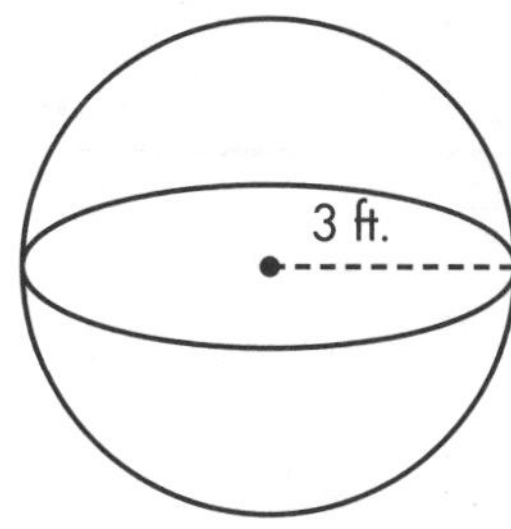 $V =$ ______ $ft.^3$	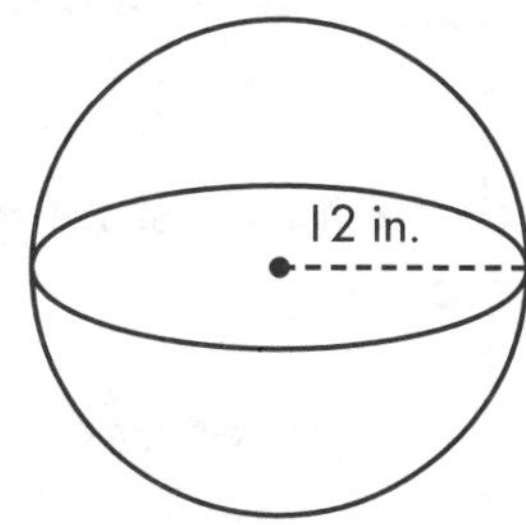 $V =$ ______ $in.^3$	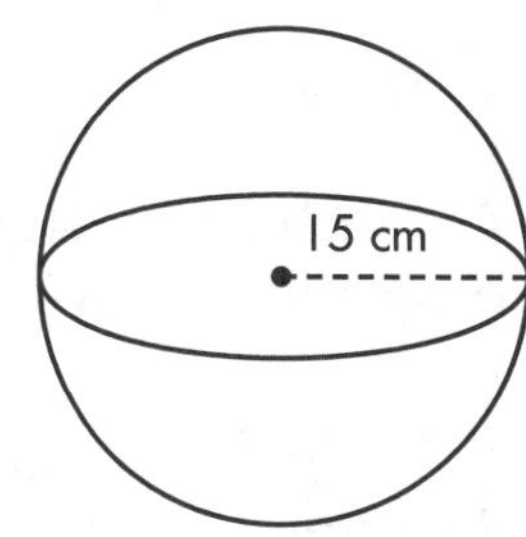 $V =$ ______ cm^3

NAME ____________________

Lesson 5.13 Problem-Solving with Volume

SHOW YOUR WORK

Solve each problem. Use 3.14 for π. Round answers to the nearest hundredth.

1. Jermaine has a mailing cylinder for posters that measures 18 inches long and 6 inches in diameter. What volume can it hold?

   The cylinder can hold ____________ cubic inches.

2. An oatmeal container is a cylinder measuring 16 centimeters in diameter and 32 centimeters tall. How much oatmeal can the container hold?

   The container can hold ____________ cubic centimeters of oatmeal.

3. Trina is using 2 glasses in an experiment. Glass A measures 8 centimeters in diameter and 18 centimeters tall. Glass B measures 10 centimeters in diameter and 13 centimeters tall. Which one can hold more liquid? How much more?

   Glass ____________ can hold ____________ more cubic centimeters of liquid.

4. Paul completely filled a glass with water. The glass was 10 centimeters in diameter and 17 centimeters tall. He drank the water. What volume of water did he drink?

   Paul drank ____________ cubic centimeters of water.

5. An ice-cream cone has a height of 6 inches and a diameter of 3 inches. How much ice cream can this cone hold?

   The cone can hold ____________ cubic inches of ice cream.

6. A beach ball that is 10 inches in diameter must be inflated. How much air will it take to fill the ball?

   It will take ____________ cubic inches of air to fill the ball.

1.
2.
3.
4.
5.
6.

NAME ___________________________

Check What You Learned

Geometry

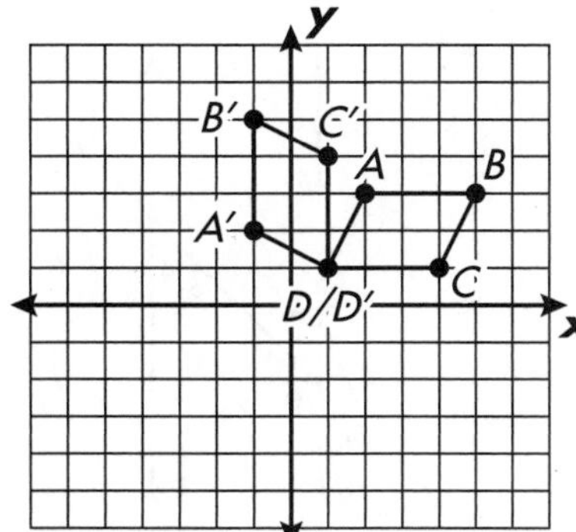

1. What are the coordinates of the preimage?

   A(________), B(________), C(________), D(________)

2. What are the coordinates of the image?

   A′(________), B′(________), C′(________), D′(________)

3. What transformation did you perform? ____________

Write the steps each figure must go through to be transformed from figure 1 to figure 2.

a | **b**

4.

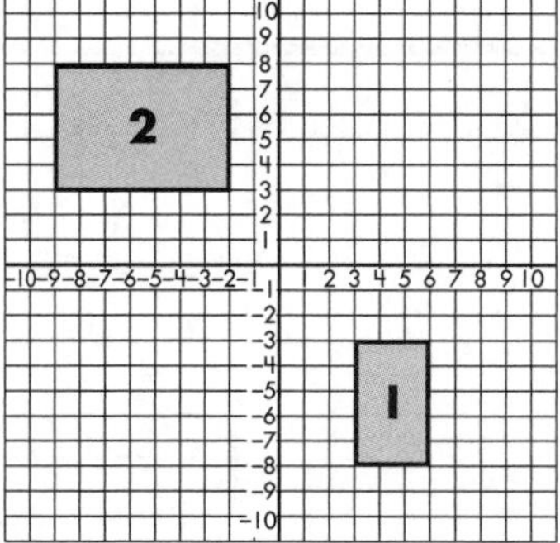

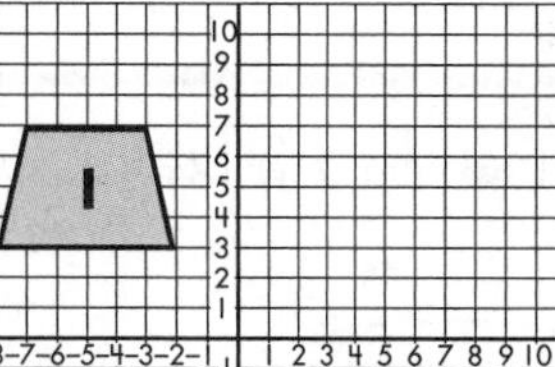

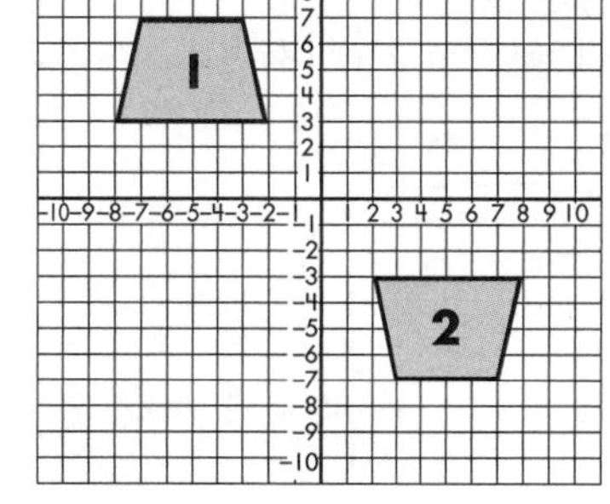

a
Step 1: ___________________________
Step 2: ___________________________
Step 3: ___________________________

b
Step 1: ___________________________
Step 2: ___________________________

Draw similar right triangles to show that each line has a constant slope.

5.

Triangle 1 Legs:
______ & ______
Triangle 2 Legs:
______ & ______

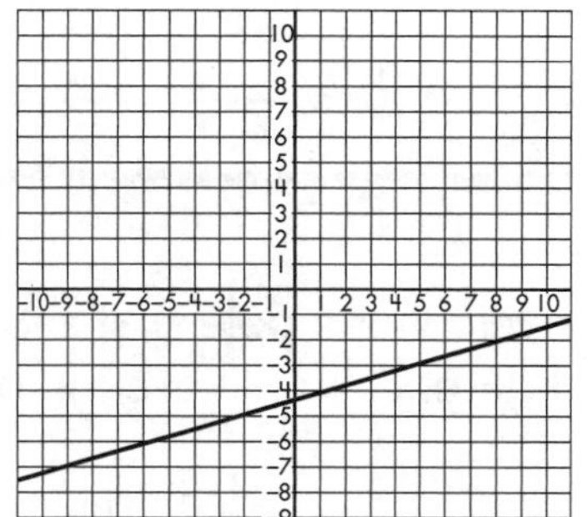

Triangle 1 Legs:
______ & ______
Triangle 2 Legs:
______ & ______

NAME ______________________

Check What You Learned

Geometry

Answer each question using letters to name each line and numbers to name each angle.

6. Which 2 lines are parallel? ____________

7. What is the name of the transversal? ____________

8. Which angles are acute? ____________

9. Which angles are obtuse? ____________

10. Which pairs of angles are vertical angles? ______________

11. Which pairs of angles are alternate exterior angles? ______________

12. Which pairs of angles are alternate interior angles? ______________

Find the volume of each figure. Use 3.14 for π. Round answers to the nearest hundredth.

13.

a

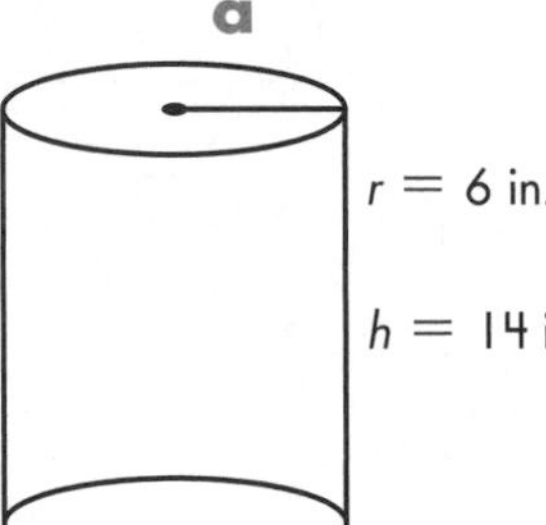

$V =$ ________ in.^{3}

b

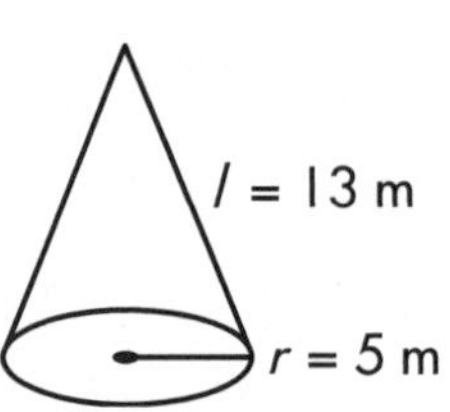

$V =$ ________ m^3

c

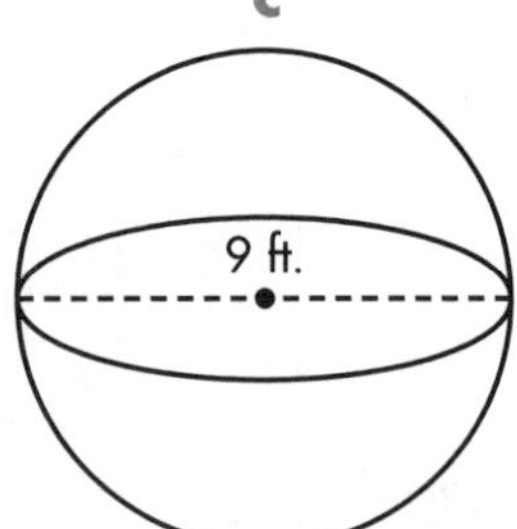

$V =$ ________ ft.^{3}

Use the Pythagorean Theorem to find the unknown lengths.

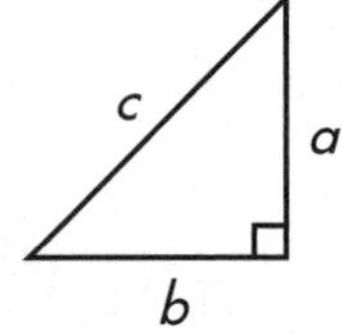

14. If $a = 7$ and $b = 10$, $c = \sqrt{}$ ________ or about ____________.

15. If $a = 11$ and $c = 18$, $b = \sqrt{}$ ________ or about ____________.

Solve each problem.

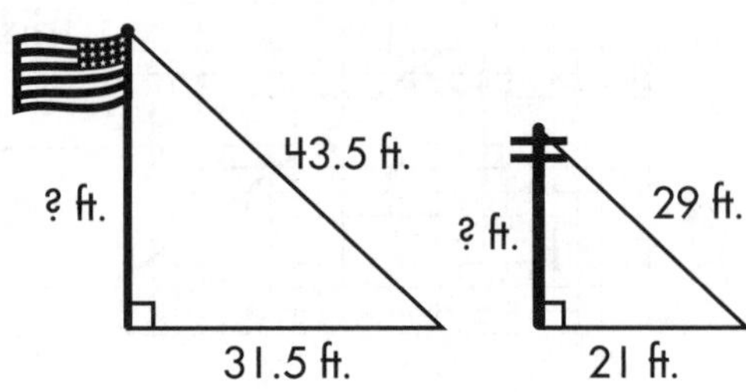

16. A flagpole and a telephone pole cast shadows as shown in the figure. How tall are the poles?

    The flagpole is ____________ feet tall.

    The telephone pole is ____________ feet tall.

Check What You Know

Statistics and Probability

Answer the questions by interpreting data from the graph.

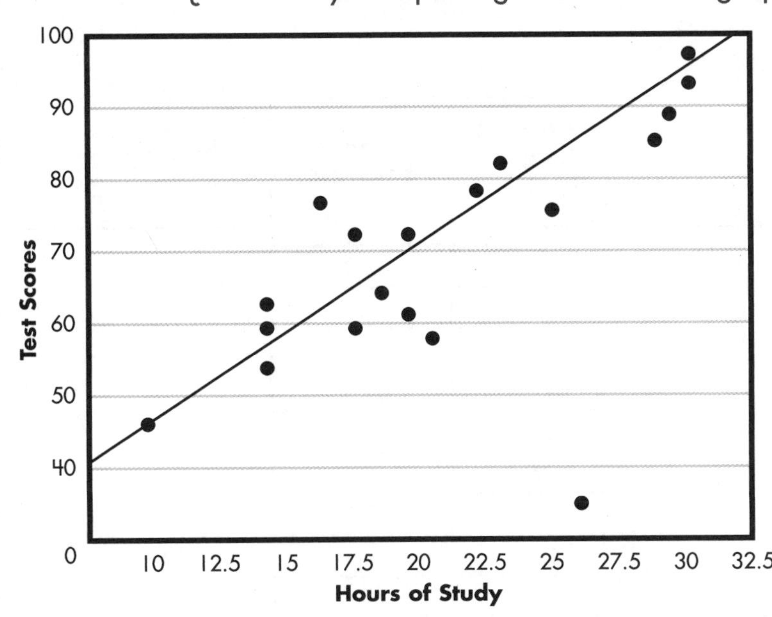

1. What two sets of data are being compared by this scatter plot?

   ____

2. Is the correlation positive or negative?

   ____

3. What is a possible explanation for the outliers?

   ____

Use the data set below to create a scatter plot with a line of best fit. Then, answer the questions.

4.

Dog Sizes	
Height (cm)	**Mass (kg)**
41	4.5
40	5
35	4
38	3.5
43	5.5
44	5
37	5
39	4
42	4
44	6
31	3.5

5. What two sets of data are being compared by this scatter plot? ______________________

6. Is the correlation between the data sets positive or negative? ______________________

7. What is a possible explanation for the outliers? ______________________

8. If a dog has a mass of 3 kg, predict the height of the dog. ______________________

NAME ______________________

Check What You Know

Statistics and Probability

Use each set of bivariate data to create a scatter plot, trend line, and an equation that approximates the data set.

9.

a

Time	Speed
20	34
33	46
22	38
39	53
40	52
37	49
46	60
44	58
24	36

equation: ______________

b

Advertising Budget (hundred thousands)	Profit Increase (%)
11	2.2
14	2.2
15	3.2
17	4.6
20	5.7
25	6.9
25	7.9
27	9.3

equation: ______________

Use the data set to complete the frequency table and answer the questions.

Gas mileage of a number of cars was collected as follows: 12, 17, 12, 14, 16, 18, 16, 18, 12, 16, 17, 15, 15, 16, 12, 15, 16, 16, 12, 14, 15, 12, 15, 15, 19, 13, 16, 18, 16, and 14.

	Mileage Range	Frequency	Cumulative Frequency	Relative Frequency
10.	11.5–13.4			
11.	13.5–15.4			
12.	15.5–17.4			
13.	17.5–19.5			

14. How many cars were included in the data set? ______________

15. What is the most common gas mileage range for this set of cars? ______________

16. What is the least common gas mileage range for this set of cars? ______________

 Lesson 6.1 Interpreting Scatter Plots

A **scatter plot** shows the relationship between two sets of data. It is made up of points. The points are plotted by using the values from the two sets of data as coordinates.

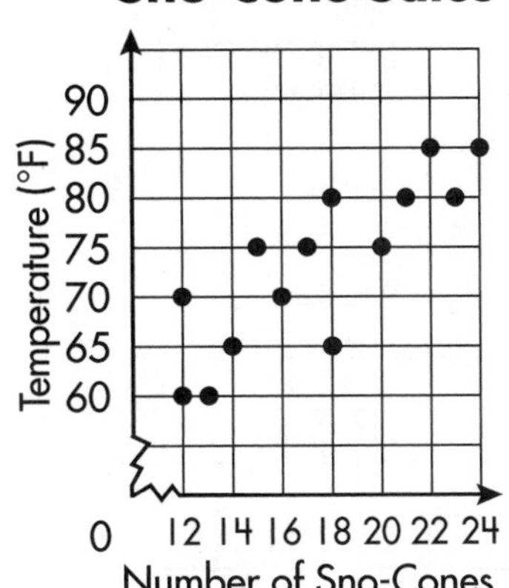

This scatter plot shows the relationship between the temperature and the number of sno-cones sold. As one value increases, the other appears to increase as well. This indicates a *positive* relationship.

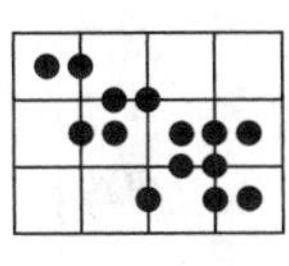

A *negative* relationship would show that more sno-cones are sold as the temperature decreases.

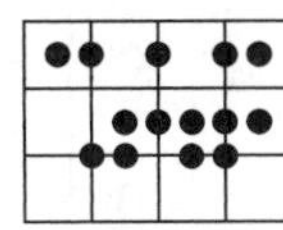

No relationship would show no clear trend in the data.

Use the scatter plot above to complete the data table. Include the coordinates for all 14 points.

1.

Sno-Cones	12	12	13	14										
Temperature	60	70	60	65										

Does each scatter plot below indicate a *positive* relationship, a *negative* relationship, or *no relationship*?

2.

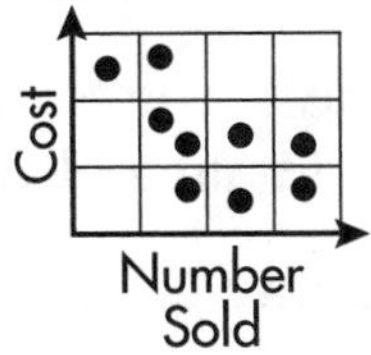

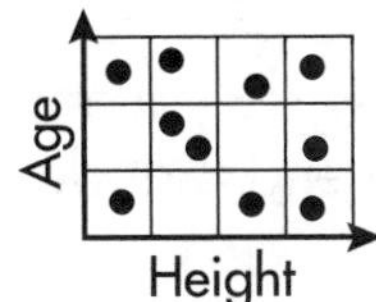

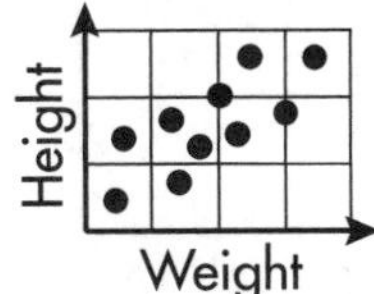

______________ ______________ ______________

Use the data below to create a scatter plot on the grid. Be sure to include all labels.

3.

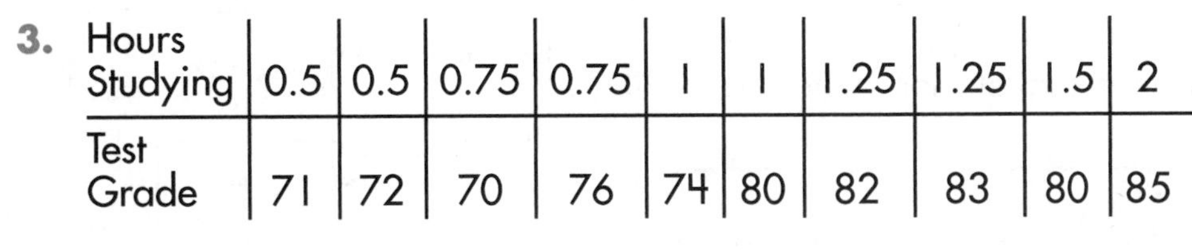

Hours Studying	0.5	0.5	0.75	0.75	1	1	1.25	1.25	1.5	2
Test Grade	71	72	70	76	74	80	82	83	80	85

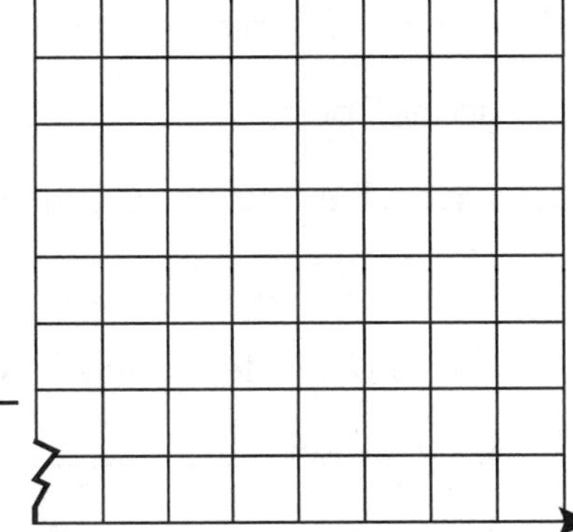

NAME ____________________

Lesson 6.1 Interpreting Scatter Plots

A **scatter plot** is a graph that shows the relationship between two sets of data. To see the relationship clearly, a **line of best fit**, or trend line, can be drawn. This is drawn so that there are about the same number of data points above and below the line.

This scatter plot shows the relationship between average high temperature and a family's gas use for heating fuel each month.

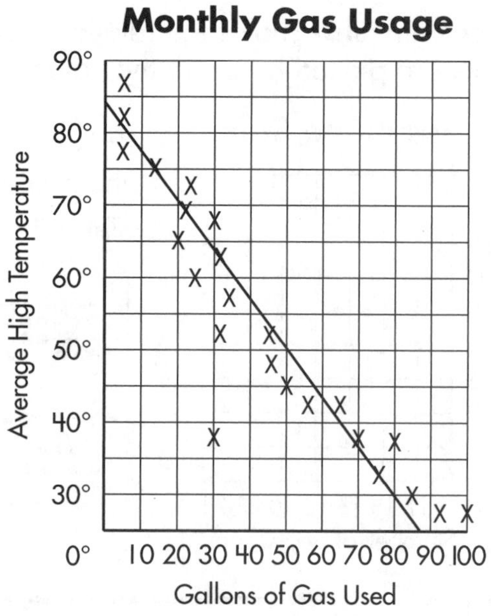

Answer the questions by interpreting data from the scatter plots.

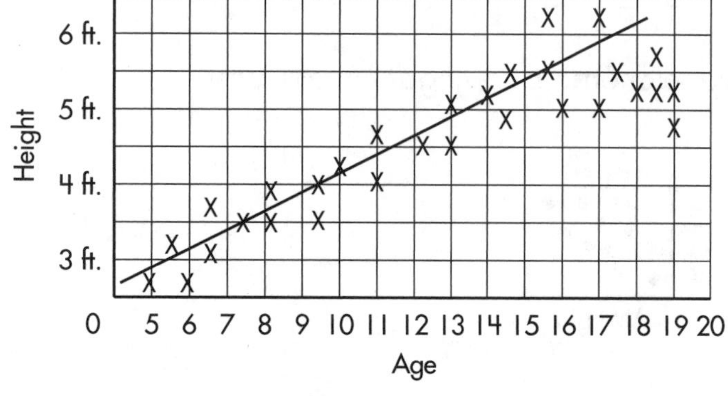

1. Which two sets of data are being compared by this scatter plot? ____________
2. Is the correlation positive or negative? ______
3. How many people were polled? ______
4. How do you explain the data points at the end that do not follow the line of best fit? ____________________

5. Which two pieces of data are being compared by this scatter plot? ____________________
6. Draw the line of best fit. Is the correlation positive or negative? ____________
7. There are a few outliers for this scatter plot. What do they show? ____________________
8. What is a possible explanation? ____________________

____

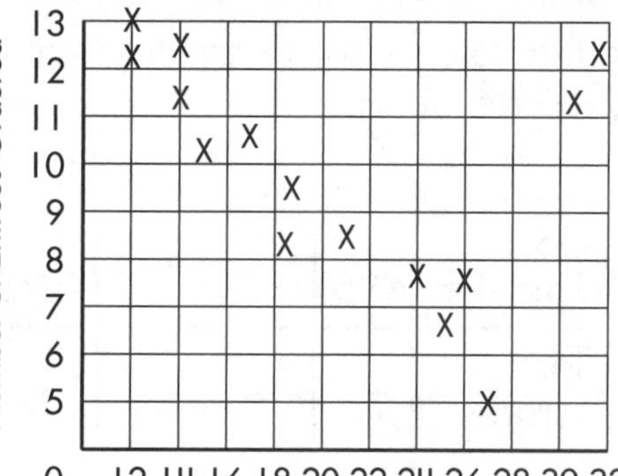

NAME ______________________

Lesson 6.2 Constructing Scatter Plots

A **scatter plot** is a way of displaying bivariate data, or two sets of data. A scatter plot can show the relationship between the bivariate data. Scatter plots can show if the values increase or decrease relative to each other and if there are any outliers in the data.

Meat (per 100 g)	**Fat** (g)	**Calories**
Beef	6.5	180
Chicken	1.9	138
Lamb	5.7	167
Pork	4.9	165
Turkey	1.5	146
Crab	1.5	125
Trout	7	160

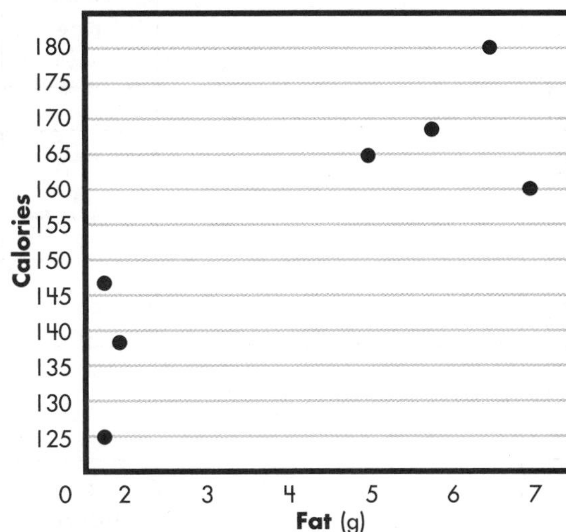

Step 1: Set up the *x*-axis of a graph with intervals for one set of the data and the *y*-axis for the other set.

Step 2: Use the data sets as ordered pairs to create points on the scatter plot.

Use the data sets below to create scatter plots.

a

1.

Hours Babysitting	**Money Earned** ($)
1	10
2	20
3	35
4	50
5	70

b

Hours Studied	**Grade Earned**
0	75
2	90
1	85
2	95
3	100

2.

Stories Tall	**Height** (m)
110	442
102	381
55	312
75	310
76	287

Height (in.)	**Weight** (lb.)
44	47
50	57
38	32
39	42
41	36
45	49
48	62
51	47

NAME ____________________

Lesson 6.2 Constructing Scatter Plots

Use the data sets below to create scatter plots.

a **b**

1.

Study Time (min.)	Test Score
20	60
65	85
30	70
90	100
45	88
30	77

Age (yrs.)	Height (in.)
11	55
10	55
8	49
6	45
10	52
11	59

2.

Weight (lb.)	Mileage (mi./gal.)
2750	29
3125	23
2100	33
4082	18
3640	21
2241	25

Hours Worked	Sales ($)
4	575
7	825
2	660
8	450
9	925
8	950
6	700
3	350

3.

City	Avg. Temp. (°F)	Avg. Precip. (in.)
Atlanta	53	5.9
Boston	38	4.1
Buffalo	33	3.0
Dallas	56	2.4
Kansas City	42	2.1
Los Angeles	60	2.4
Nashville	49	5.6

Time (min.)	Depth of Water in a Pool (in.)
2	7
4	8
6	13
8	19
10	20
12	24
14	32
16	37

NAME ____________________

Lesson 6.3 Fitting Lines to Scatter Plots

When bivariate data is graphed on a scatter plot, it may have a positive or negative association. A trend line can be used to make predictions about values that are not included in the data set. The accuracy of the prediction will depend on how closely the trend line fits the data points.

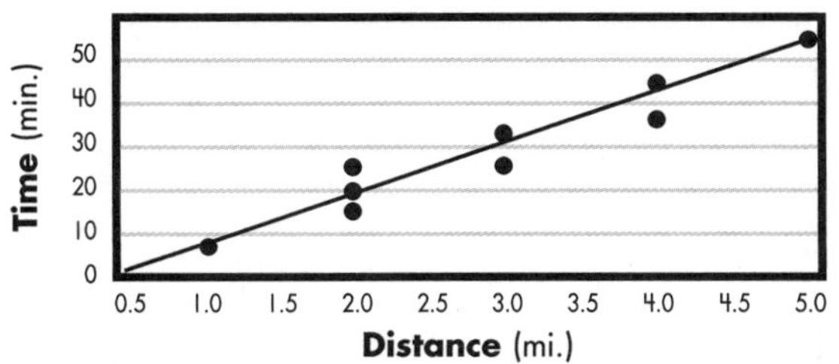

Create a trend line by using a straight edge to draw a line across the points on a scatter plot. Attempt to have the same number of points above and below the trend line while ignoring outliers.

Based on this trend line, at a distance of 3.5 miles, the time should be about 37 minutes.

Create a trend line for each scatter plot shown below.

a | **b**

1.

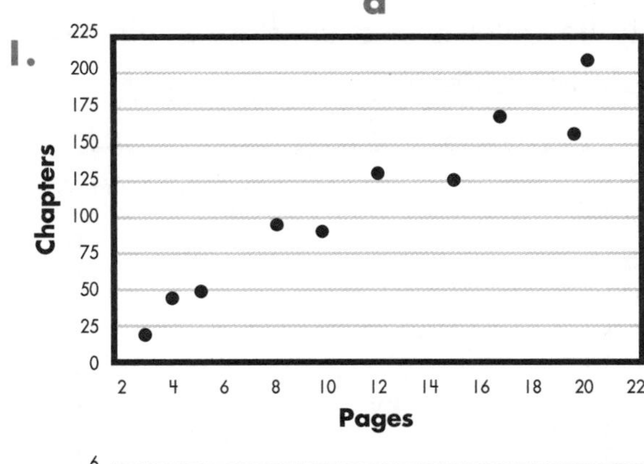

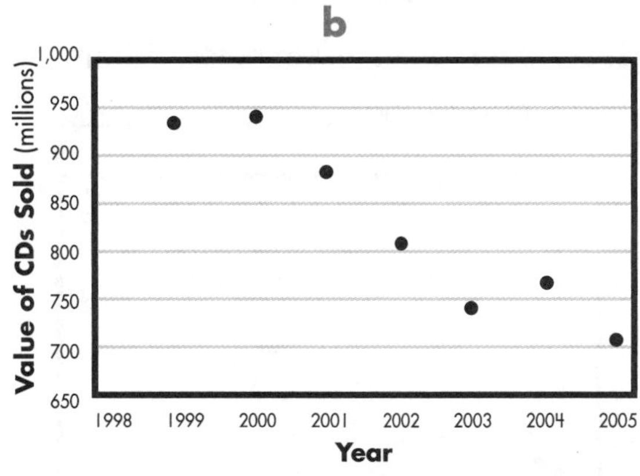

2.

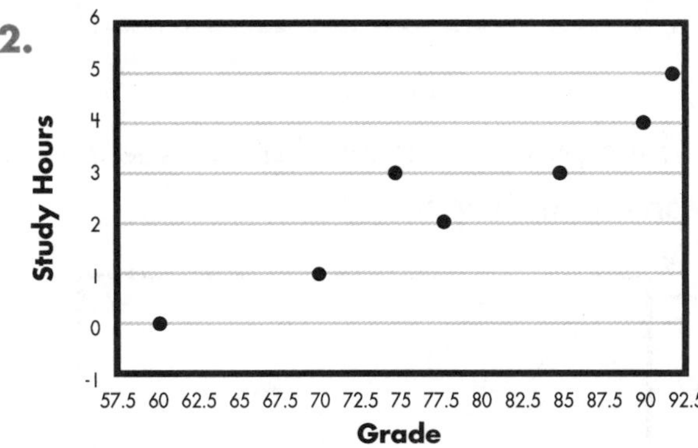

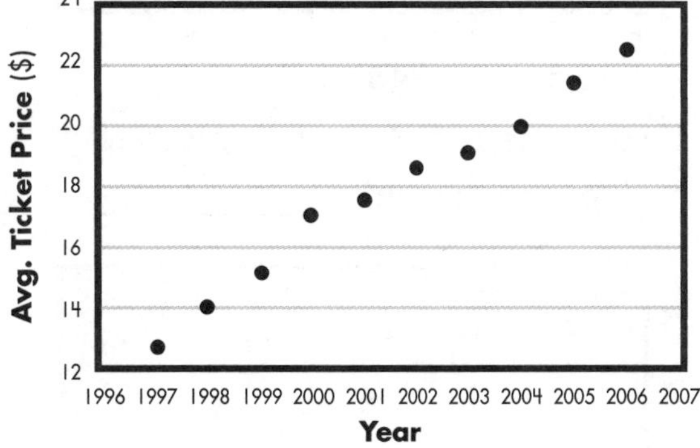

3.

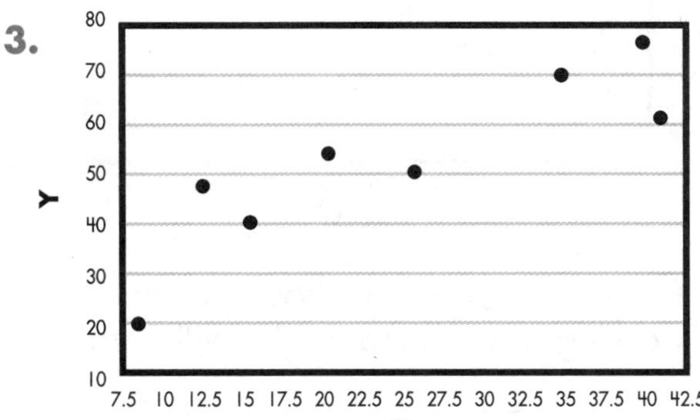

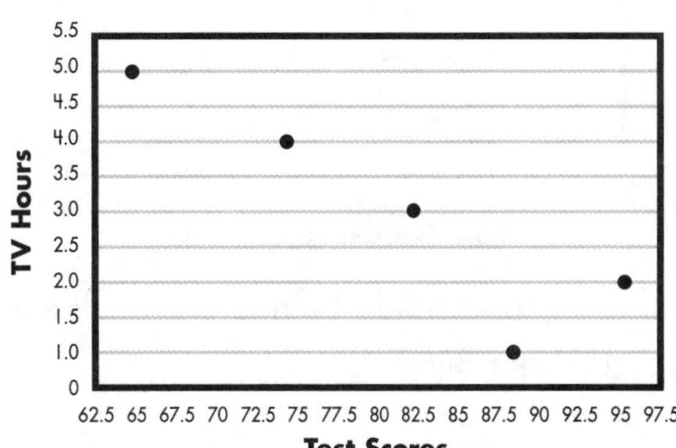

NAME ______________________

Lesson 6.3 Fitting Lines to Scatter Plots

Create a trend line for each scatter plot shown below. Then, make a prediction about the value of one variable given one value of the other variable.

a | **b**

1.

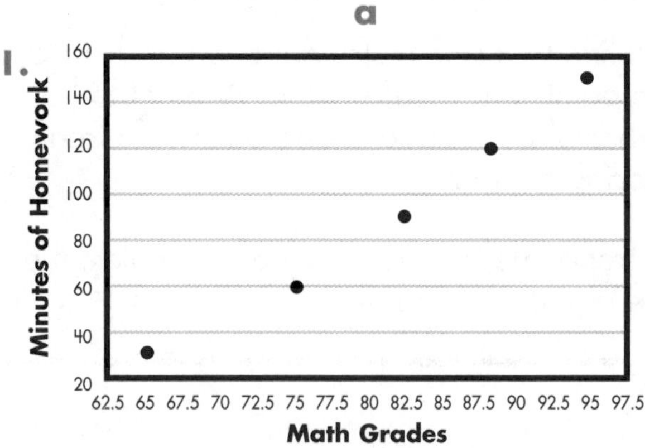

If a student does 80 minutes of homework, predict his grade. ______________

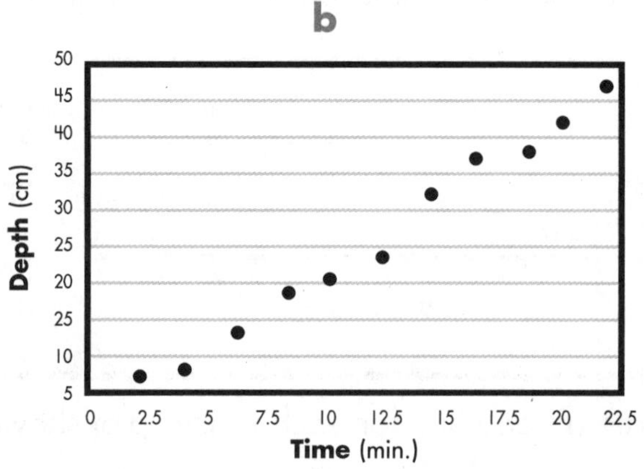

If the water is measured at 13 minutes, predict its depth. ______________

2.

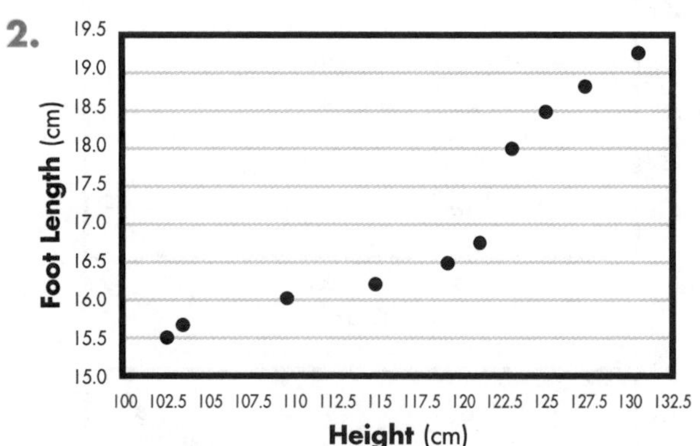

If someone is 106 cm tall, predict his/her foot length. ______________

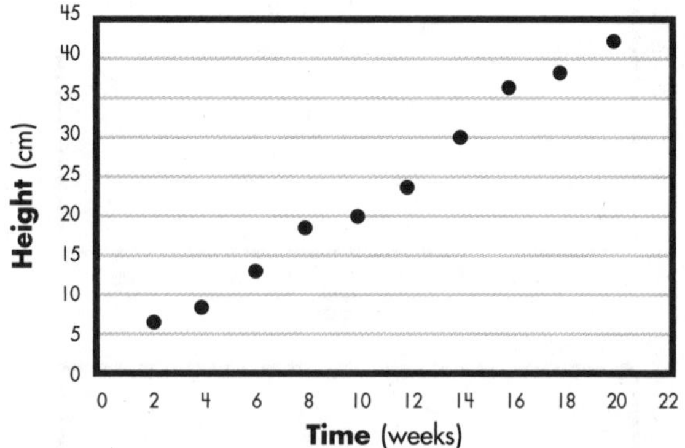

If the plant is measured at 15 weeks, predict its height. ______________

3.

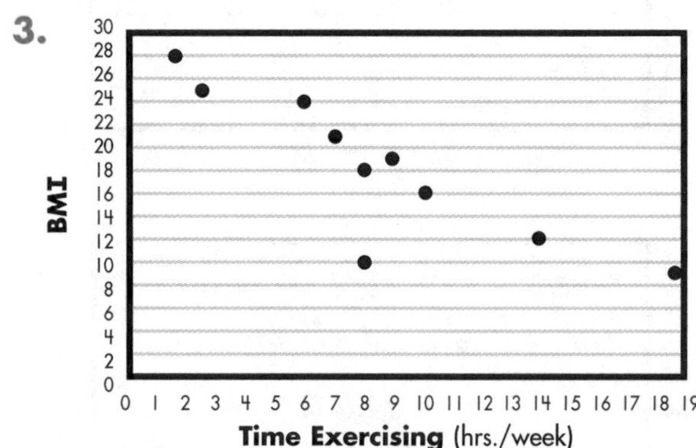

If a person spends 17 hours a week exercising, predict her BMI. ______________

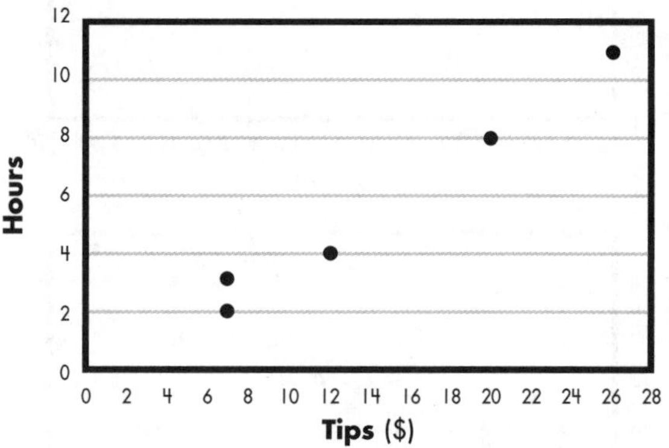

If a server spends 12 hours a week working, predict the tips he will earn.

____

NAME ______________________

Lesson 6.4 Creating Equations to Solve Bivariate Problems

When given a set of bivariate data with a fairly consistent rate of change, a scatter plot with a trend line can be used to create an equation that will approximate the relationship between the two sets of data.

Temp. (°F)	Ice Cream Sales ($)
57.6	215
61.5	325
53.4	185
59.4	332
65.3	406
71.8	522
66.9	412

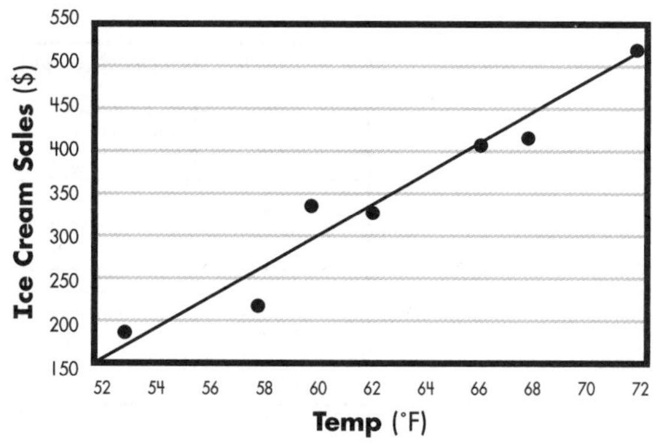

Step 1: Use the data set to create a scatter plot with a trend line.

Step 2: Use the 2 points of data closest to the trend line to find the slope of the trend line.

Step 3: Use one point of data with the calculated slope to find the y-intersect of the trend line.

Step 4: Use the calculated slope and y-intersect to state the equation in linear form, $y = mx + b$.

$m = \frac{522 - 406}{71.8 - 65.3} = \frac{116}{6.5} = 17.85$

$406 = (17.85)(65.3) + b$

$y = 17.85x - 759.61$

$b = -759.61$

Use each set of bivariate data to create a scatter plot, trend line, and an equation that approximates the data set.

1.

a

x	y
2	5
4	15
5	25
1	2
7	20
4	8
6	10
1	1
3	12

equation: ______________

b

Hours	Wages ($)
8	300
6	200
10	500
9	400
4	100
12	700
14	1000
5	150
2	50

equation: ______________

NAME ____________________

Lesson 6.4 Creating Equations to Solve Bivariate Problems

Use each set of bivariate data to create a scatter plot, trend line, and an equation that approximates the data set.

a

1.

Hours	Test Score
18	59
16	67
22	74
27	90
15	62
28	89
18	71
19	60
22	84
30	98

equation:

____

b

Population (hundred thousands)	Number of Schools
110	4
130	4
130	6
140	5
150	6
160	8
170	7
180	8
190	9

equation:

____

2.

Temp. (°F)	Ice Cream Sales ($)
57	125
60	175
53	100
59	130
65	275
71	405
66	295
77	735
73	525
62	200

equation:

____

Amount of Time in the Sun (hours)	Sunflower Height (cm)
2	15
4	19
6	25
3	17
5	22
7	30
2	14
4	20
5	23
6	24

equation:

____

NAME ______________________

Lesson 6.4 Creating Equations to Solve Bivariate Problems

Use each set of bivariate data to create a scatter plot, trend line, and an equation that approximates the data set.

a

1.

Time (hours)	Cost of Job ($)
5	1000
7	1000
5	1500
8	1200
10	2000
13	2500
15	2800
20	3200
25	4000

equation: ______________

b

Time (hours)	Score
4	15
5	16
5	20
10	12
15	8
10	8
20	5
15	4
15	12

equation: ______________

2.

Time (hours)	Money ($)
2	15
4	20
6	23
7	24
3	17
10	50
9	42
4	22
5	24
7	26

equation: ______________

Height (inches)	Distance (miles)
62	9.3
64	9.7
67	10.2
71	11.5
75	13.5
78	15.6
63	9.4
55	8.6
53	8.2
51	7.9

equation: ______________

NAME ____________________

Lesson 6.5 Frequency Tables

Mr. Park's class got the following scores on a recent test: 85, 88, 92, 72, 95, 84, 84, 82, 97, 67, 90, 84, 87, 90, 78, 80, 88, 90, 84, 78. He made this **frequency table** with the scores.

Score Range	Number in the Range	Cumulative Frequency	Relative Frequency
(60–69)	1	1	$\frac{1}{20}$
(70–79)	3	4	$\frac{3}{20}$
(80–89)	10	14	$\frac{10}{20}$ or $\frac{1}{2}$
(90–99)	6	20	$\frac{10}{20}$ or $\frac{1}{2}$

The chart shows that the scores ranged from the 60s to the 90s, with the most frequent scores in the 80s range. The relative frequency compares the number in each range with the total number of scores.

Complete the chart with fractions in simplest form. Then, answer the questions.

Eighth Graders' Siblings

	No. of Siblings	Frequency	Cumulative Frequency	Relative Frequency
1.	0	7	7	
2.	1	23	30	
3.	2	19	49	
4.	3+	12	61	

5. How many 8th graders were polled? ____________

6. How many different options were the students given to choose from? ____________

Complete the chart with the missing numbers. Then, answer the questions.

Scores on a Recent Science Test

	Score Range	Frequency	Cumulative Frequency	Relative Frequency
7.	(50–59)		2	
8.	(60–69)		7	
9.	(70–79)		13	
10.	(80–89)		21	
11.	(90–99)		24	

12. In what 10-point range did the most students score? ____________

13. What was the total range of points students could have received on the test? ____________

NAME ___________________________

Lesson 6.5 Frequency Tables

Use the data sets to complete the frequency table and answer the questions.

Radar was used to record the speed of cars traveling through downtown as follows: 29, 23, 30, 30, 27, 24, 30, 25, 23, 28, 25, 24, 28, 30, 23, 30, 27, 25, 29, 24, 23, 26, 30, 28, and 25.

	Speed Range	Frequency	Cumulative Frequency	Relative Frequency
1.	23–24			
2.	25–26			
3.	27–28			
4.	29–30			

5. At what speed were most cars driving? ________________

6. In which two speed ranges were the same number of cars driving? ________________

One die was rolled with the following results: 6, 5, 4, 4, 5, 6, 1, 2, 1, 6, 4, 3, 3, 3, 4, 2, 2, 5, 6, 4, 1, 2, 4, 3, 5, 5, 3, 3, 4, and 2.

	Roll	Frequency	Cumulative Frequency	Relative Frequency
7.	1			
8.	2			
9.	3			
10.	4			
11.	5			
12.	6			

13. How many times was the die rolled? ________________

14. Which number was rolled most frequently? ________________

The heights of students in inches are as follows: 66, 68, 65, 70, 67, 64, 70, 64, 66, 70, 72, 71, 69, 69, 64, 67, 63, 70, 71, 63, 68, 67, 65, 69, 65, 67, 66, 69, 64, and 69.

	Height Range	Frequency	Cumulative Frequency	Relative Frequency
15.	63–64			
16.	65–66			
17.	67–68			
18.	69–70			
19.	71–72			

20. At what height are most students? ________________

21. How many students were measured? ________________

NAME ______________________

Lesson 6.5 Frequency Tables

Use the data sets to complete the frequency table and answer the questions.

At a blood drive, the blood types of the donors is tracked as follows: A, B, B, AB, O, O, O, B, AB, B, B, B, O, A, O, A, O, O, O, AB, AB, A, O, B, and A.

	Blood Type	Frequency	Cumulative Frequency	Relative Frequency
1.	A			
2.	B			
3.	O			
4.	AB			

5. Which blood type was most common? ______________

6. How many donors came to the blood drive? ______________

Record high temperatures from around the country are recorded as follows: 112, 100, 127, 120, 134, 118, 105, 110, 109, 112, 110, 118, 117, 116, 118, 122, 114, 114, 105, 109, 107, 112, 114, 115, 118, 117, 118, 122, 106, 110, 116, 108, 110, 121, 113, 120, 119, 111, 104, 111, 120, 113, 120, 117, 105, 110, 118, 112, 114, and 114.

	Temp. Range	Frequency	Cumulative Frequency	Relative Frequency
7.	100–109			
8.	110–119			
9.	120–129			
10.	130+			

11. What was the most common temperature range? ______________

12. What was the least common temperature range? ______________

The ages of the 50 wealthiest people in the USA are: 49, 57, 38, 73, 81, 74, 59, 76, 65, 69, 54, 56, 69, 68, 78, 65, 85, 49, 69, 61, 48, 81, 68, 37, 43, 78, 82, 43, 64, 67, 52, 56, 81, 79, 85, 40, 85, 85, 59, 80, 60, 71, 57, 61, 69, 61, 83, 90, 87, and 74.

	Age Range	Frequency	Cumulative Frequency	Relative Frequency
13.	35–44			
14.	45–54			
15.	55–64			
16.	65–74			
17.	75+			

18. What is the largest age group of wealthy people? ______________

19. What is the age difference between the oldest person and the youngest? ______________

NAME ______________________

Check What You Learned

Statistics and Probability

Answer the questions by interpreting data from the graph.

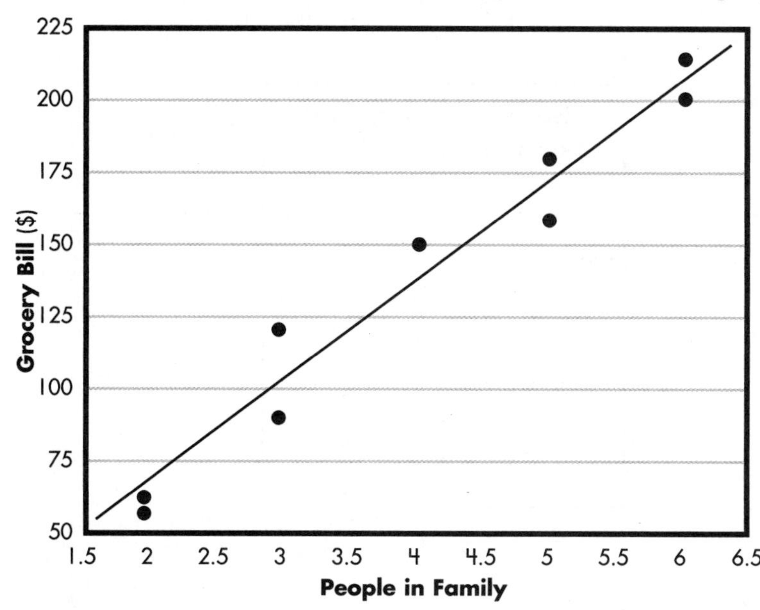

1. What two sets of data are being compared by this scatter plot?

____

2. Is the correlation positive or negative?

____

3. Why might there be no outliers in this data?

____

CHAPTER 6 POSTTEST

Use the data set below to create a scatter plot with a line of best fit. Then, answer the questions.

4.

Diameter (cm)	Circumference (cm)
3	10
5	16
10.8	32.5
13	40
10	32.3
6.8	21
4.5	18

5. What two sets of data are being compared by this scatter plot? ______________________
6. Is the correlation between the data sets positive or negative? ______________________
7. Why might there be no outliers in this data? ______________________
8. If the diameter is 12, predict the circumference. ______________________

NAME ______________________

Check What You Learned

Statistics and Probability

Use each set of bivariate data to create a scatter plot, trend line, and an equation that approximates the data set.

9.

a

Time Testing (min.)	Test Grade
31	64
38	66
46	82
49	90
20	52
35	66
40	79
52	95

equation: ______________

b

Hours Worked	Paycheck ($)
12	54
13	56
16	65
17	64
20	100
10	50
12	55
18	70

equation: ______________

Use the data set to complete the frequency table and answer the questions.

The height of students is collected as follows: 70, 68, 60, 63, 73, 66, 71, 66, 72, 64, 68, 62, 70, 64, 67, 65, and 69.

	Height Range	Frequency	Cumulative Frequency	Relative Frequency
10.	60–63			
11.	64–67			
12.	68–71			
13.	72–75			

14. How many students were included in the data set? ______________

15. What are the most common height ranges for this set of students? ______________

16. What is the least common height range for this set of students? ______________

NAME ____________________

Final Test Chapters 1–6

Evaluate each expression. Simplify fractions.

	a	b	c
1.	$\sqrt{81}$ = ________	$\sqrt[3]{343}$ = ________	$\sqrt{\frac{16}{25}}$ = ________
2.	$\sqrt[3]{\frac{27}{216}}$ = ________	$\sqrt{1}$ = ________	$\sqrt[3]{0}$ = ________

Approximate the value to the hundredths place.

3. The value of $\sqrt{5}$ is between ____________ and ____________.

4. The value of $\sqrt{13}$ is between ____________ and ____________.

Create a number line to show each set of values in order from least to greatest.

5. π, $\sqrt{10}$, -3, $\frac{7}{4}$

Find the value of each expression.

	a	b	c
6.	2^2 = ________	5^8 = ________	3^6 = ________
7.	3^{-3} = ________	10^{-4} = ________	2^{-6} = ________

Write each number in scientific notation or standard form.

8.	103.6 = ________	4.2×10^{-1} = ________	0.082 = ________
9.	5.86×10^2 = ________	19,300 = ________	7.6×10^{-2} = ________
10.	3,604 = ________	5×10^{-3} = ________	0.0063 = ________

Rewrite the multiplication or division expression using a base and an exponent.

11.	$3^4 \times 3^3$ = ________	$2^{-6} \times 2^{-2}$ = ________	$5^{-3} \div 5^{-6}$ = ________
12.	$4^{10} \div 4^{-4}$ = ________	$8^2 \times 8^{-3}$ = ________	$10^{-6} \div 10^4$ = ________
13.	$6^{-3} \times 6^{-3}$ = ________	$11^{-7} \div 11^3$ = ________	$7^{-3} \times 7^2$ = ________

NAME ________________

Final Test Chapters 1–6

Determine if the slope, or rate of change, is *constant* or *variable*. Show your work.

14. Mike is on his way to school. The table below shows how far he has traveled and how long he has been traveling.

Distance Traveled (mi.)	$\frac{1}{2}$	$\frac{3}{4}$	$\frac{3}{4}$	4
Time Traveled (min.)	10	12	15	25

The rate of change for this situation is ____________.

Use the slope-intercept form of equations to draw lines on the grids below.

15.

a $y = 4x + 2$

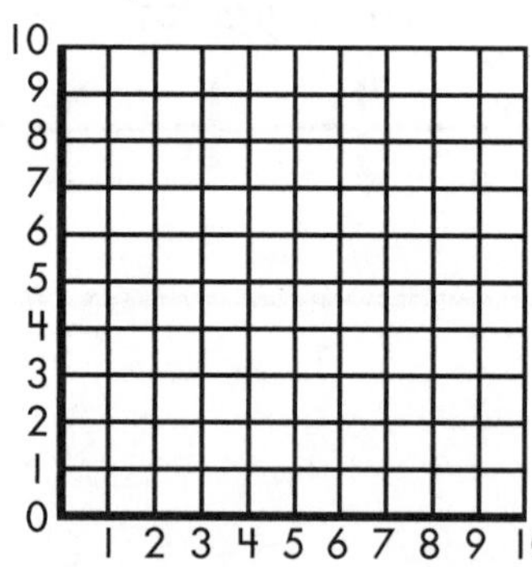

b $y = -\frac{3}{4}x + 7$

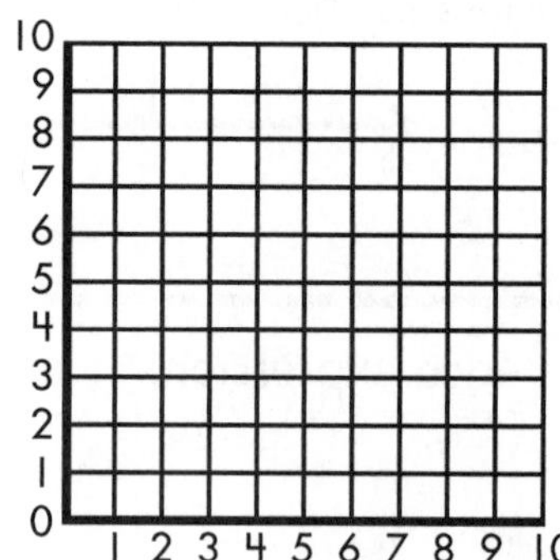

Find the value of the variable in each equation.

	a	b	c
16.	$3n + 2 = 23$ ________	$\frac{14}{m} + 6 = 8$ ________	$3t = 48$ ________
17.	$p \div 5 = 21$ ________	$x + 54 = 72$ ________	$49 - a = 36$ ________
18.	$15b - 2 = 58$ ________	$\frac{n}{12} + 4 = 9$ ________	$108 \div m = 6$ ________

Use substitution or elimination to solve each system of equations.

19.

$y = -\frac{1}{2}x + 18$

$y = -x + 20$

$x =$ ______, $y =$ ______

$y = x - 11$

$4x + \frac{4}{5}y = 68$

$x =$ ______, $y =$ ______

$-8x + 2y = -48$

$6x - 2y = 28$

$x =$ ______, $y =$ ______

NAME ______________________

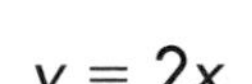

Final Test Chapters 1–6

Use slope-intercept form to graph each system of equations and solve the system.

a

20. $y = -2x - 3$

$y = 2x$

x: ______;

y: ______

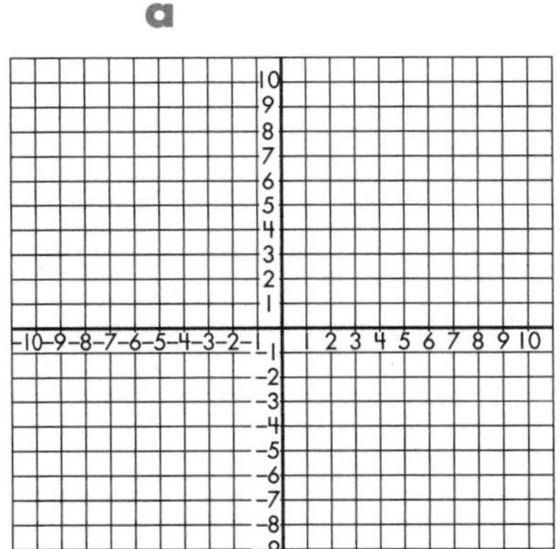

b

$y = \frac{3}{4}x - 3$

$y = -\frac{1}{2}x + 2$

x: ______;

y: ______

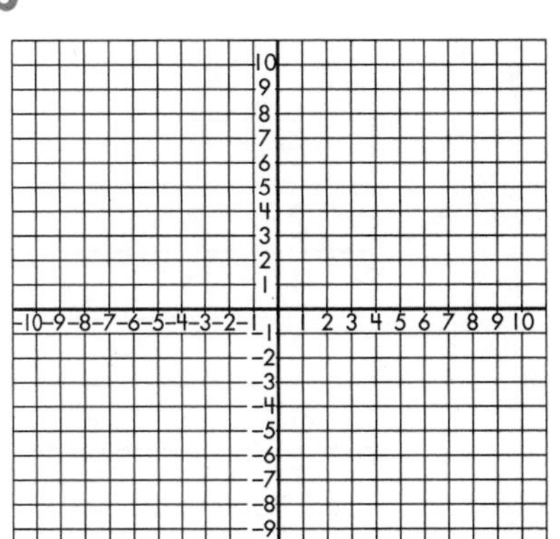

Decide if each table represents a function by stating *yes* or *no*.

21.

a

input	output
2	21, 25
5	27
8	30

____

b

input	output
2	−2
4	−2
5	0, 2
9	2, 4

____

c

input	output
−3	1
1	0
3	2
5	3

____

Find the rate of change for each function below.

22.

input	output
−1	0
1	4
3	8

rate of change: ______________

input	output
−2	−3.5
2	4.5
6	12.5

rate of change: ______________

input	output
4	9
6	14
8	19

rate of change: ______________

Find the initial value for each problem.

23. Joan is filling her bathtub. After 2 minutes of running the water, there are 10 gallons of water in the bathtub. How much water will be in the tub after 5 minutes?

Initial Value: ______________

24. Paul lives 7 miles from the park. After 5 minutes of bicycling, he still has 6 miles left before he gets to the park. How far will he have traveled after 20 minutes of bicycling?

Initial Value: ______________

NAME ______________________

Final Test Chapters 1–6

Complete each function table for the given function.

25.

a $y = 4x - 11$

x	y
23	
47	
54	
63	
75	

b $y = 22x + 2$

x	y
0	
3	
6	
8	
13	

c $y = \frac{1}{15}x - 4$

x	y
45	
90	
105	
165	
225	

Construct a function model, or equation, for each situation in the form of $y = mx + b$.

26.

a

input	output
0	9
1	12
2	15

Function model:

y = ____________

b

input	output
2	8
4	11
6	14

Function model:

y = ____________

c

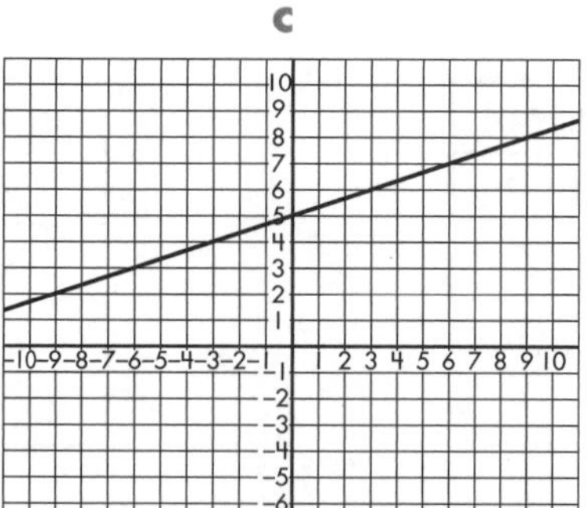

Function model:

y = ____________

Compare the rate of change for the equations and tables shown below and decide which has a greater rate of change by writing *equation* or *table*.

27.

a $y = 2x + 4$ or

x	0	1	2
y	3	9	15

____

b $y = 6x + 7$ or

x	0	1	2
y	5	10	15

____

c $y = -7x + 4$ or

x	0	1	2
y	4	8	12

____

NAME ______________________

Final Test Chapters 1–6

Sketch each linear function.

28.

a $y = x + 6$

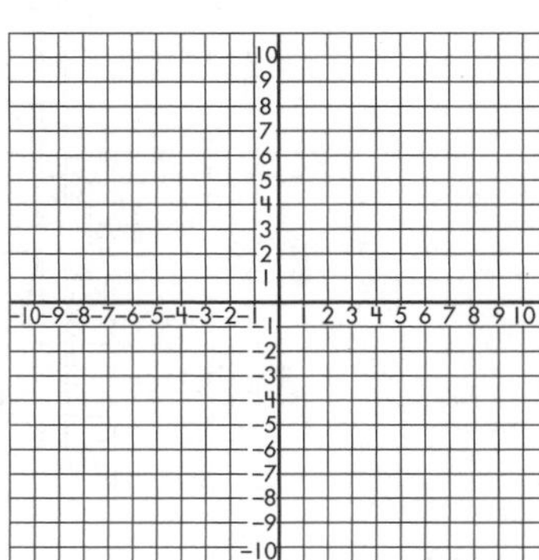

b $y = 3x + 1$

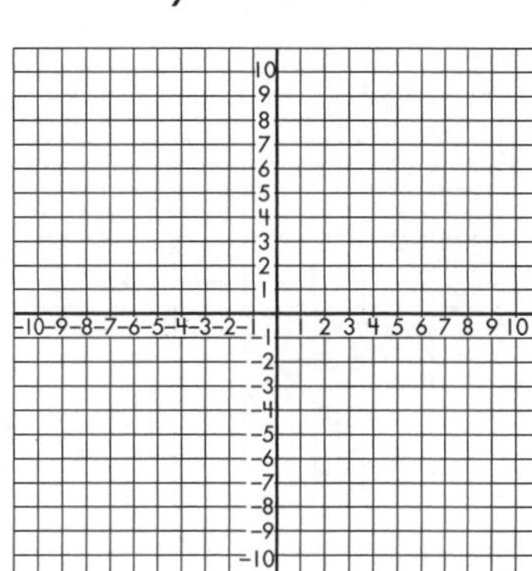

Complete the function table for each function. Then, graph the function.

29.

$-y = \frac{x}{2} + 3$

x	y

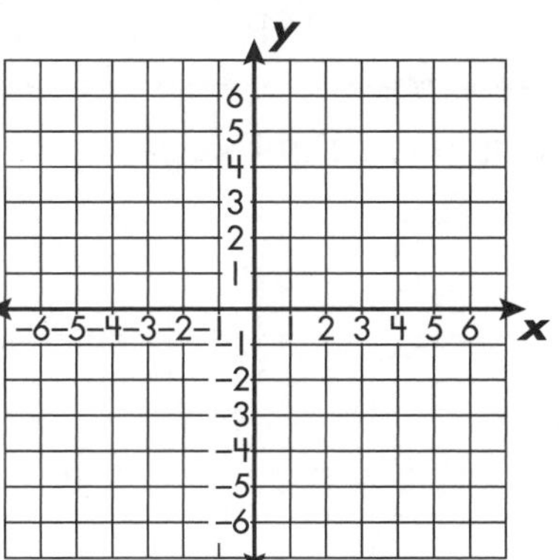

$y = 4x - 4$

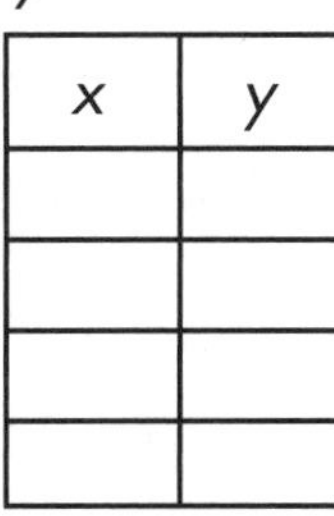

x	y

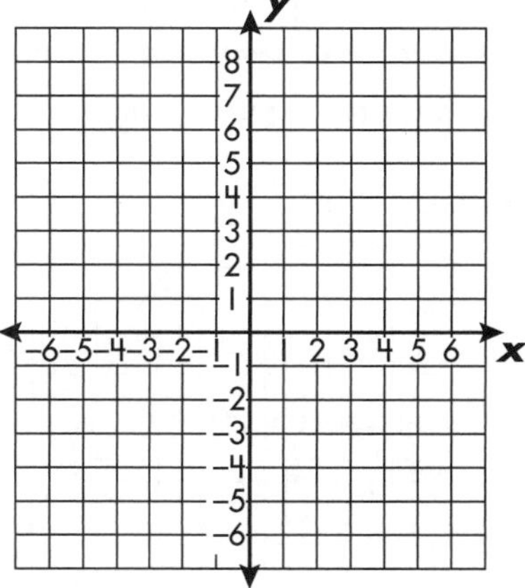

State if the figures below represent a *rotation*, *reflection*, or *translation*.

30.

a

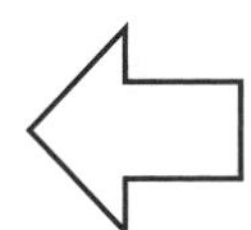

____

b

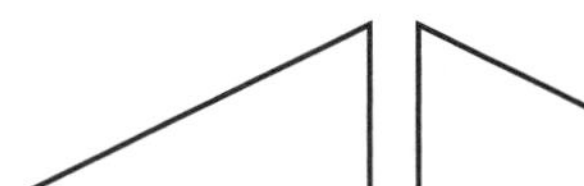

____

c

____

NAME ______________________________

Final Test Chapters 1–6

Write the steps each figure must go through to be transformed from figure 1 to figure 2.

31.

a

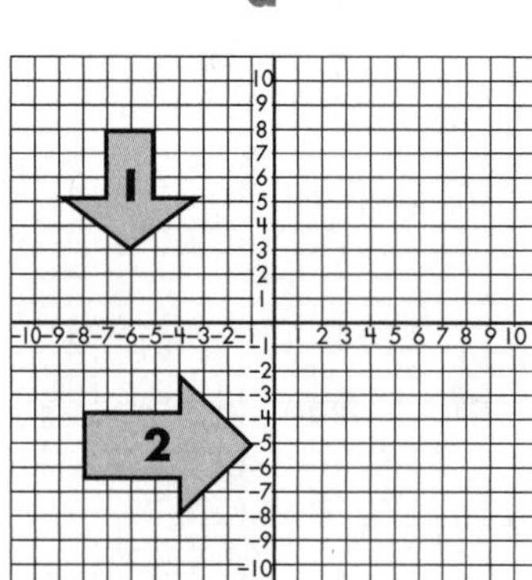

Step 1: ______________________________

Step 2: ______________________________

Step 3: ______________________________

b

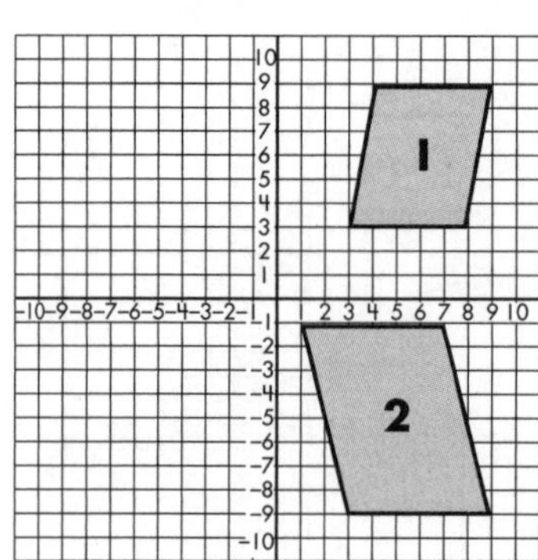

Step 1: ______________________________

Step 2: ______________________________

Step 3: ______________________________

Use similar right triangles to prove that each line has a constant slope.

32.

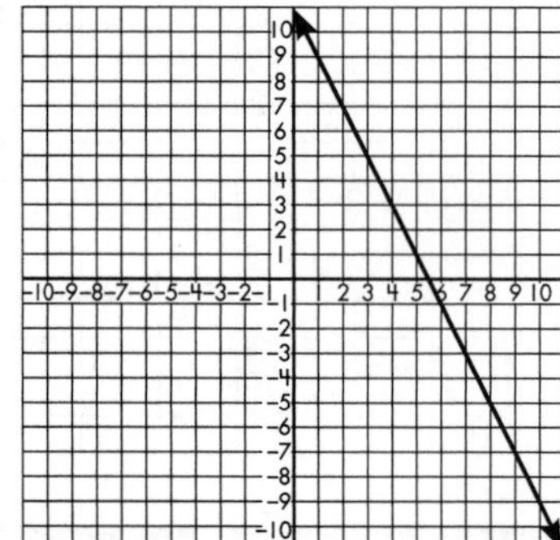

Triangle 1 Legs:

______ & ______

Triangle 2 Legs:

______ & ______

Proportionality Test:

$\frac{\_\_}{\_\_} = \frac{\_\_}{\_\_}$

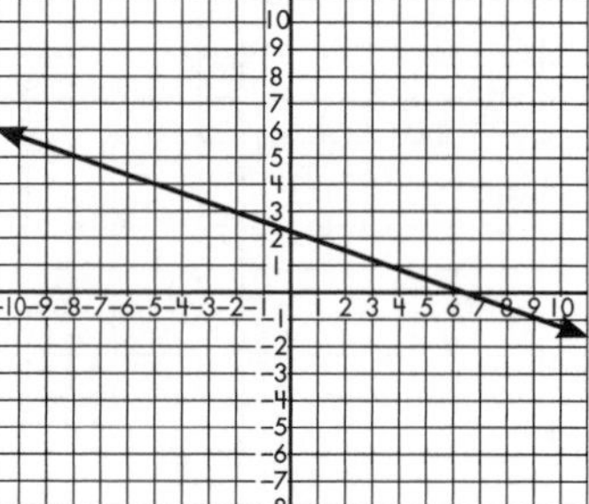

Triangle 1 Legs:

______ & ______

Triangle 2 Legs:

______ & ______

Proportionality Test:

$\frac{\_\_}{\_\_} = \frac{\_\_}{\_\_}$

Answer each question using letters to name each line and numbers to name each angle.

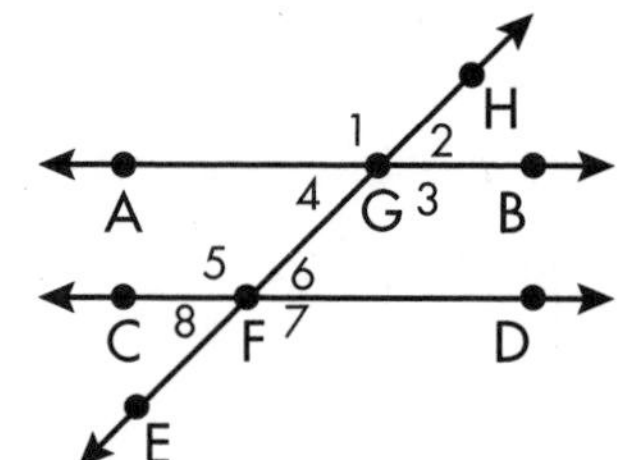

33. Which 2 lines are parallel? ____________

34. What is the name of the transversal? ____________

35. Which angles are obtuse? ____________________

36. Which pairs of angles are alternate exterior angles? ____________________

37. Which pairs of angles are alternate interior angles? ____________________

CHAPTERS 1–6 FINAL TEST

NAME ____________________

Final Test Chapters 1–6

Use the Pythagorean Theorem to find the unknown lengths.

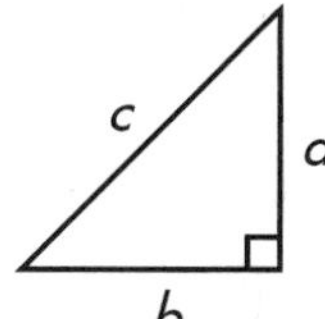

38. If $a = 8$ and $b = 9$, $c = \sqrt{\_\_\_\_}$ or about ________.

39. If $a = 15$ and $b = 10$, $c = \sqrt{\_\_\_\_}$ or about ________.

Find the volume of each figure.

40.

a

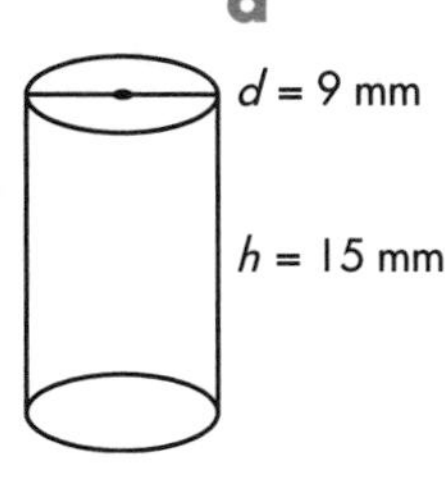

$V =$ ________ mm³

b

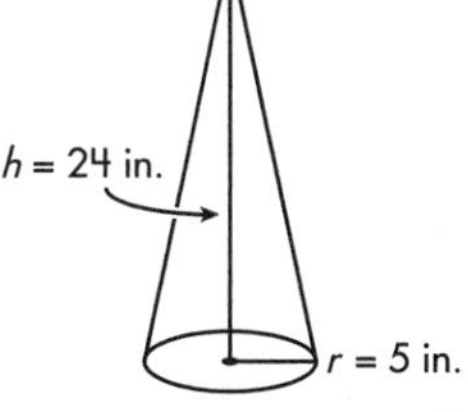

$V =$ ________ in.³

c

9 ft.

$V =$ ________ ft.³

Answer the questions by interpreting data from the graph.

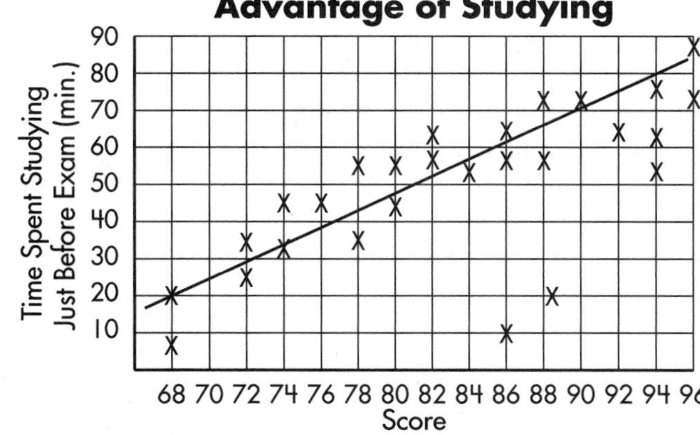

41. What two sets of data are being compared by this scatter plot? ____________

42. Is the correlation positive or negative? ____________

43. What is a possible explanation for the outliers? ____________

Answer the questions by interpreting data from the graph.

Number of Pets My Classmates Have

	No. of Pets	Frequency	Cumulative Frequency	Relative Frequency
44.	0	5		$\frac{5}{28}$
45.	1	10		$\frac{5}{14}$
46.	2	7		$\frac{1}{4}$
47.	3	5		$\frac{5}{28}$
48.	4 or more	1		$\frac{1}{28}$

49. How many students were polled? ________

50. What was the most frequent response? ________ How many gave that response? ________

NAME ______________________________ DATE ______________

Scoring Record for Chapter Posttests, Mid-Test, and Final Test

		Performance			
Chapter Posttest	Your Score	Excellent	Very Good	Fair	Needs Improvement
1	____ of 66	60–66	53–59	46–52	45 or fewer
2	____ of 36	32–36	29–31	25–28	24 or fewer
3	____ of 36	32–36	29–31	25–28	24 or fewer
4	____ of 39	35–39	31–34	27–30	26 or fewer
5	____ of 38	34–38	30–33	27–29	26 or fewer
6	____ of 27	24–27	22–24	19–21	18 or fewer
Mid-Test	____ of 99	90–99	80–89	70–79	69 or fewer
Final Test	____ of 152	137–152	122–136	107–121	106 or fewer

Record your test score in the Your Score column. See where your score falls in the Performance columns. Your score is based on the total number of required responses. If your score is fair or needs improvement, review the chapter material.

Grade 8 Answers

Pretest, page 5

	a	b	c
1.	343	32,768	16
2.	6,561	1	1,679,616
3.	$\frac{1}{64}$	$\frac{1}{243}$	$\frac{1}{2,401}$
4.	$\frac{1}{32}$	$\frac{1}{729}$	$\frac{1}{1000}$
5.	2,401	$\frac{1}{81}$	1,953,125
6.	4^3	6^{-2}	8^{-2}
7.	9^5	5^{-4}	3^{-10}
8.	8^5	6^{11}	4^3
9.	7^3	4^{11}	9^{11}
10.	2^{12}	3^6	12^{14}
11.	5^6	10^3	11^7
12.	7^3	6^9	12^2

Pretest, page 6

	a	b	c
13.	9,545	0.008596	0.009318
14.	8,124,000	87,430	296,100
15.	10,428	0.078543	0.0004937
16.	239,600	0.000008352	38,500,000
17.	395.7	9,389,000	0.00004109
18.	4.357×10^{-1}	6.686×10^{-3}	1.333×10^5
19.	7.614×10^{-1}	1.087×10^{-2}	5.177×10^5
20.	8.9232×10^5	4.282×10^5	1.283×10^{-2}
21.	7.83×10^5	4.642×10^{-4}	4.782×10^8
22.	5.389×10^7	4.1832×10^9	2.8737×10^{-4}

Lesson 1.1, page 7

	a	b	c
1.	3 × 3 × 3	5 × 5 × 5 × 5 × 5	6
2.	2 × 2 × 2 × 2 × 2 × 2 × 2 × 2 × 2 × 2 × 2 × 2	3 × 3 × 3 × 3 × 3 × 3 × 3 × 3	3 × 3 × 3 × 3 × 3 × 3
3.	4 × 4 × 4 × 4 × 4 × 4 × 4	4 × 4 × 4 × 4 × 4	8 × 8 × 8
4.	24^3	2^4	
5.	3^5	5^2	
6.	5^6	4^3	
7.	512	6,561	100

Lesson 1.1, page 8

	a	b	c
1.	9 × 9	58	4 × 4 × 4
2.	5 × 5 × 5 × 5	8 × 8	3 × 3 × 3 × 3
3.	75 × 75	6 × 6	10 × 10 × 10 × 10 × 10 × 10 × 10 × 10 × 10 × 10
4.	8^1	13^2	
5.	6^4	5^4	
6.	2^7	3^3	
7.	86^3	4^5	
8.	10^5	15^5	
9.	7	81	100,000
10.	16,807	125	4,096
11.	16	32	4,782,969
12.	1,296	1,728	343

Lesson 1.2, page 9

	a	b	c
1.	49	512	64
2.	100	6,561	161,051
3.	4,913	15,625	1,296
4.	9,261	65,536	248,832
5.	8^5; 32,768	3^6; 729	2^4; 16
6.	7^2; 49	9^2; 81	16^2; 256
7.	6^5; 7,776	4^6; 4,096	3^4;81
8.	10^2; 100	8^1; 8	7^3; 343
9.	5^5; 3,125	10^7;10,000,000	15^3; 3,375
10.	2^5; 32	3^2; 9	6^3; 216

Lesson 1.2, page 10

	a	b
1.	4^8	9^5
2.	3^5	5^3
3.	8^4	2^2
4.	5^4	9^4
5.	10^4	6^3
6.	4	7^2
7.	11^7	6^6
8.	8^2	5^5
9.	12^{11}	11^6
10.	3^8	4^3
11.	5^2	6^{12}
12.	4^6	3^{12}
13.	6	15^5
14.	9^{15}	7^{10}
15.	2^6	4^{12}

Lesson 1.3, page 11

	a	b	c
1.	$\frac{1}{3^2}$; 0.1111	$\frac{1}{6^3}$; 0.0046	$\frac{1}{8^2}$; 0.0156
2.	$\frac{1}{7^3}$; 0.0029	$\frac{1}{3^3}$; 0.0370	$\frac{1}{9^2}$; 0.0123
3.	$\frac{1}{4^3}$; 0.0156	$\frac{1}{5^2}$; 0.04	$\frac{1}{2^3}$; 0.125
4.	$\frac{1}{2^4}$; 0.0625	$\frac{1}{10^3}$; 0.001	$\frac{1}{1^4}$; 1
5.	0.00098	0.03125	0.00412
6.	0.00077	0.00006	0.01235
7.	0.01563	0.00292	0.125
8.	0.0625	0.01563	0.03704
9.	0.0625	0.04	0.00463
10.	0.00412	0.00391	0.125

Lesson 1.3, page 12

	a	b
1.	3^{-10}	9^2
2.	4^5	5^{-1}
3.	12^{-7}	4^{-2}
4.	7^9	2^{-6}
5.	11^1	6^{-9}
6.	8^{-8}	12^{-5}
7.	7	5^{-1}
8.	2^8	3^{-16}
9.	6^7	7^{-7}
10.	9	10^{-7}
11.	8^{-2}	2^{-14}
12.	3^{-9}	8^{-10}
13.	10^{-5}	4^{-7}

14.	9^{-3}	11^{6}
15.	6^{-8}	5^{-16}
16.	12^{-6}	4^{-7}

Lesson 1.4, page 13

	a	b	c
1.	1.3×10^{-2}	4.105×10^{3}	2.73×10
2.	8.104×10^{2}	6.84×10^{-1}	1.7×10^{-2}
3.	6×10^{-4}	4.275×10^{2}	3.6054×10^{4}
4.	5.021×10^{4}	5×10^{-4}	2.5621×10^{2}
5.	3.625×10	8.92×10^{-1}	6.5×10^{-4}
6.	2.7×10^{-2}	1.4163×10^{3}	4.9×10^{-3}
7.	0.0026	846,000	0.465
8.	90,200	0.0515	8,450
9.	0.000725	1,060	0.0000906
10.	0.0097	30,200	15,600

Lesson 1.4, page 14

	a	b	c
1.	3.25×10^{1}	6.708×10^{3}	3.87×10^{2}
2.	5.69×10^{-1}	6.7345×10^{4}	2.7×10^{-2}
3.	7.9×10^{-2}	5.1×10^{1}	6.791×10^{3}
4.	9.825×10^{1}	2.385×10^{3}	4.13×10^{-1}
5.	7.831×10^{3}	4.18×10^{2}	7.5183×10^{1}
6.	4×10^{-4}	7.3014×10^{3}	1.8×10^{-3}
7.	5.624×10^{3}	2.365×10^{1}	9.65×10^{-1}
8.	4.5×10^{-3}	5.23×10^{2}	3.55×10^{-1}
9.	913,000	0.00402	24,300
10.	0.1124	8,480	0.0512
11.	9,470	.000328	.00673
12.	0.000053	41,300	37,800
13.	3,120	132,900	869
14.	.00045	.0000098	356,000
15.	.0542	.0000000908	2,700
16.	730	12,500	.000000088

Posttest, page 15

	a	b	c
1.	2,187	65,536	25
2.	5,159,780,352	1,024	4,096
3.	$\frac{1}{729}$	$\frac{1}{64}$	$\frac{1}{78,125}$
4.	$\frac{1}{10,000}$	$\frac{1}{216}$	$\frac{1}{32,768}$
5.	$\frac{1}{262,144}$	2,401	$\frac{1}{19,683}$
6.	10,000,000	$\frac{1}{81}$	256
7.	8^{5}	5^{-8}	6^{6}
8.	4^{2}	3^{7}	12^{-6}
9.	5^{11}	8^{-8}	5^{5}
10.	9^{-7}	7^{11}	6^{2}
11.	7^{-4}	9^{-4}	3^{-12}
12.	10	8^{9}	7^{6}

Posttest, page 16

	a	b	c
13.	0.00304	426	0.00081
14.	650,000	0.024	71.5
15.	0.00003286	8,273,400	0.000007362
16.	82,300,000	0.004602	238,200
17.	91,200,000	0.007292	0.0008153
18.	1.985×10^{3}	1.032×10^{1}	4.141×10^{2}
19.	3.954×10^{-4}	9.545×10^{1}	8.524×10^{3}
20.	2.3939×10^{5}	3.121×10^{-3}	4.31×10^{4}
21.	2.83×10^{-2}	2.73×10^{-4}	3.476×10^{6}
22.	3.712×10^{7}	3.742×10^{5}	5.283×10^{-3}

Pretest, page 17

	a	b	c
1.	5	3	10
2.	$\frac{2}{4}$	9	$\frac{3}{5}$
3.	7	9	4
4.	6	$\frac{3}{8}$	$\frac{4}{9}$
5.	3; 4		
6.	4; 5		
7.	6; 7		
8.	2; 3		
9.	1; 2		
10.	4; 5		
11.	8	81	7
12.	216	11	1,000

Pretest, page 18

	a	b	c
13.	=	<	<
14.	<	>	<
15.	>	<	<

Check number lines for remaining items.

16. $\sqrt{18}, 4\pi, 14$
17. $\sqrt{12}, \sqrt{15}, \sqrt{21}$
18. $2, \sqrt{5}, 5$

Lesson 2.1, page 19

	a	b	c
1.	rational	irrational	rational
2.	rational	rational	rational
3.	rational	rational	rational
4.	irrational	rational	rational
5.	irrational	irrational	rational

Lesson 2.2, page 20

	a	b	c
1.	4	8	5
2.	10	1	3
3.	6	9	2
4.	9	10	9
5.	4	5	4
6.	5	6	6
7.	8	9	8
8.	6	7	7

Lesson 2.2, page 21

	a	b	c
1.	8	6	7
2.	10	5	1
3.	3	2	13
4.	11	9	20
5.	8	9	9
6.	10	11	10
7.	9	10	9
8.	13	14	13
9.	1	2	2

Grade 8 Answers

	a	b	c
10.	7	8	7
11.	11	12	11
12.	8	9	9
13.	11	12	11
14.	5	6	5

Lesson 2.3, page 22

	a	b	c
1.	12	9	35
2.	15	8	25
3.	20	5	7
4.	2	4	10
5.	3	6	40
6.	50	70	60
7.	1	100	30
8.	80	90	200

Lesson 2.3, page 23

	a	b	c
1.	$\frac{1}{4}$	$\frac{2}{3}$	8
2.	0	$\frac{4}{5}$	1
3.	$\frac{2}{6}$	$\frac{5}{7}$	4
4.	2	3	2
5.	4	5	5
6.	7	8	8
7.	5	6	5
8.	10	11	11

Lesson 2.4, page 24

	a	b	c
1.	$\frac{4}{13}$	9	$\frac{4}{25}$
2.	5	$\frac{5}{8}$	8
3.	$\frac{1}{2}$	8	6
4.	4	7	1

Lesson 2.4, page 25

	a	b	c
1.	625	25	216
2.	20	6,859	49
3.	14	324	6
4.	518	196	343

Lesson 2.5, page 26

	a	b	c
1.	<	<	>
2.	>	=	<
3.	=	<	>
4.	<	>	<
5.	<	=	<
6.	<	<	<
7.	<	<	<
8.	=	<	>

Lesson 2.6, page 27

1. 2.6; 2.7
2. 3.1; 3.2
3. 5.0; 5.1
4. 2.9; 3.0
5. 4.6; 4.7
6. 8.0; 8.1
7. 8.8; 8.9
8. 9.3; 9.4

Lesson 2.6, page 28

1. 2.82; 2.83
2. 3.31; 3.32
3. 9.48; 9.49
4. 4.16; 4.17
5. 4.32; 4.33
6. 5.19; 5.20
7. 3.20; 3.21
8. 4.79; 4.80

Lesson 2.7, page 29

Check number lines for all responses.

1. $\sqrt{75}$, π^2, 10
2. $\sqrt{\frac{7}{2}}$, 2, $\sqrt{7}$
3. $\sqrt{10}$, 3.5, 2^2
4. $\sqrt{15}$, 4, 5.2
5. $\frac{1}{3}$, 0.45, $\sqrt{1}$
6. $\sqrt{72}$, 9, 8^2

Lesson 2.7, page 30

	a	b
1.	<	>
	3.5 + 2; 10 + 1.5	4 + 1.5; 2 + 2
2.	>	<
	12 + 2.5; 3.5 + 6	2 + 6; 8 + 1.5
3.	>	<
	15 + 3.5; 3.5 + 12	2.5 + 3; 7 + 1.5
4.	<	>
	4 + 1.5; 1.5 + 7	1.5 + 5; 3 + 2.5

Posttest, page 31

	a	b	c
1.	6	4	11
2.	$\frac{3}{6}$	12	$\frac{10}{11}$
3.	8	10	5
4.	6	$\frac{4}{8}$	$\frac{2}{9}$

5. 3.4; 3.5
6. 4.2; 4.3
7. 6.7; 6.8
8. 2.7; 2.8
9. 1.9; 2.0
10. 5.4; 5.5

	a	b	c
11.	49	8	9
12.	12	64	729

Posttest, page 32

	a	b	c
13.	>	>	=
14.	>	<	<
15.	=	<	<

Check number lines for items 13-15.

16. $\sqrt{38}$, 2π, $\sqrt{52}$
17. 2.75, $\sqrt[3]{27}$, $\sqrt{18}$
18. 1.4; $\frac{3}{2}$; $\sqrt{3}$

Grade 8 Answers

Pretest, page 33

	a	b	c
1.	10		
2.	14	6	32
3.	4	72	52
4.	23	48	11

5a.

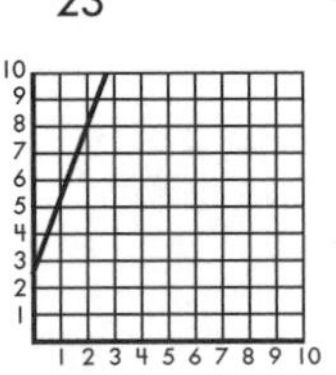

5b.

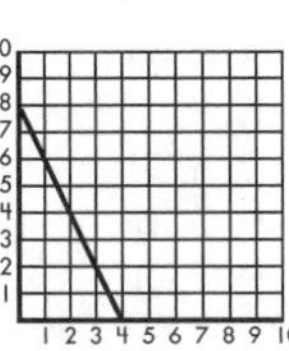

6. **a**

x	y
0	−3
1	−1
2	1
3	3

b

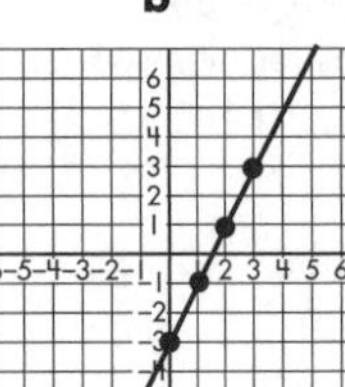

Pretest, page 34

	a	b
7.	8, −1	0, −2
8.	1, −2	−6, 0

9a.

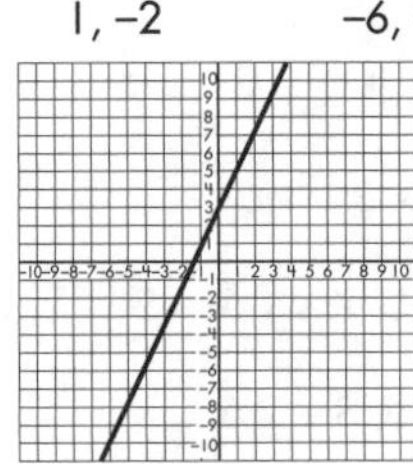

0; 3

9b.

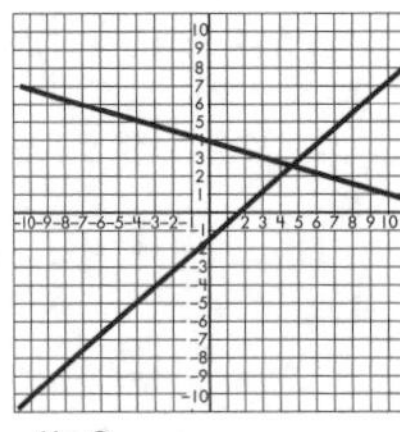

4; 2

10. $b + c = 80$; $2b + 4c = 270$; 25; 55

Lesson 3.1, page 35

1. 5
2. 4.2

Lesson 3.1, page 36

1. constant
2. variable

Lesson 3.1, page 37

1. variable
2. constant
3. constant

Lesson 3.2, page 38

1a.

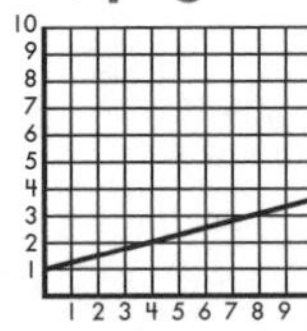

1b.

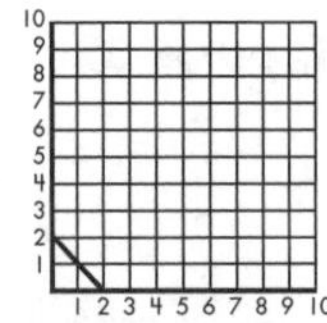

2a.

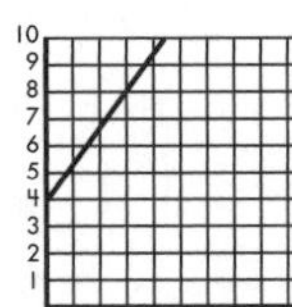

2b.

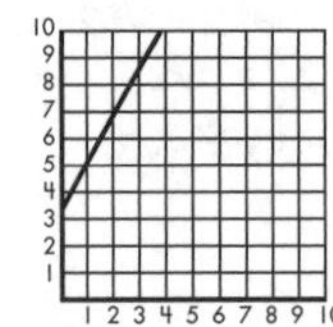

Lesson 3.2, page 39

	a	b
1.	$y = -x + 7$	$y = \frac{1}{2}x + 4$
2.	$y = -\frac{3}{2}x + 6$	$y = \frac{2}{3}x$

Lesson 3.2, page 40

	a	b	c
1.	$y = \frac{4}{3}x + 3$	$y = -2x + 4$	$y = -\frac{1}{2}x + 7$
2.	$y = 3x - 5$	$y = \frac{2}{5}x$	$y = -\frac{3}{4}x - 2$
3.	$y = -4x + 6$	$y = \frac{5}{2}x - 3$	$y = \frac{1}{2}x + 1$

Lesson 3.3, page 41

	a	b	c
1.	13	12	37
2.	15	14	55
3.	22	48	35
4.	21	18	24
5.	28	33	28
6.	23	9	14
7.	12	32	8
8.	39	24	16
9.	8	55	22
10.	7	15	7
11.	5	14	56
12.	4	41	6

Lesson 3.3, page 42

	a	b	c
1.	7	64	6
2.	28	11	6
3.	8	2	5
4.	80	5	15
5.	77	200	90
6.	4	12	13
7.	42	11	15
8.	24	12	63
9.	13	54	3
10.	72	12	72

Lesson 3.3, page 43

	a	b	c
1.	1	4	9
2.	84	136	11
3.	5	198	17
4.	8	6	72
5.	17	12	16
6.	15	9	60
7.	9	7	7
8.	52	36	7
9.	10	5	3
10.	198	1	8
11.	60	13	15
12.	15	4	20

Lesson 3.4, page 44

	a	b	c
1.	7	15	36
2.	3	5	120
3.	48	10	11

4.	81	13	72
5.	8	120	272
6.	14	45	20
7.	60	8	42
8.	18	56	11
9.	65	96	21

Lesson 3.4, page 45

	a	**b**	**c**
1.	10	−4	−9
2.	6	−4	15
3.	8	−3	−17
4.	0	−3	−21
5.	16	15	−4
6.	24	18	−17
7.	−2	−8	16
8.	−2	−3	6
9.	−20	−28	−23
10.	7	5	3
11.	$-\frac{4}{3}$	$\frac{1}{2}$	$9\frac{1}{9}$
12.	1	−5	−84
13.	$2\frac{2}{5}$	−1,960	7,812
14.	$1\frac{3}{4}$	$15\frac{2}{3}$	56
15.	4,048	1,242	−7
16.	−3,150	2,565	104

Lesson 3.4, page 46

	a	**b**
1.	5	3
2.	16	3
3.	-9	−8
4.	7	−7
5.	8	$-23\frac{2}{3}$
6.	12	−10
7.	−8	−12
8.	5	12
9.	7	$-2\frac{1}{4}$
10.	5	0
11.	$-4\frac{5}{19}$	$-7\frac{3}{8}$
12.	$30\frac{3}{4}$	$-7\frac{1}{3}$

Lesson 3.5, page 47

Answers in tables may vary.

1a.

x	y
0	−3
2	−1
4	1
6	3

1b.

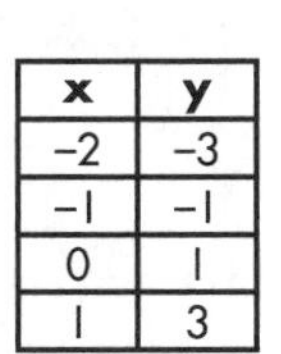

x	y
−2	−3
−1	−1
0	1
1	3

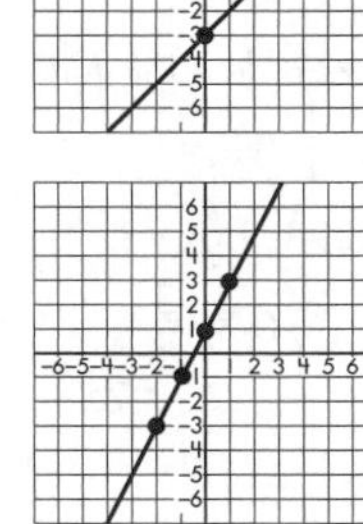

2a.

x	y
−2	−3
0	−2
2	−1
4	0

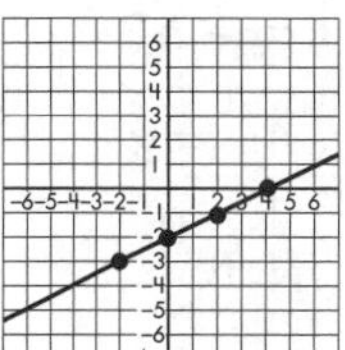

2b.

x	y
−4	−2
−1	−1
2	0
5	1

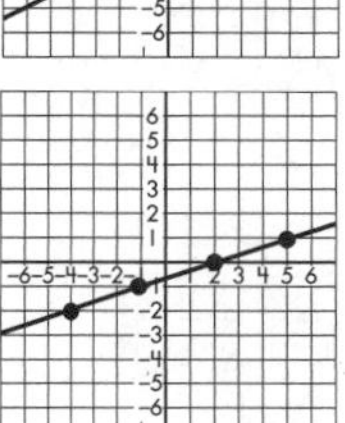

Lesson 3.5, page 48

1a.

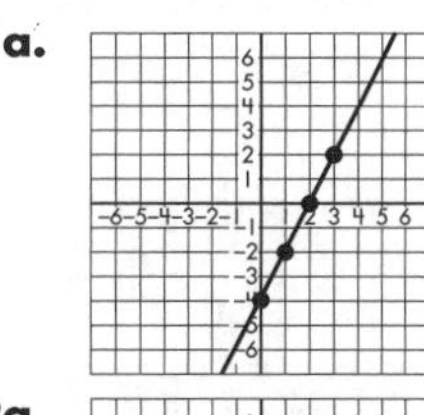

1b.

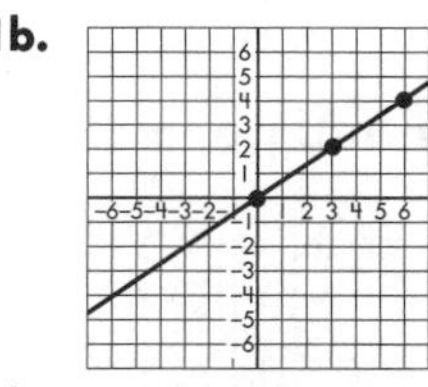

2a.

2b.

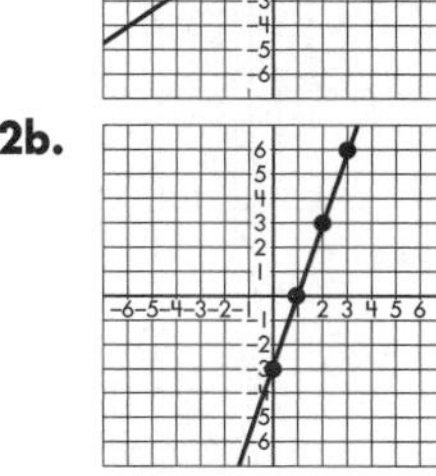

3a.

3b.

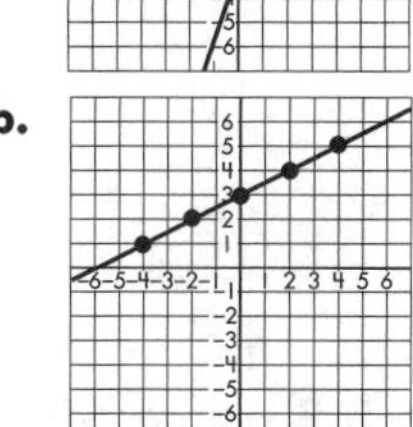

Lesson 3.6, page 49

	a	**b**
1.	yes	no
2.	no	yes

Lesson 3.7, page 50

	a	**b**
1.	3; 2	4; 5
2.	−3; −7	0; −5
3.	3; −3	2; 5

Lesson 3.7, page 51

	a	**b**
1.	6; −6	7; −1
2.	10; −1	−1; −1
3.	−1; 3	−1; −8

Lesson 3.7, page 52

	a	**b**
1.	9; 1	−1; −2
2.	1; 3	5; 6
3.	$-\frac{1}{2}; 3\frac{1}{2}$	9; 5
4.	$g = 4, f = 3$	$b = 4, t = 1$
5.	$x = 1\frac{1}{2}, y = 1$	$h = 6, e = 1$

Grade 8 Answers

Lesson 3.8, page 53

1a.

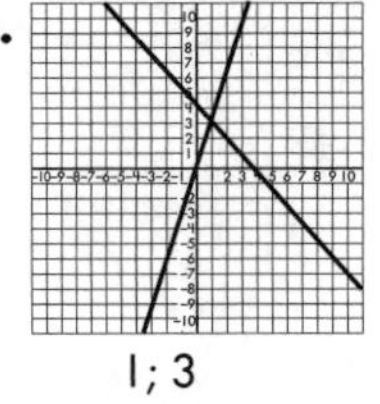

1; 3

1b.

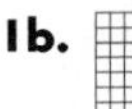

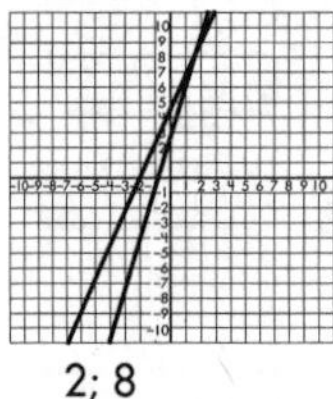

2; 8

2a.

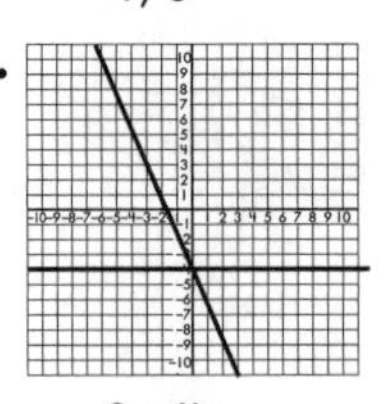

0; –4

2b.

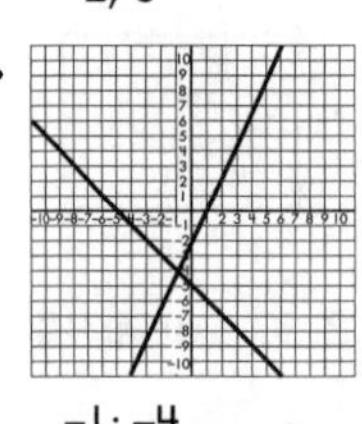

–1; –4

Lesson 3.8, page 54

1a.

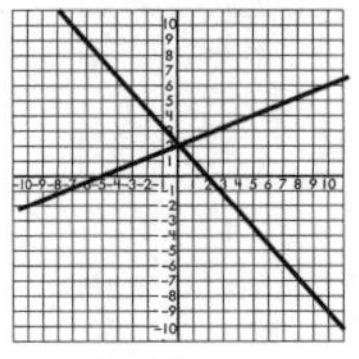

0; 2

1b.

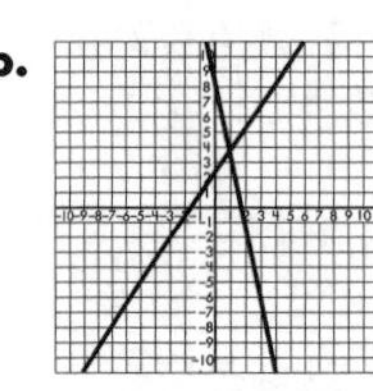

1; 4

2a.

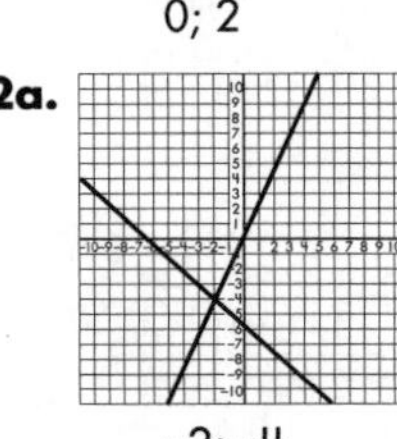

–2; –4

2b.

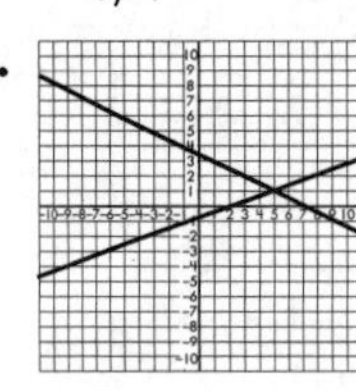

5; 1

Lesson 3.8, page 55

1a.

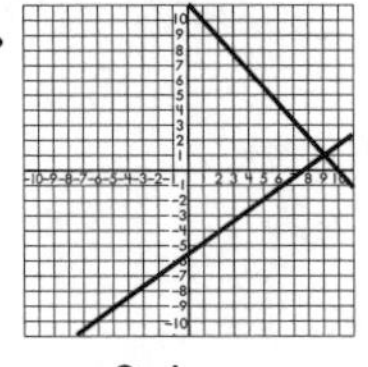

9; 1

1b.

1; 3

2a.

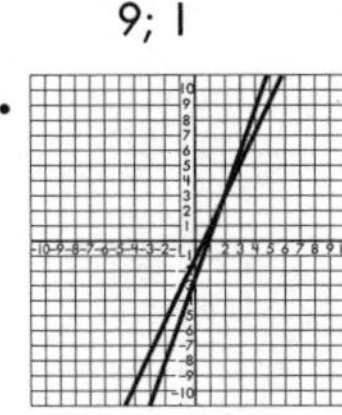

2; 3

2b.

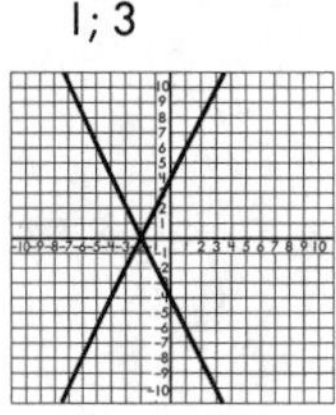

–2; 0

3a.

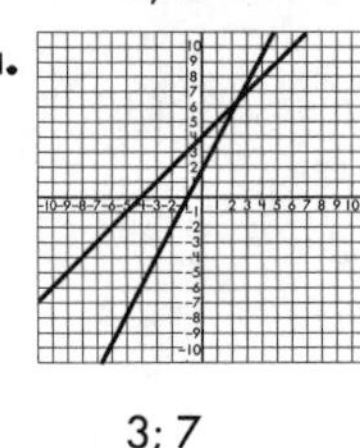

3; 7

3b.

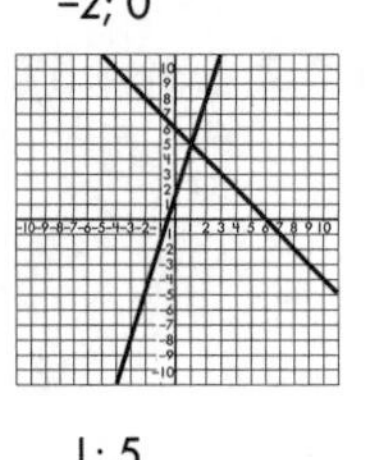

1; 5

Lesson 3.9, page 56

1. $w + s = 172$; $(\$1.10)w + (\$2.35)s = \$294.20$; 88; 84
2. $t + f = 40$; $2t + 4f = 100$; 30; 10

Lesson 3.9, page 57

1. $q + d = 57$; $(\$0.25)q + (\$0.10)d = \$12.00$; 42; 15
2. $c + t = 125$; $\$3c + \$5t = \$425$; 100; 25
3. $a + c = 2{,}200$; $4a + 1.5c = \$5{,}050$; 1,500; 700

Posttest, page 58

	a	b	c
1.	20		
2.	25	45	18
3.	43	20	8
4.	7	13	56

5a.

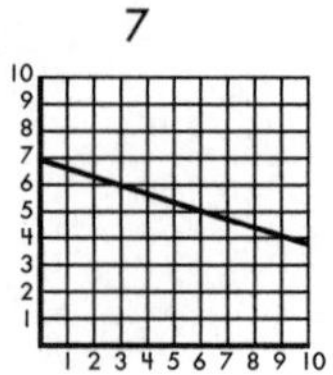

5b.

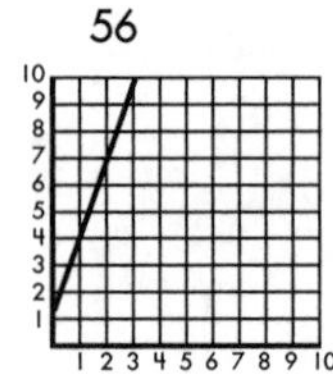

6a. 8; 6; 3; 0; –2

6b.

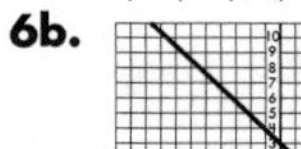

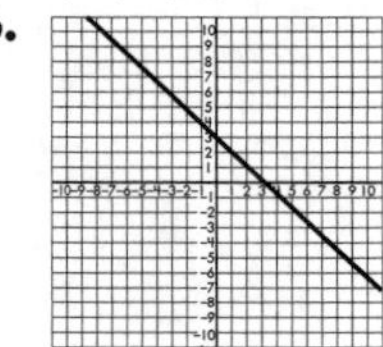

Posttest, page 59

	a	b
7.	–1; –5	–5; –3
8.	–6, 4	2, 0

9a.

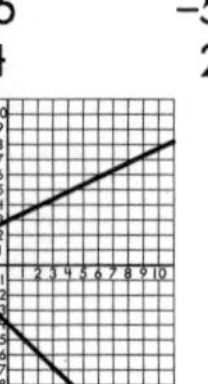

–5; 1

9b.

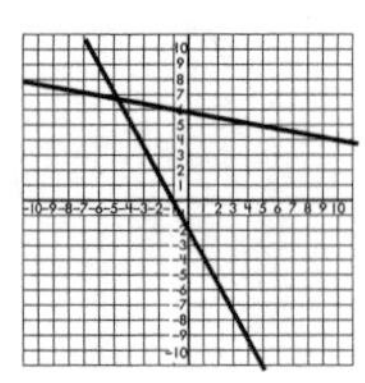

–5; 7

10. $t + x = 15$; $2t + 3x = 33$; 12; 3

Mid-Test, page 60

	a	b	c
1.	7	0	$\frac{1}{4}$
2.	$\frac{2}{3}$	$\frac{1}{3}$	8
3.	11	7	3

4. 1.73; 1.74
5. 3.87; 3.88
6. 8.83; 8.84

Check number line for items 7–9.

7. $-1.75, -\frac{1}{2}, \sqrt{2}, \pi$
8. $0.05, 0.98, 1\frac{1}{4}, \sqrt{3}$
9. $0.25, \sqrt{\frac{1}{4}}, 0.7, \frac{3}{4}$

10.	16	25	512

Grade 8 Answers

11.	$\frac{1}{6,561}$	$\frac{1}{1,728}$	$\frac{1}{32,768}$

	a	b	c
12.	1.565×10^1	9.247×10^3	4.22×10^2
13.	7.5×10^{-1}	1.5295×10^4	3.4×10^{-2}

Mid-Test, page 61

	a	b	c
14.	$\frac{2}{5}$	8	$\frac{3}{7}$
15.	81	225	729
16.	\$1.50		
17.	15	10	−12
18.	3	20	−3
19.	3	2	$1\frac{2}{5}$
20.	−3; −6	−5; 9	3; −3

Mid-Test, page 62

21.

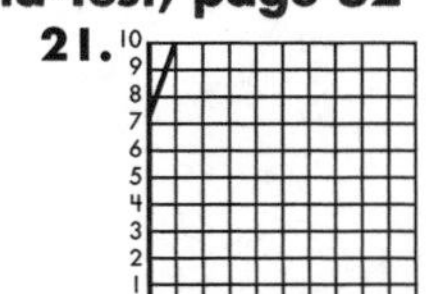

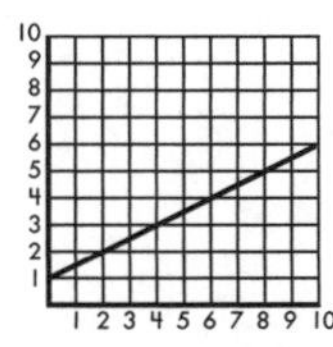

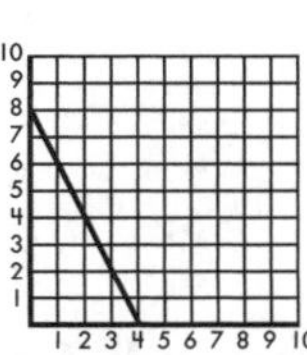

22.

x	y
−2	−1
0	−2
2	−3
4	−4

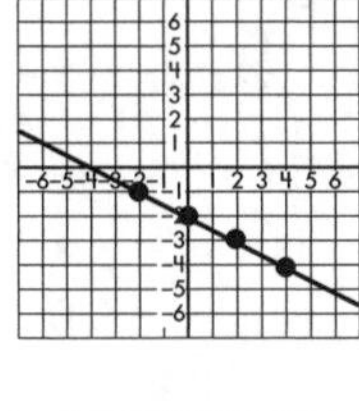

24.

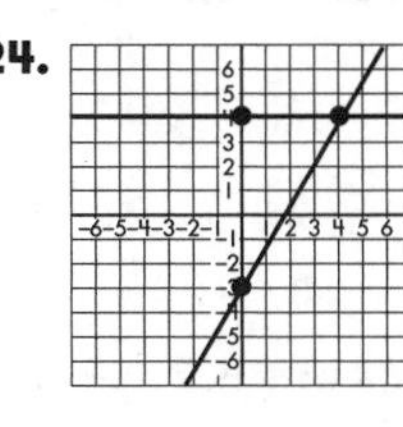

23.

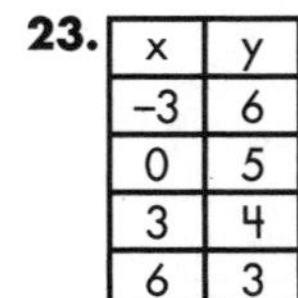

x	y
−3	6
0	5
3	4
6	3

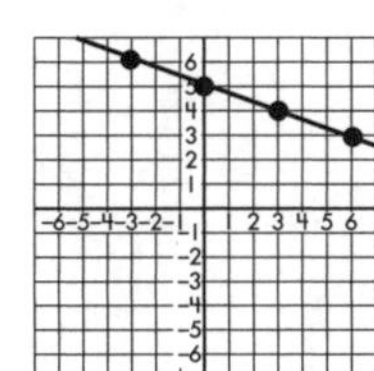

25.

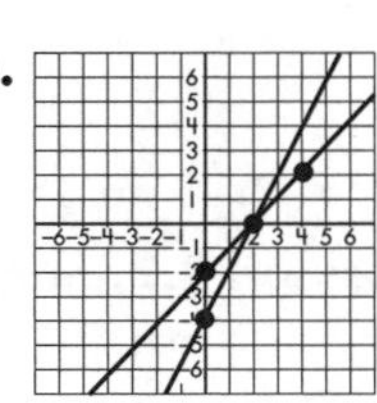

Mid-Test, page 63

	a	b	c
26.	5^3	4^6	3^{12}
27.	15^3	7^2	6^3
28.	10^7	2^4	7^3
29.	rational	irrational	irrational
30.	rational	irrational	irrational
31.	rational	rational	rational
32.	$\sqrt{36} < 6.5$	$1.4 < \sqrt{2}$	$\frac{1}{2} < 0.55$
33.	$3.9 > \sqrt{10}$	$\sqrt{5} < 4$	$\sqrt{8} < 3$
34.	$1 > \sqrt{\frac{16}{25}}$	$\sqrt[3]{343} < 7.2$	$\sqrt[3]{6} < 2$

Pretest, page 64

	a	b	c
1.	no	yes	yes

2.

a: y	b: y	c: y
−274	−82	−153
−202	−61	−69
86	−47	−45
158	18	123
212	36	147

	a	b
3.	31, 85, $y = 9x + 4$	4, 5, $y = \frac{1}{7}x - 5$
4.	−2, 2, nonlinear	6, 6, linear

Pretest, page 65

	a	b	c
5.	1	$\frac{1}{9}$	$\frac{5}{4}$
6.	−1	2	3
7.	$y = \frac{3}{4}x - 1$	$y = \frac{1}{6}x$	$y = \frac{1}{3}x + 4$
8.	equation		

Lesson 4.1, page 66

	a	b	c
1.	yes	yes	no
2.	no	yes	no

Lesson 4.2, page 67

1.

a: y	b: y	c: y
	−2	−7
	0	−5
6	4	−2
9	8	0
11	14	3
14	18	8

2.

a: y	b: y	c: y
6	−2	−6
1	−1	−4
−2	1	−2
−3	2	0
6	3	1

3.

a: y	b: y	c: y
−7	−2	0
−4	−1	1
2	1	2
8	2	4
17	3	5

Lesson 4.2, page 68

1.

a: y	b: y	c: y
−94	−9	−27
−58	−2	−15
−22	3	−8
41	8	7
104	13	18

2.

a: y	b: y	c: y
−12	−48	−7
−6	−38	−3
5	−20	8
11	20	14
17	42	15

3.

y
−72
−51
−30
−9
12

y
−14
−7
−2
8
15

y
−63
−24
57
81
102

Lesson 4.2, page 69

1. Values chosen for x may vary but should create a whole number value for y.

a

x	y
2	−6
4	−5
6	−4
8	−3
10	−2

b

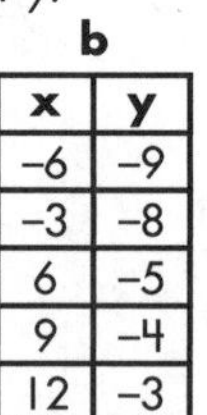

x	y
−6	−9
−3	−8
6	−5
9	−4
12	−3

c

x	y
−9	−1
−4	0
1	1
6	2
11	3

2. Values chosen for x may vary but should create a whole number value for y.

x	y
−1	−12
0	−3
1	6
2	15
3	24

x	y
−2	2
0	0
2	2
4	8
6	18

x	y
−6	3
0	2
6	1
12	0
18	−1

	a	b	c	d
3.	$x - 1$	$-3x$	$\frac{x}{2} + 1$	x^2

Lesson 4.3, page 70

	a	b
1.	4, 5, $y = \frac{1}{12}x$	5, 8, $y = x + 3$
2.	44, 60, $y = 8x - 12$	30, 110, $y = 10 + 10$
3.	40, 75, $y = 7x + 5$	0, 10, $y = \frac{1}{4}x - 2$

Lesson 4.3, page 71

	a	b
1.	32, 67, $y = 7x - 3$	4, 14, $y = \frac{1}{4}x + 2$
2.	6, 13, $y = \frac{1}{5}x + 3$	7, 18, $y = 11x - 4$
3.	22, 42, $y = 4x - 6$	6, 13, $y = \frac{1}{7}x + 4$

4a. 12, 18, $y = x + 6$

4b. 2, 4, $y = \frac{1}{3}x + 1$

Lesson 4.4, page 72

	a	b
1.	$\frac{3}{5}$, $\frac{3}{5}$, linear	$\frac{7}{4}$, $\frac{7}{4}$, linear
2.	2, 18, nonlinear	−1, 1, nonlinear
3.	$\frac{3}{2}$, $\frac{3}{2}$, linear	2,000, 2,080, nonlinear

Lesson 4.5, page 73

	a	b	c
1.	2	4	2
2.	$\frac{1}{2}$	−8	−15
3.	$\frac{1}{3}$	$\frac{1}{6}$	$\frac{3}{2}$

Lesson 4.5, page 74

	a	b	c
1.	1	$\frac{1}{9}$	$\frac{5}{3}$
2.	4	1	−1
3.	4	2	$\frac{2}{3}$
4.	$\frac{1}{2}$	$\frac{5}{6}$	5

Lesson 4.6, page 75

	a	b	c
1.	5	0	−8
2.	−6	11	8
3.	5	8	−4

Lesson 4.6, page 76

1. 6
2. 0
3. 3
4. 50
5. 25
6. 10

Lesson 4.7, page 77

	a	b	c
1.	$y = 3x$	$y = \frac{1}{3}x$	$y = 6x$
2.	$y = 2x - 2$	$y = \frac{3}{2}x - 2$	$y = x - 8$
3.	$y = x - 3$	$y = 4x - 1$	$y = 2x + 6$

Lesson 4.7, page 78

	a	b
1.	$y = \frac{5}{9}x - 4$	$y = -\frac{2}{3}x - 3$
2.	$y = \frac{1}{4}x + 3$	$y = -\frac{5}{3}x - 2$

Lesson 4.7, page 79

	a	b	c
1.	$y = 2x - 2$	$y = -\frac{1}{2}x + 7$	$y = 2x$
2.	$y = 3x + 1$	$y = -\frac{3}{2}x + 3$	$y = \frac{1}{2}x + 2\frac{1}{2}$
3.	$y = 2x - 1$	$y = x + 2$	$y = \frac{1}{2}x + 5$
4.	$y = 3x + 10$	$y = 5x + 3$	$y = -\frac{1}{2}x + 5$

Lesson 4.8, page 80

Answers may vary.

1. The biggest increase in visitors was between months 2 and 3. The number of visitors was at its greatest at month 5. The number of visitors increased until month 5 and then decreased.
2. Grace learned words quickly in the first weeks. Grace learned fewer new words as time increased. By the end of her studying period, Grace was learning very few new words.
3. The family moved at a constant pace, but more slowly at the beginning of the trip. The family moved at almost the same pace at just before they stopped moving and shortly after they started moving again. The family stopped moving during the middle of the trip.

Grade 8 Answers

Lesson 4.9, page 81

1a.
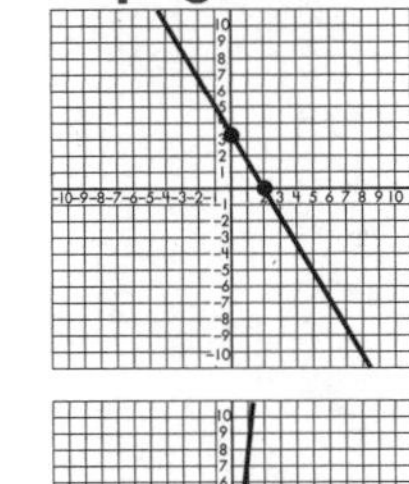

1b.
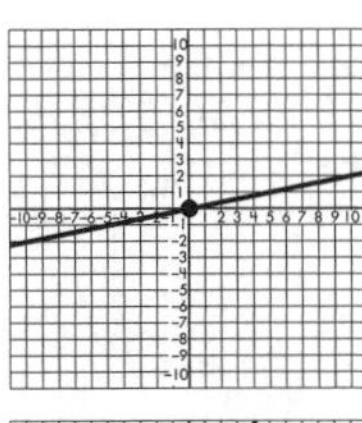

2a.
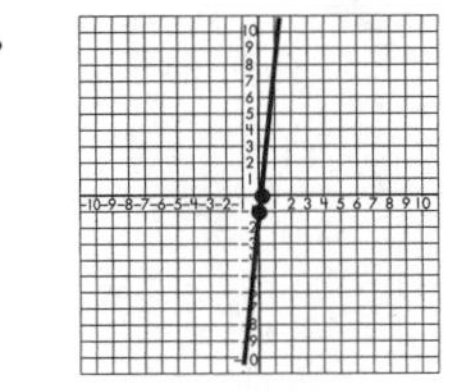

2b.
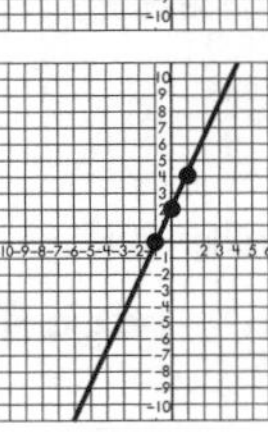

Lesson 4.9, page 82

1a.
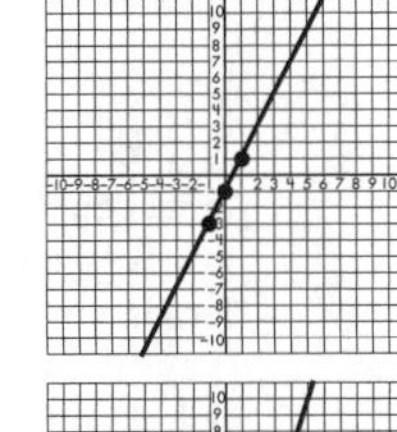

1b.
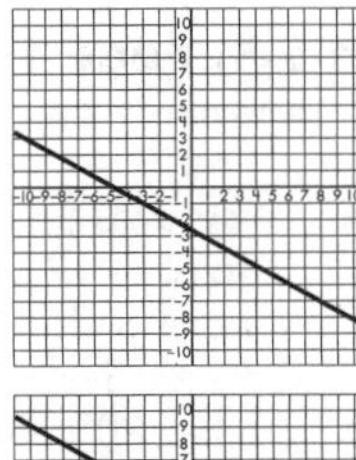

2a.
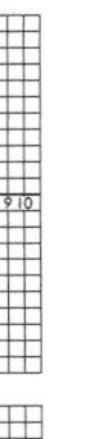

2b.

3a.

3b.

Lesson 4.9, page 83

1a.
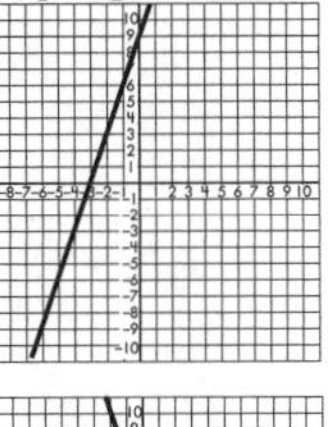

1b.
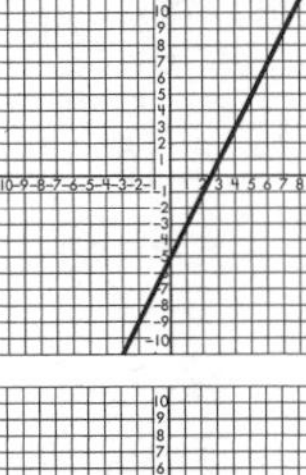

2a.
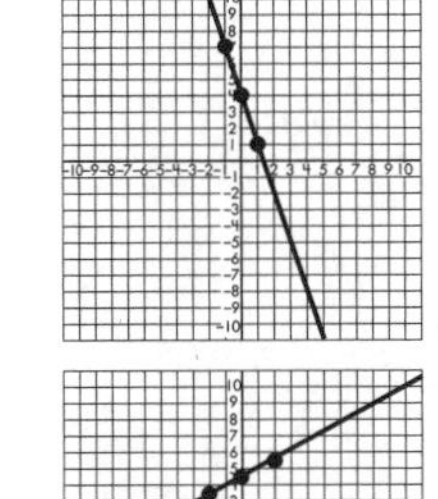

2b.

3a.
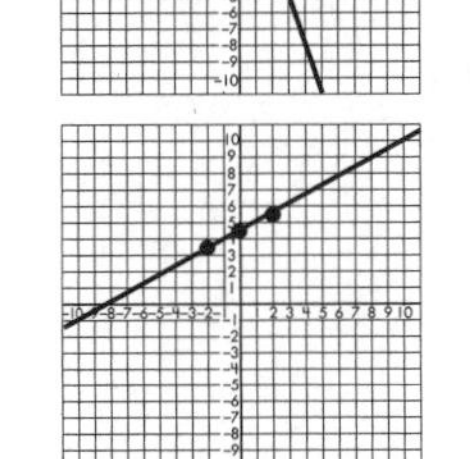

3b.
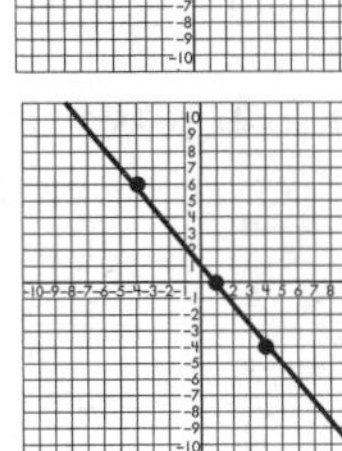

Lesson 4.10, page 84

	a	b
1.	table	equation
2.	equation	table
3.	table	equation
4.	equation	equation

Lesson 4.10, page 85

	a	b
1.	table	equal
2.	equation	table
3.	equation	equal

Lesson 4.10, page 86

	a	b	c
1.	graph	equal	equation
2.	equal	graph	equation

Posttest, page 87

	a	b	c
1.	no	yes	yes
2.	54	17	5
	66	45	7
	81	61	12
	99	105	15
	111	133	18
3.	0; 6; $y = x - 6$	0; −2; $y = -x + 7$	
4.	4; 4; linear	2; 18; nonlinear	

Posttest, page 88

	a	b	c
5.	4	4	$\frac{1}{2}$
6.	5		
7.	$y = 3x - 7$	$y = 10x + 6$	$y = -\frac{2}{3}x + 3$

8.

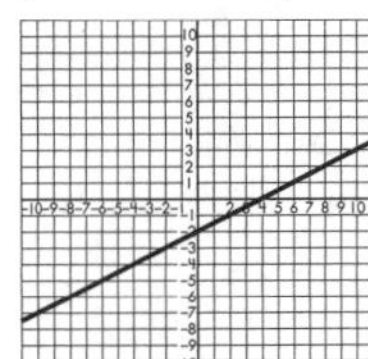

Pretest, page 89

1. (−4,−1); (−1,−1); (−1, −5)
2. (0,4); (3,4); (3, 0)
3. translation

	a	b	c
4.	congruent	similar	not

5. Answers will vary but should reflect proportionality.

Pretest, page 90

6. ($\overleftrightarrow{EF}$)
7. ∠2,∠3,∠6,∠7
8. ∠1,∠4,∠5,∠8
9. ∠1/∠4,∠2/∠3,∠5/∠8,∠6/∠7
10. ∠1/∠8,∠2/∠7
11. ∠3/∠6,∠4/∠5

	a	b	c
12.	445.1	489.84	113.04
13.	√289;17		
14.	√120; 11		
15.	√319; 18		

Grade 8 Answers

Lesson 5.1, page 91

	a	b	c
1.	yes	no	yes
2.	yes	no	no
3.	no	no	yes

Lesson 5.1, page 92

	a	b	c
1.	yes	yes	no
2.	no	yes	no
3.	no	yes	yes

Lesson 5.1, page 93

	a	b	c
1.	yes	no	no
2.	no	yes	yes
3.	yes	no	yes

Lesson 5.1, page 94

	a	b	c
1.	reflection	rotation	translation
2.	reflection	rotation	reflection
3.	translation	reflection	translation
4.	reflection	translation	rotation

Lesson 5.2, page 95

	a	b	c
1.	yes	yes	no
2.	no	yes	yes
3.	yes	no	yes

Lesson 5.3, page 96

	a	b	c
1.	translation	translation	reflection
2.	reflection	dilation	rotation
3.	translation	rotation	dilation

Lesson 5.3, page 97

1. (−4, 1), (−1, 1), (−1, −4), (−2, −4)
2. (−4, 1), (−1, 1), (−1, 4), (−2, 4)
3. reflection
4. (−5, 1), (−1, 1), (−1, 4)
5. (−2, −2), (2, −2), (2, 1)
6. translation

Lesson 5.3, page 98

1. (−4, 3), (0, 3), (−2, 1), (−6, 1)
2. 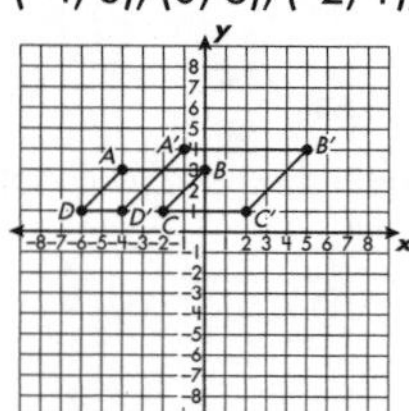
3. dilation
4. (2, 3), (5, 1), (1, 0)
5. 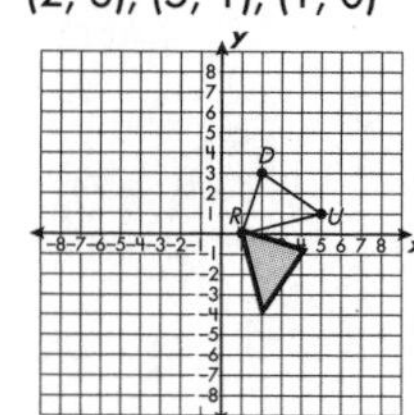
6. rotation
7. (2,5), (5,3), (5,1), (0,0)
8. 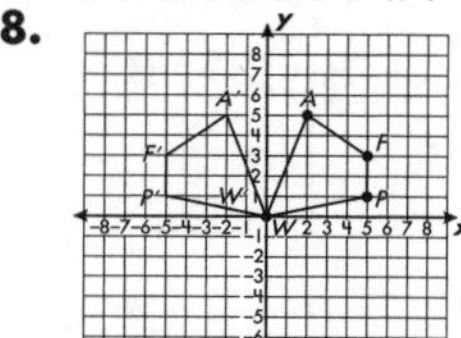
9. reflection

Lesson 5.4, page 99

	a	b	c
1.	congruent	not	similar
2.	not	congruent	similar

Lesson 5.4, page 100

Order of steps may vary.

	a	b
1.	rotate 90°; dilate by 2; translate +9 on the *y*-axis and −10 on the *x*-axis	reflect on the *x*-axis translate +6 on the *x*-axis
2.	rotate 90°; dilate by 2; translate by −12 on the *y*-axis	reflect on the *x*-axis rotate 90°; dilate by 2

Lesson 5.5, page 101

Answers may vary.

	a	b
1.	1, 2 2, 4 $\frac{1}{2} = \frac{2}{4}$	2, 1 4, 2 $\frac{2}{4} = \frac{1}{2}$
2.	2, 3 4, 6 $\frac{2}{4} = \frac{3}{6}$	3, 2 6, 4 $\frac{3}{6} = \frac{2}{4}$

Lesson 5.5, page 102

Answers may vary.

	a	b
1.	1, 5 2, 10 $\frac{1}{2} = \frac{5}{10}$	2, 3 4, 6 $\frac{2}{4} = \frac{3}{6}$
2.	1, 3 2, 6 $\frac{1}{2} = \frac{3}{6}$	2, 2 6, 6 $\frac{2}{6} = \frac{2}{6}$

	a	b
3.	1, 2 2, 4 $\frac{1}{2} = \frac{2}{4}$	6, 2 12, 4 $\frac{6}{12} = \frac{2}{4}$

Lesson 5.6, page 103

1. $\overleftrightarrow{RS}$; corresponding
2. $\overleftrightarrow{AB}$; alternate interior
3. $\overleftrightarrow{RS}$; corresponding
4. $\overleftrightarrow{TU}$; alternate exterior

5. $\overleftrightarrow{TU}$; alternate interior
6. $\overleftrightarrow{CD}$; alternate exterior
7. $\overleftrightarrow{TU}$; alternate exterior
8. $\overleftrightarrow{TU}$; corresponding
9. $\overleftrightarrow{AB}$; alternate interior
10. $\overleftrightarrow{CD}$; alternate interior
11. $\overleftrightarrow{RS}$; corresponding
12. $\overleftrightarrow{TU}$; corresponding

Lesson 5.6, page 104

1. ∠1/∠2, ∠3/∠4, ∠5/∠6, ∠7∠8
   ∠1/∠4, ∠2/∠3, ∠5/∠8, ∠6/∠7
2. ∠4 and ∠6
3. ∠2/∠8
4. ∠1/∠2, ∠2/∠4, ∠6/∠8, ∠8/∠7
   ∠7/∠5, ∠3/∠1, ∠5/∠6, ∠3/∠4
5. ∠3/∠6, ∠4/∠5
6. ∠1/∠8, ∠2/∠7
7. ∠1/∠4, ∠2/∠3; ∠5/∠8, ∠6/∠7

Lesson 5.6, page 105

1. 45°
2. 78°
3. 76°
4. 83°
5. 115°
6. 96°
7. 35°
8. 102°
9. 70°
10. 80°
11. 75°
12. 85°
13. 80°
14. 110°
15. 70°
16. 95°
17. No, because these angles are on different transversals.

Lesson 5.7, page 106

1. yes; yes
2. no; no
3. no; no
4. yes; yes
5. no; no
6. yes; yes
7. no; no
8. no; no
9. yes; yes
10. no; no
11. no; no
12. no; no
13. Once you identify any three values that solve the Pythagorean Theorem, any multiple of those three numbers will also solve the theorem.

Lesson 5.8, page 107

1. √97; 9.85
2. √74; 8.6
3. √45; 6.71
4. √85; 9.22
5. √61; 7.81
6. √34; 5.83
7. √85; 9.22
8. √100; 10
9. √53; 7.28
10. √89; 9.43

Lesson 5.8, page 108

1. √256; 16
2. √100; 10
3. √39; 6.24
4. √120; 11
5. √624; 25
6. √81; 9
7. √81; 9
8. √5929; 77
9. √3025; 55
10. √288; 17

Lesson 5.8, page 109

1. 21
2. 9
3. 8.66
4. 65
5. 15.3

Lesson 5.9, page 110

	a	b	c
1.	12.53	11.18	10.30
2.	14.32	12.17	12.37

Lesson 5.9, page 111

	a	b	c
1.	9.85	8.54	9.90
2.	9.06	6.40	6.71
3.	8.54	8.60	8.49

Lesson 5.10, page 112

	a	b	c
1.	942	502.4	1,607.68
2.	678.24	549.5	1.13
3.	552.64	14.13	1,256

Lesson 5.10, page 113

	a	b	c
1.	16,076.8	3,538.78	747.76
2.	1,582.56	8,440.32	87.92
3.	26,660.01	2,034.72	4,876.92
4.	4,710	549.5	452.16

Lesson 5.11, page 114

	a	b	c
1.	200.96	376.8	39.25
2.	769.3	50.24	314
3.	94.2	9,231.6	47.1

Lesson 5.11, page 115

	a	b	c
1.	167.47	2,786.23	25.12
2.	314	1,526.04	103.62
3.	29.31	29.31	200.96
4.	16.49	678.24	949.85

Grade 8 Answers

Lesson 5.12, page 116

	a	b	c
1.	267.95	381.51	1,766.25
2.	2,143.57	523.33	4,186.67
3.	904.32	1,436.03	113.04

Lesson 5.12, page 117

	a	b	c
1.	523.33	4,186.67	904.32
2.	267.95	4.19	1,436.03
3.	2,143.57	33.49	3,052.08
4.	113.04	7,234.56	14,130

Lesson 5.13, page 118

1. 508.68
2. 6,430.72
3. B; 116.18
4. 1,334.5
5. 14.13
6. 523.33

Posttest, page 119

1. (2, 3); (5, 3); (4, 1); (1, 1)
2. (–1, 2); (–1, 5); (1, 4); (1, 1)
3. rotation

4a. rotate 90°; translate up and to the left; dilate by 2

4b. reflect on the *x*-axis; translate to the right

5. Answers will vary but should reflect proportionality.

Posttest, page 120

6. $\overleftrightarrow{MN}$ and $\overleftrightarrow{OP}$
7. $\overleftrightarrow{QR}$
8. ∠1, ∠4, ∠5, ∠8
9. ∠2, ∠3, ∠6, ∠7
10. ∠1/∠4, ∠2/3, ∠5/∠8, ∠6/∠7
11. ∠1/∠8, ∠2/∠7
12. ∠3/∠6, ∠4/∠5

	a	b	c
13.	1,582.56	314	381.51

14. √149; 12.2
15. √203; 14.2
16. 30; 20

Pretest, page 121

1. Test Scores and Hours of Study
2. positive
3. a student was not studying effectively
4. 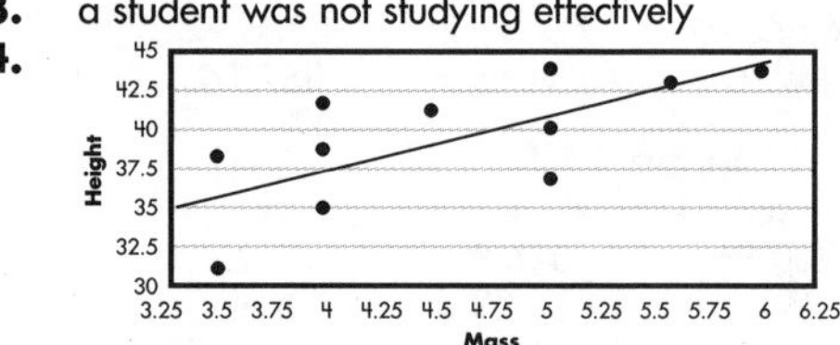

5. Height of dogs and Mass of dogs
6. positive
7. some dogs have a thinner build depending on their breed
8. $20\frac{2}{7}$ centimeters

Pretest, page 122

9a. 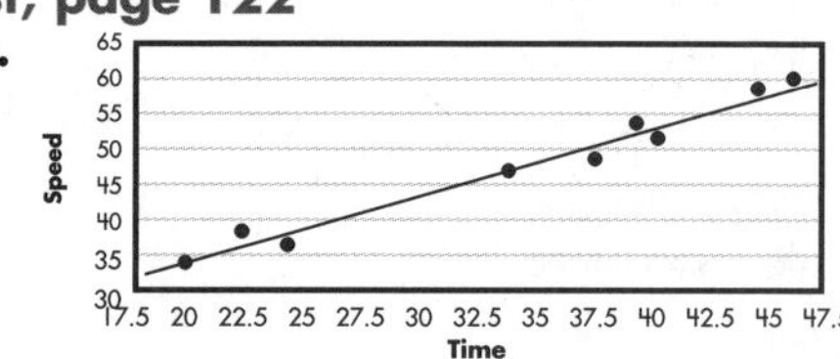

$y = \frac{6}{7}x + 17\frac{5}{7}$

9b. 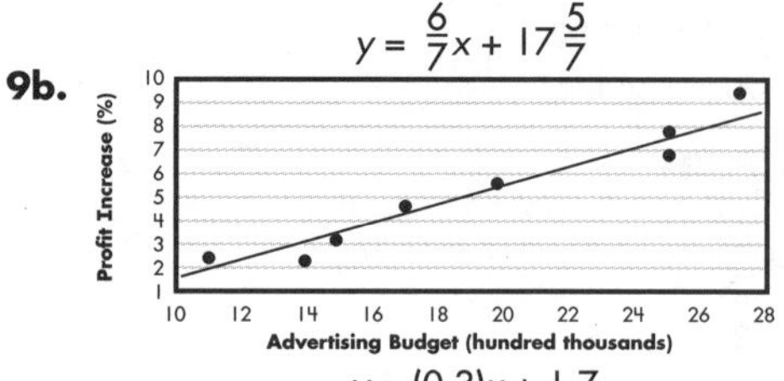

$y = (0.3)x + 1.7$

10. 7; 7; 23.3%
11. 9; 16; 30%
12. 10; 26; 33.3%
13. 4; 30; 13.3%
14. 30
15. 15.5–17.4
16. 17.5–19.5

Lesson 6.1, page 123

1.

15	16	17	18	18	20	21	22	23	24
75	70	75	65	80	75	80	85	80	85

2. negative; no relationship; positive
3. 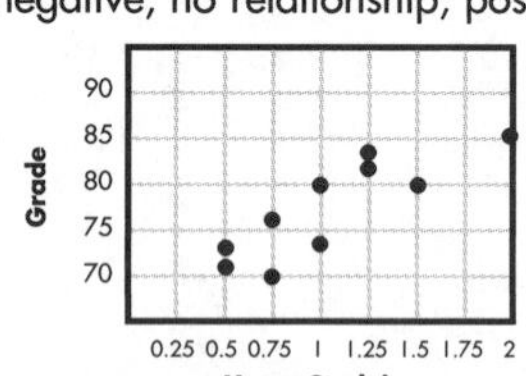

Note: student answers may vary depending on intervals chosen for axis labels.

Lesson 6.1, page 124

1. age and height
2. positive
3. 30
4. People stop growing after a certain age.
5. Price of Entrée and Number Ordered
6. negative
7. Some expensive entrees are still popular.
8. Possible answer: People will pay a lot for certain house specialties.

Lesson 6.2, page 125

1a. 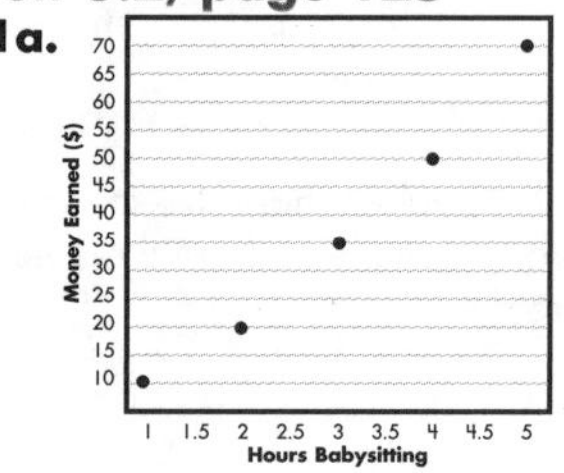

1b. 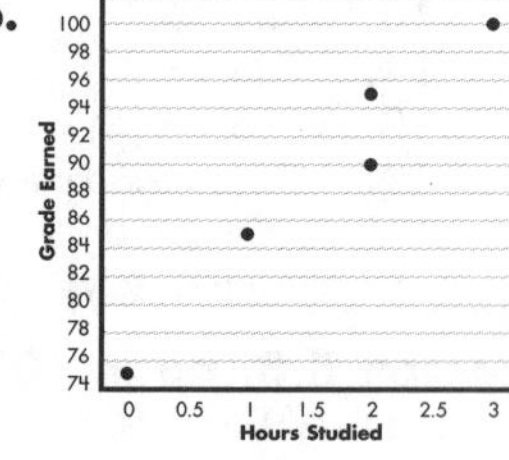

Grade 8 Answers

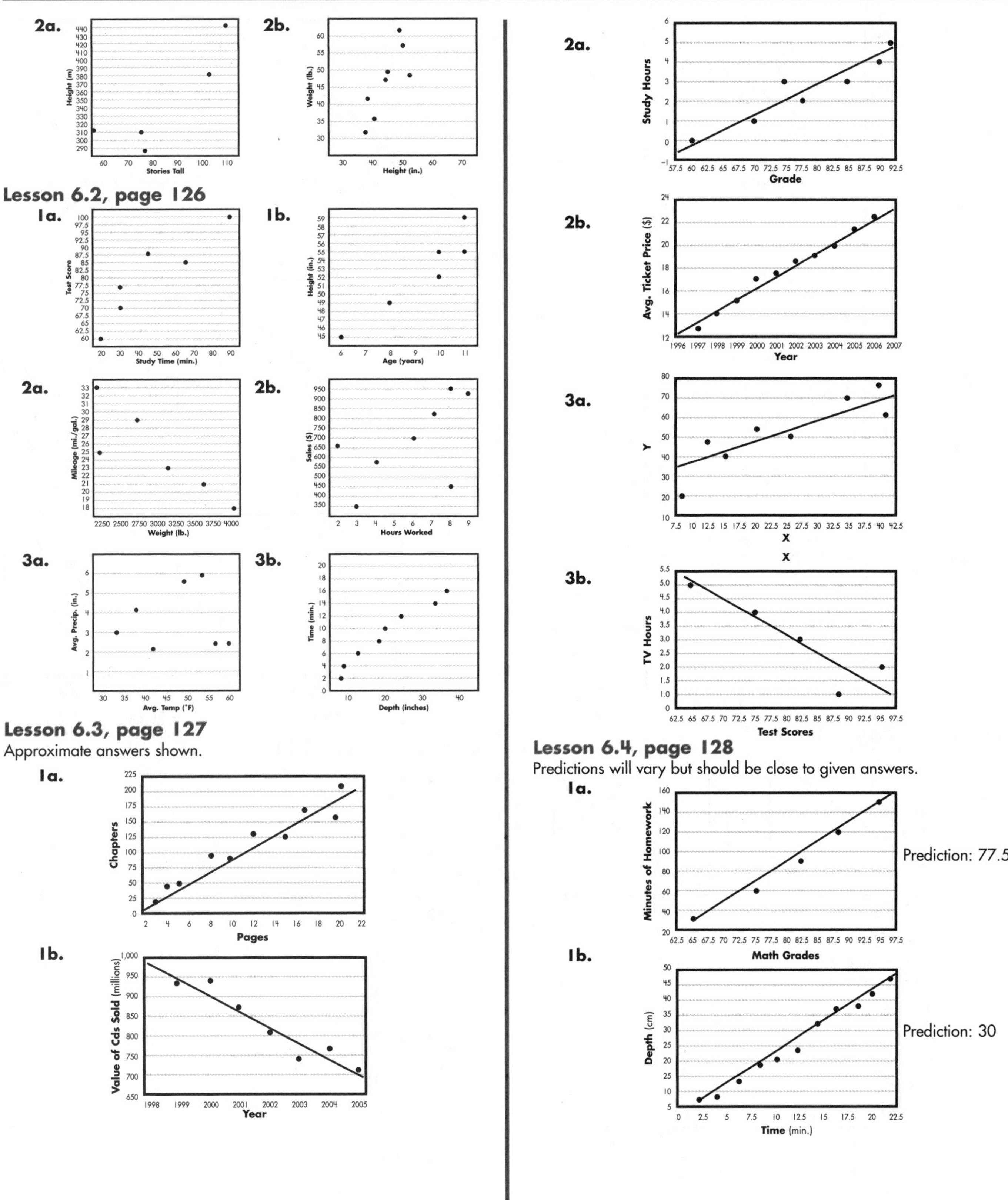

Lesson 6.2, page 126

Lesson 6.3, page 127

Approximate answers shown.

Lesson 6.4, page 128

Predictions will vary but should be close to given answers.

Grade 8 Answers

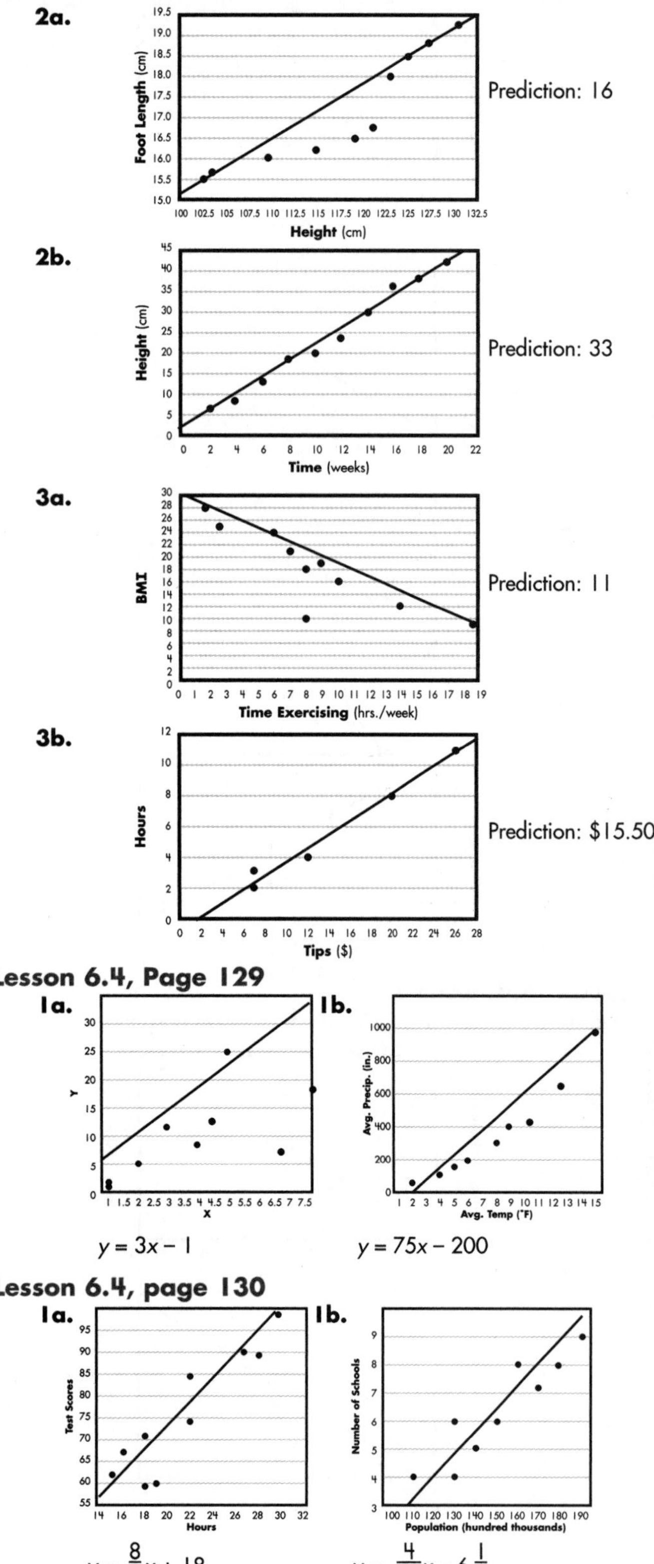

Lesson 6.4, Page 129

1a. X, Y

$y = 3x - 1$

1b. Avg. Precip. (in.), Avg. Temp (°F)

$y = 75x - 200$

Lesson 6.4, page 130

1a. Test Scores, Hours

$y = \frac{8}{3}x + 18$

1b. Number of Schools, Population (hundred thousands)

$y = \frac{4}{50}x - 6\frac{1}{5}$

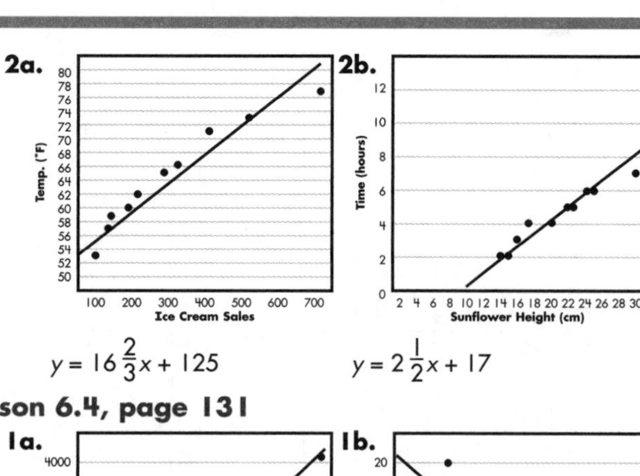

2a. $y = 16\frac{2}{3}x + 125$

2b. $y = 2\frac{1}{2}x + 17$

Lesson 6.4, page 131

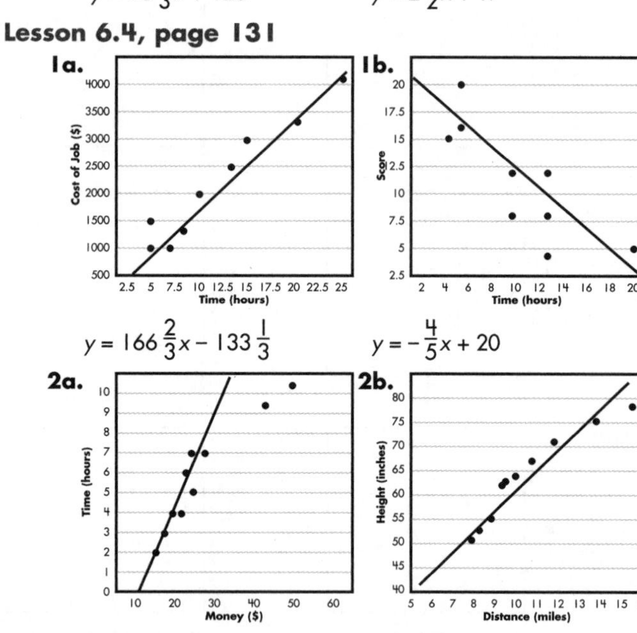

1a. $y = 166\frac{2}{3}x - 133\frac{1}{3}$

1b. $y = -\frac{4}{5}x + 20$

2a. $y = 2x + 15$

2b. $y = 4.28x + 8$

Lesson 6.5, page 132

1. $\frac{7}{61}$
2. $\frac{23}{61}$
3. $\frac{19}{61}$
4. $\frac{12}{61}$
5. 61
6. 4
7. 2; $\frac{1}{12}$
8. 5; $\frac{5}{24}$
9. 6; $\frac{1}{4}$
10. 8; $\frac{1}{3}$
11. 3; $\frac{1}{8}$
12. 80–89
13. 50–99

Grade 8 Answers

Lesson 6.5, page 133

1. 7; 7; $\frac{7}{25}$
2. 5; 12; $\frac{1}{5}$
3. 5; 17; $\frac{1}{5}$
4. 8; 25; $\frac{8}{25}$
5. 29–30
6. 25–26 and 27–28
7. 3; 3; $\frac{1}{10}$
8. 5; 8; $\frac{1}{6}$
9. 6; 14; $\frac{1}{5}$
10. 7; 21; $\frac{7}{30}$
11. 5; 26; $\frac{1}{6}$
12. 4; 30; $\frac{2}{15}$
13. 30
14. 4
15. 6; 6; $\frac{1}{5}$
16. 6; 12; $\frac{1}{5}$
17. 8; 20; $\frac{4}{15}$
18. 7; 27; $\frac{7}{30}$
19. 3; 30; $\frac{1}{10}$
20. 67-68
21. 30

Lesson 6.5, page 134

1. 5; 5; $\frac{1}{5}$
2. 7; 12; $\frac{7}{25}$
3. 9; 21; $\frac{9}{25}$
4. 4; 25; $\frac{4}{25}$
5. 0
6. 25
7. 10; 10; $\frac{1}{5}$
8. 31; 41; $\frac{31}{50}$
9. 8; 49; $\frac{4}{25}$
10. 1; 50; $\frac{1}{50}$
11. 110-119
12. 130+
13. 5; 5; $\frac{1}{10}$
14. 5; 10; $\frac{1}{10}$
15. 11; 21; $\frac{11}{50}$
16. 13; 34; $\frac{13}{50}$
17. 16; 50; $\frac{8}{25}$
18. 75+
19. 53

Posttest, page 135

1. Grocery Bill and People in the Family
2. Positive
3. Because the cost of groceries per person is fairly consistent.
4.

5. Diameter and Circumference
6. positive
7. Because the circumference of a shape is highly dependent on its diameter.
8. 36

Posttest, page 136

9a.

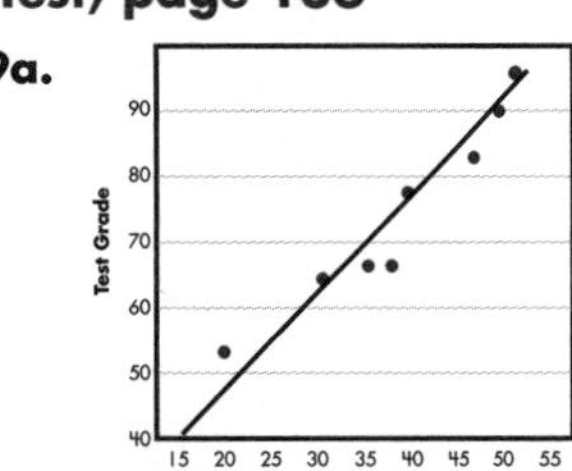

$y = \frac{13}{9}x + 19\frac{5}{9}$

9b.

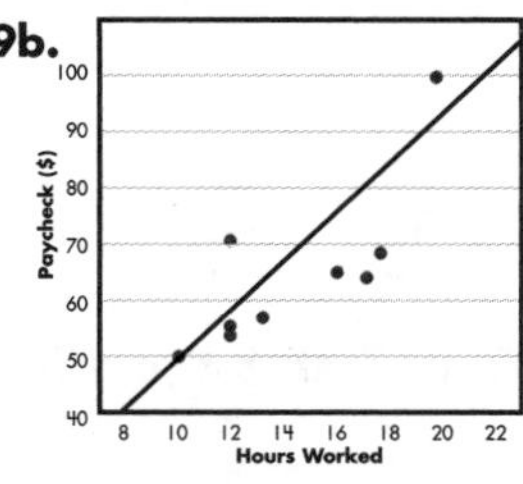

$y = \frac{5}{2}x + 25$

10. 3; 3; 17.6%
11. 6; 9; 35.3%
12. 6; 15; 35.3%
13. 2; 17; 11.8%
14. 17
15. 64–67 and 68–71
16. 72–75

Final Test, page 137

	a	b	c
1.	9	7	$\frac{4}{5}$
2.	$\frac{1}{2}$	1	0

3. 2.23; 2.24
4. 3.60; 3.61
5. 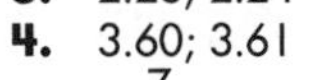 $-3, \frac{7}{4}, \pi, \sqrt{10}$

	a	b	c
6.	4	390,625	729
7.	$\frac{1}{27}$	$\frac{1}{10{,}000}$	$\frac{1}{64}$
8.	1.036×10^2	0.42	8.2×10^{-2}
9.	586	1.93×10^4	0.076
10.	3.604×10^3	0.005	6.3×10^{-3}
11.	3^7	2^{-8}	5^3

12.	4^{14}	8^{-1}	10^{-10}
13.	6^{-6}	11^{-10}	7^{-1}

Final Test, page 138

14. variable

15a.

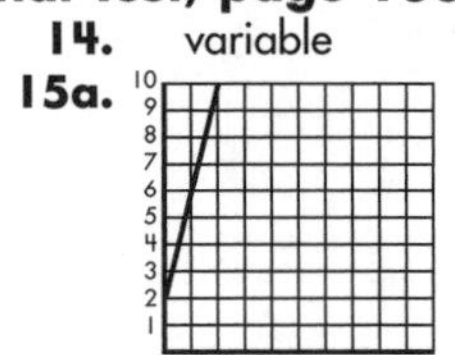

15b.

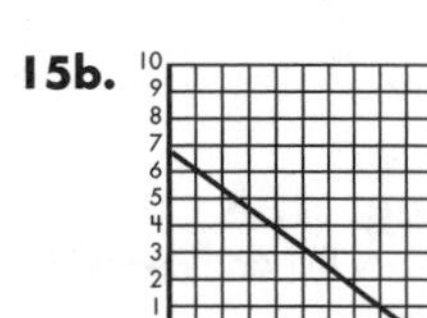

	a	b	c
16.	7	7	16
17.	105	18	13
18.	4	60	18
19.	4; 16	16; 5	10; 16

Final Test, page 139

20a.

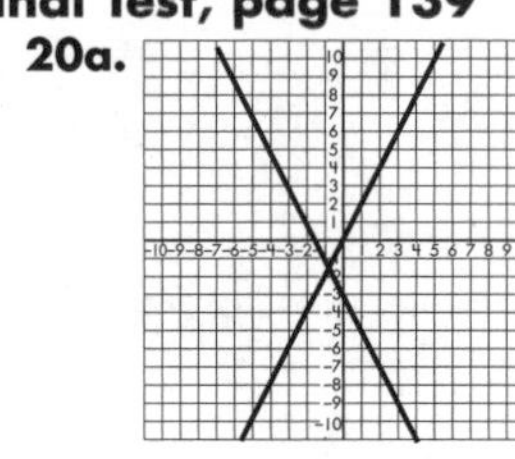

$-\frac{3}{4}; -1\frac{1}{2}$

20b.

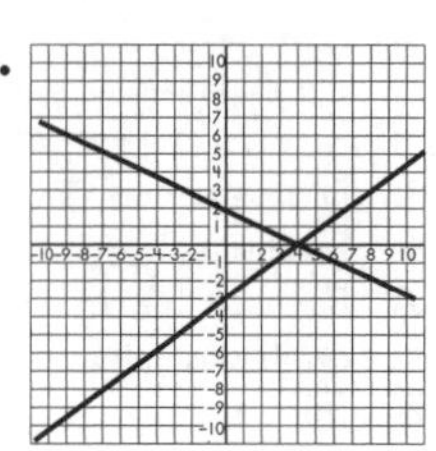

4; 0

	a	b	c
21.	no	no	yes
22.	2	2	$\frac{5}{2}$
23.	0		
24.	7		

Final Test, page 140

	a	b	c
25.	81	2	−1
	177	68	2
	205	134	3
	241	178	7
	289	288	11
26.	$y = -\frac{5}{3}x + 3\frac{2}{3}$	$y = \frac{3}{2}x + 5$	$y = \frac{1}{3}x + 5$
27.	table	equation	equation

Final Test, page 141

28a.

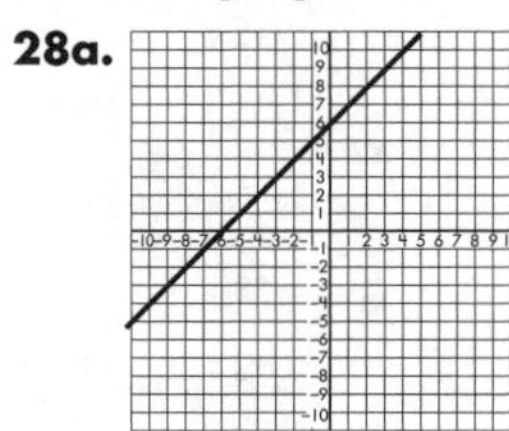

28b.

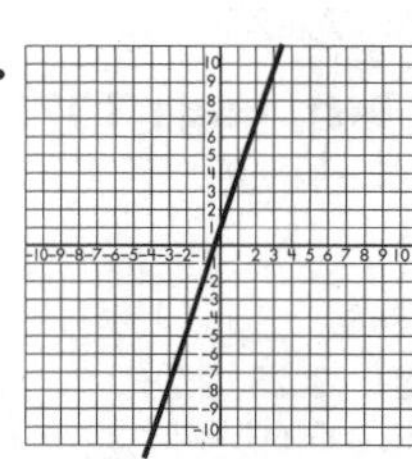

29a.

x	y
−2	2
0	3
2	4
4	5

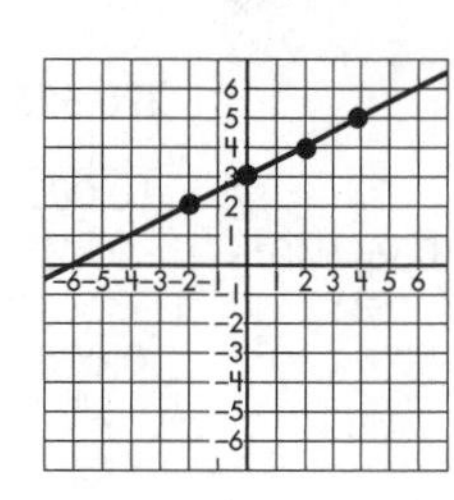

29b.

x	y
0	−4
1	0
2	4
3	8

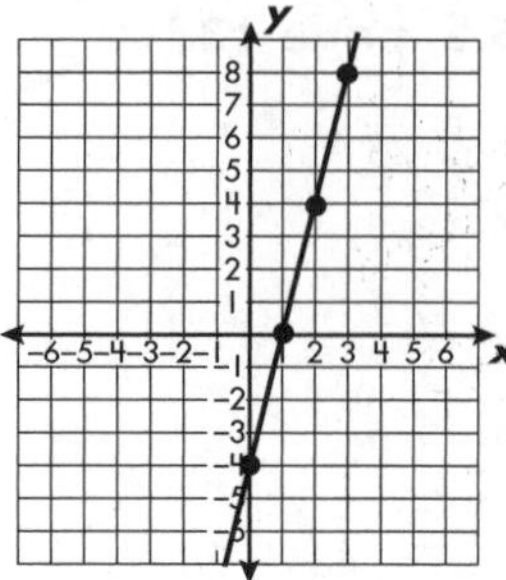

	a	b	c
30.	rotation	reflection	translation

Final Test, page 142

31a. rotate 90°; translate on x-axis; dilate by 2

31b. reflect on x-axis; translate on x-axis; dilate by 2

Answers may vary.

	a	b
32.	2, 1	1, 3
	4, 2	2, 6
	2 × 2 = 4	1 × 6 = 6
	1 × 4 = 4	2 × 3 = 6

33. $\overleftrightarrow{AB}$ and $\overleftrightarrow{CD}$

34. $\overleftrightarrow{EH}$

35. ∠1, ∠3, ∠5, ∠7

36. ∠1 and ∠7, ∠2 and ∠8

37. ∠4 and ∠6, ∠5 and ∠3

Final Test, page 143

38. √145; 12.04

39. √325; 18.03

	a	b	c
40.	953.78	628	381.51

41. Time Spent Studying and Test Scores

42. positive

43. Possible Answer: Students studied earlier.

44. 5

45. 15

46. 22

47. 27

48. 28

49. 28

50. 1; 10